CONVERSING WITH THE FUTURE

Visions of the Year 2020

Conversing With The Future

Visions of the Year 2020

By
Jenna Catherine

Wild Flower Press
P.O. Box 190
Mill Spring, NC 28756

Library of Congress Cataloging-in-Publication Data
Catherine, Jenna, 1943—
Conversing with the future: visions of 2020/
by Jenna Catherine.
p. cm.

ISBN 0-926524-45-3
1. Twenty-first century—Miscellanea.
2. Time travel.
3. Telepathy
I. Title.
BF1045.T55C37   1997
133.3--dc21

97-38504
CIP

Cover Artwork: Maynard Demmon
Manuscript editor: Brian Crissey

Printed in the United States of America.

Address all inquiries to:
Wild Flower Press
an imprint of Blue Water Publishing, Inc.
P. O. Box 190
Mill Spring, NC 28756
U.S.A.

Blue Water Publishing, Inc., is committed
to using recycled paper.

DEDICATION

To Carlene Sampson,
with deep affection

Conversing with the Future

Introduction

by Dolores Cannon

Time travel is possible. It can be achieved. However, it does not happen with time machines that are so popular in Science Fiction. Instead it is accomplished with the marvelous use of the human mind. Jenna Catherine is a time traveler, and so am I. We are just using different methods to achieve the same results. She is visiting the future through her own mind, while I am gaining my information through other people's minds. I know time travel is possible, because I have done it, and reported about it in my books. For almost twenty years I have been a hypnotherapist. But I do not practice the "normal" type of hypnosis, such as is used for help with habits, and pain control. My type of hypnosis focuses on past-life regression and past-life therapy. This is where you take the subject into other lifetimes to discover the answers to problems in this lifetime. This, of course, brings up the belief in reincarnation and that our other lives influence our present life. During my years of therapy I discovered a doorway through time, which I call a "time tunnel". This time tunnel allows passage not only to the past, but to the future, as though time does not exist. Our concept of time is no barrier. While in trance the person literally becomes another personality and relives whatever period of history they find themselves in. I am the guide to take them through the experience. Thus I consider myself the reporter, the investigator, the researcher and the accumulator of evidence.

While working in this fascinating field I had the strangest adventure of all when I was contacted by the "living" Nostradamus, and given the assignment of translating and interpreting (with his invaluable help) all of the known quatrains, or prophecies. (There are almost 1000 of them, and they resulted in the three volume set, "Conversations With Nostradamus, Volumes I, II, and III.) Thus, as Jenna Catherine has done, I have explored the future. Many people have said they do not like to read Nostradamus' predictions, because they are so filled with doom and gloom. But Nostradamus said he was giving me the "worst possible" scenario. He said, "If I tell you the most horrible things man can do to himself, will you do something to stop it?"

He said the future is not one unchangeable scenario set in concrete. He saw it as many probabilities and possibilities branching off in many directions. These possibilities were influenced by the actions of mankind, actions that would decide which path we would go down. Our own actions would decide which future world would become our reality.

I have also done the same type of time travel when, instead of working with individual subjects, I have regressed or progressed whole roomfuls of people as a group. Upon awakening they reported what they saw in the future worlds they visited. There were many scenarios from the worst to the best, and all varying degrees in-between. I have performed this experiment all over the world, and many people have seen similar futures, which makes me believe these are becoming the most probable realities.

Jenna Catherine reveals an idyllic, Utopian future world of peace and love. Could such a perfect world exist on the timelines? Nostradamus said it is indeed possible, if mankind wants to create this type of world. He said we first had to get through the Time of Troubles, the decade of the 1990s. Then after the turn of the century we would enter the 1000 years of peace. He saw in that future time that people would learn how to raise their consciousness en mass to a higher level. They would be functioning from and utilizing their psychic abilities to a remarkable degree. Their world would hold no bounds. But how do we assure that this is the future world we create? Nostradamus said that people underestimate the power of their minds. You have created everything that is within your life. You may not want to admit that, because much in our lives is far from ideal. But once you realize that you do create your own reality, then you can just as easily uncreate the unpleasant things in your life. If you create your life, then you create the future you will live in. He said if you realize that your mind can create a world of peace and harmony, then all you have to do is focus and concentrate on creating that reality. He also said that if the power of one person's mind is that powerful, imagine the power of group mind. Our energy is so scattered, but once we learn to focus it the power of group concentration is tremendous. This is because the power is not only multiplied, it is squared, and this power can truly create miracles.

Jenna Catherine's positive future world is on the time lines, because she has seen it. First comes the vision, the dream, before the creation. She has given us the blueprint. Now that we know it exists in time, we can strive for it and attain it. Then that perfect world will become our reality.

—Dolores Cannon

Prologue

Hello, my name is Jenna. Since we're going to be communicating tele-pathically, call me whatever you want...or don't call me anything. It doesn't matter. Just feel my essence, as I will yours, and we will get to know one another. That's the way it works with telepathy. I know you are reading these words right now, but I encourage you to feel the ideas behind them—the whole ideas, not just the words which are like labels. The labels are just little thingamajigs that confine energy. You probably learned that to have effective communication you must have a common reference...well, that's what these words are...but I encourage you to transcend them. Just kind of bounce off them. Then together, along with Paul & Rebecca, the other two "characters" of this book, you and I will pool our energies so that you will increase your awareness. That is one goal of this book, to illustrate to you that the best way to know more, or tap in to your unconscious, possibly even universal intelligence, is to actually *add* others' ideas to your arsenal, rather your mind. If you stay open to the possibilities of all of the proposed ideas in this book—not *deciding* what is true or untrue based on something you know from the past—you will be amazed at what takes place in your mind. You will tap into your own wisdom, having considered mine. Mine will trigger yours! Also, you will do some time traveling yourself, most likely to the future since it is the subject of this book, and you will actually converse with it—your future.

This is quite different from how we relate to the future now. Right now most of us think of the future as fearful, hardly "talking" to it, or interacting with it, and are usually preparing ourselves in some way to protect our-selves from it. This is because we haven't learned to allow things to just be, instead having to know exactly if something is true or not. This is what keeps the future out of our minds in the first place—our compulsion to define. When we do that, we don't allow our own energy to flow. If you realized what you do to yourself when you decide something is untrue, you would never do it again. You close down your heart, you close down your mind, and you isolate yourself from life. You don't interact with much of anything—except maybe your false beliefs—and you miss your whole thrust in life—your spirit...so please, consider putting what you intuit into a new category, a "maybe-true" category...do this with all ideas. If you consider them possible...as opposed to untrue, you've taken a giant step toward expanding your own awareness. After all, when you do that, you are saying *you* are possible, possible of doing anything.

When you allow something to be, even an idea, without judgment (true or untrue), there is a natural conversation that occurs between you and that idea...there is an energy exchange. You can know about the idea itself, i.e., the future, or a society like the one you'll read about here in this book, in the year 2020. When two beings surrender to each other (or anything surrenders to anything), there is an energy exchange. Each entrains with the other, and there is resonance. Telepathy happens, as it is a natural product of resonance. At this point much enters the conscious mind. With people, we know a lot about each other. Into our minds pops the essence of the other, and we conceptualize it using ideas. Some refer to this as direct experience. Humans don't do this very well right now because of our unresolved emotional issues (we don't trust for openers), which keep us from truly surrendering not only to other people but to everything in our environments, including our own thoughts. As a result, our thoughts dominate us, leaving us more aware of our thoughts than what they're about. Now that's a little odd, don't you think? A barrier of definition separating us from what's real? If all of us would surrender to what's in our minds—our thoughts, allowing them to move, rather than controlling and dominating us—the whole world would change, starting with enormous changes in perception. We would not be so locked into what we have learned. The single biggest act, in my opinion, that keeps us in an unaware state, is our propensity to decide whether something is true or not, before it happens, always referencing it to the past, rather than allowing truth to emerge in the actual experience. This is what I mean by not allowing our thoughts to dominate us. It may be that if we allow a certain vagueness to enter our minds, our deeper truths would clear up in a hurry.

Using the future as a Frame of Reference

Most of us use the past as our sole reference. It would never occur to people to use their future experiences. Hopefully, this book will open the door to that possibility, using what you know about yourself in the future to affect you now. You do have a future, after all, and it is not so terrifying that your primary thoughts about it need be, "Will I have enough money," "Will I be healthy," and/or "Will I be alone?" My suggestion is that you relate to the future itself, as an idea, not your thoughts about it, which paralyze you and keep you from it. The hard part is imagining it in the first place because we are so used to putting what we know into space and we don't really know where our futures will be. So we stop thinking right there. The future doesn't have the kind of form that we are used to in terms of what we know. It hasn't even physically manifested yet, but there is a subtle form there, the idea of it, vague as it may seem to you. Consider the possibility that you can take that vagueness and clear it up, much as you can with a telephoto lens. The time has come to embrace the future, using it as inspiration and a guide.

How do you know what you know?

I'll bet you think it out, analyze, categorize, reason, selectively remember, bring into your mind what makes you feel good about yourself, incorporate what you were taught…oh, there's all sorts of things we do to know, to create "truth," and it happens so fast, convincing us it is truth. You bet it's truth, just like we want it. Well, there are other ways of knowing, and the future is a big part of it. When you can grasp yourself as a future being—feeling emotionally safe there, the future becomes apparent to you! Let me explain.

You have some experiences in the future. How do you do that? You imagine yourself there. Get over your bias about your imagination, as if you are just making it up. There is a tremendous bias in our society about making things up, as if truth were clear cut. It isn't. Truth is a process. It is not something you memorize but something you allow, something that leads you! As soon as you make something up, you allow a vagueness to enter your mind. There is confusion because you don't know if it is true, and you feel compelled to know, before going on. That is the old way of processing information. You don't have to ever decide truth. Allow something external to affect you, such as an idea, mix with it, and allow truth to emerge on its own in the moment. This book is about a new way of relating to ideas, not defining them, which will allow more into your conscious mind. It is a book about being visionary, living your potential, instead of always looking backwards, which is what you do now to have "meaning." But before you can feel crystal-clear information—with all of your cells tingling, the way people know truth in 2020—you may have to allow other information into your mind, information that leaves you fumbling and filled with self-doubt. That is the hard part, not knowing for sure about truth, or who you are. Our thoughts keep us from knowing who we are, our true feelings and the doubts we have about ourselves...not exactly where most people spend their time. But you will have to go into your self-doubt to get into your future. It is not so hard, really.

Introducing Paul

Believe me, I had much doubt about myself when I began communicating telepathically for the first time. About ten years ago in 1987, I wanted to write a new age investment book. I wrote one all right, but it didn't turn out to be an investment book at all. I discovered Paul, a spirit guide, who turned out to be far more interesting than amassing investment tips from the other side. Before I knew it, he was giving me assignments on how to fine tune my telepathy and instructing me how to time travel! He would send me messages like this: Okay, I want you to think of something, then describe to me everything you felt before, during and after that thought. I'd send back, what do you mean before I was aware of the thought?! And then we'd take off from there, working on these assignments together. Other examples: "See how long you can maintain the feeling of love, then let's talk about it. Compare the energy of two ideas, starting with the weight of the ideas." The weight?...I'd reply dumbfoundedly. But I did the assignments designed to expand my awareness, over a period of years, finding the whole concept irresistible, learning from a loving guide who was patient and so knowledgeable. He was also remarkably funny, as evidenced by our very first communication. One day I was thinking to myself that I had to go to the bathroom, and his reply was a concise, "Well, by all means then, go." I was hooked right then in spite of my doubt about communicating telepathically, which came up from time to time. I had the "Is this true?" disease myself for a while, wondering how much of this was my "imagination." But I allowed myself to be affected by something external—Paul—instead of just aligning with my critical mind, which helped me open up and understand the process too. Regarding time travel, through a series of exercises Paul taught me how to expand my mind to such an extent that somewhere deep within me came impressions as vivid or more vivid than anything I had ever experienced before. I became fascinated with this, learning a great deal about the decade of the 1990s and also about some of the early years of the twenty-first century. But the 1990s were not very inspiring— fairly bleak, actually—and I longed for something more uplifting.

The idea of 2020

About this time, my attorney was on a committee that was studying the legal system in Colorado in 2020. He and his committee were trying to project into the future to prepare themselves. I offered to time travel there to find out what was going on. I welcomed this chance to get away from the dismal world conditions of the late 1990s. But I had never before traveled so far ahead. I was shocked when I saw what society was like in 2020. It was filled with joyous, loving people throughout the world—all living together in fabulous harmony! This was quite a contrast to the emotionally depressed, "lost" people of the 1990s. I decided to investigate further. If I could sense what was going on in the legal system in 2020, why not take another look at another segment of society? So I took another look, this time at mental health in 2020. Again, people were flowing tremendously—vastly more attuned with their thoughts and feelings than today—and I couldn't believe the kinds of things that were offered in the field of mental health. Extremely innovative and progressive. Hmmmm...I became more curious. Next it was on to humor and entertainment in 2020. Again, good news. By this time, I began to realize what we were in store for, in 2020—and I was excited about it. In addition, I looked at communication and the media, business and economics, learning and education, as well as a typical day in 2020. In short, although I was initially skeptical that so much change could possibly have occurred in such a short period of time—about 27 years—I ended up sensing an entire society, by being there, and so I wrote about it, the subject of this book. By being there, or time travel, I am talking about knowing information from afar, across space and time, without physical means of gathering it, such as a telephone, television, radio, computer or using one's mind to do it. I am not talking about physically being in the future, rather bringing the past AND the future (that's the new part) into the now with one's mind. There is an absolute sensation of being there when this is done. It is no longer an impression of it but much more of a sensation of it, with the future literally becoming now. If we allow our environment to sparkle, it will. This is not the way most people today sense their environment, as sparkling, but it is the way they perceive it in the future. Everything around them glistens. Time travel is common in the society of 2020, about which you'll read. And this is what I did to gather information for the book. Incidentally, I threw out the entire chapter on the legal system when I realized later there wasn't any, one of the hazards, I guess of the future. Sometimes things happen so fast that by the time you've sensed something, it has already evolved into something else—in this case disappeared.

Enter Rebecca

Meanwhile, about the time I was checking out the legal system in 2020 for my attorney, I had a most unusual experience. A "human" contacted me telepathically. I had always wanted to interview some of these people I saw in the future but hadn't done it yet. Previously I would just take a trip, observe the people and the conditions, then record the data at my computer. However, one day I had my dear friend and collaborator over (she wanted to hear what these people were going to say), so we turned on the tape recorder so that I would interview whoever popped into my mind. I didn't expect to contact a real person—alive now, not just some elusive being trekking around the cosmos! Prior to this, I just figured I would talk to whoever was there in the future; it was as simple as that, but it was from a removed perspective.

On this particular day in October of 1991, when I turned on the recorder, there was a man there in my awareness, a man named Todd Martin, who was a farmer and who was in his fields at a futuristic time in Sacramento, California, but who didn't want to talk to me. I was able to read him perfectly, knowing a great deal about him, but he didn't seem very interested in opening up to me at all. I thought to myself, I need someone who wants to talk to *me*, and that's when it happened. Just at that moment I sensed a woman in my mind. I asked her where she was and she told me at a conference in Northern Yugoslavia, on the Adriatic. But there was something odd about it. I was very confused and turned the recorder off. "What's wrong?" my friend said. Well, there's all this emotion coming through, I told her. So? my friend continued. Well, spirit guides don't have so much emotion, I said, primarily emanating love—I don't know how to deal with it; I'm used to more flow, not this tighter energy. I had all my questions in hand in case anyone came into my awareness, to ask about conditions in the world, lifestyle, and so forth, but I was totally unprepared for someone wanting something from *me*, which is what I could feel. She wants to thank me for something, I told my friend. Well, what does she want to thank you for, my friend continued. I don't know, I said, amazed. Well, ask her, my friend demanded. Her exact words were a shock to me: "I want to thank you for the interview I did with you in Paris in 1995." "What?" I responded telepathically, realizing our conversation was taking place in 1991. Talk about confusing. I didn't know what to make of it. The lady continued: "I interviewed you in Paris for a small French newspaper about your ideas—when you gave a speech—and because of them, my career has really blossomed; and I just wanted to thank you for it." At this point I didn't know whether to say what career?…what speech?…or just turn off the recorder. I also had the impression she wanted to keep talking, which totally amazed me.

This encounter was also a big turning point for me. Previous to this, I had understood on an intellectual level what operating outside of time was all about, but now I was emotionally involved—outside of time. She told me about what I spoke of—a new method of hearing, a classic definition of love, for which I was known, she said, and the dynamics of sound in relation to time travel—all of which totally took me by surprise. We have been carrying on conversations ever since, this woman and I. I have her name, Rebecca Schoenwald. I know a great deal about her—and also a great deal about our individual futures, both of which are in the field of communications—and largely in Europe. This woman is, yes, alive today, and living in Austria; she is a woman in her early fifties, about my age, married to a husband who is "heavy set, with a black beard." And she too can time travel; it is why we have been able to share these perceptions of later years, which is what we've been doing. She has told me she is a therapist in the late 1990s, also of her innovative work in psychotherapy, a fascinating subject in itself. I am saying she functions multidimensionally—alive in 1997 but aware of other dimensions of time, just as I am. Rebecca also has been instructing me in the fine points of telepathy, emotional expression, and perception, areas in which we are highly skilled by the end of the millennium, and also at which time we are helping others in these regards. That is why we are communicating now, she reminds me frequently, to learn all these things for later. She is, however, vastly more aware than I, with detail upon detail of what we are doing together in the future. I know she is right—I can feel it in my gut—but I do not have the kind of awareness she has about our intertwined lives. It's been fascinating, to say the least.

The technicalities are amazing when she sends me her messages telepathically. Rebecca has had me running to my science dictionary (actually I went out and bought one) in order to understand her. I couldn't believe I was able to pull into my mind something I seemingly knew nothing about. Granted, I had been learning from Paul about the nature of ideas but was flabbergasted by some of her messages. Witness this one, received in 1991, telling me about herself: "I am most intrigued with the role of velocity as it affects ideas. This is similar to you but its thrust is more from the direction of mechanical energy whereas your ideas fluctuate more in accordance with volume." "I beg your pardon?" There I was again with my usual response. I knew I was in the process of learning that telepathic information was very precise, but this was ridiculous, not having ever studied physics. I hadn't a clue what that meant. She also kept asking me how I simplified things so quickly, telling me she wanted to know more about that process. I am still not clear on that, although we have had many conversations about it. What is clear to me is that she sincerely wants to learn much from me. It's a little different from Paul who is more into teaching love, whereas she and I seem to be studying very specifically perception and communication. Though loving, our relationship is more businesslike. Paul has encouraged this relationship, telling me I have much to learn since we can compare our human experiences which include emotions, something she knows more about than he does, he says.

In short, both she and Paul have pushed me to my limits, with their assignments (oh, yes, I've gotten them from her too) and their insistence and persistence in linking up with me. It's been both weird to learn like this, telepathically, and amazing—using our *futures*; whoever heard of that? It seems so strange, all this information—for *later*—preparing ourselves now for when we as people will be, among other things, more telepathic. This is quite obvious to me, both from my interactions with them, as well as my own experiences in the future. Rebecca and I are preparing skills now that actually exist in the future. If you truly get that, you don't even have to read this book, but it is not a concept easily grasped unless, of course, you are operating from tremendous knowledge about your own unconscious intent, which also could be another way of "defining" the future.

The Path

The problem is, to quote a friend of mine, How do we bridge the gap between here and there? How do we create what I have experienced in the future, this loving society of 2020? That was when I decided somebody had to work on carving a path. I knew it started with perception. But what is it we have to learn or do? I began to mull it over. Why not ask Paul and Rebecca for their advice? They were, after all, extremely knowledgeable. Paul could give very broad-based advice, as a spirit guide, and Rebecca could give very human-experience-based advice. They accepted my invitation with enthusiasm. It is in this context, then, that Paul and Rebecca are in this book, as consultants, for forming a more loving world.

After visiting 2020 in the beginning of each chapter, I then converse telepathically with Paul and Rebecca, asking them how to physically manifest this loving society that I have witnessed. We speak of 2020 as if it has already happened, as I have seen it—using it as truth, or a given—then work backwards, sorting out what it will take to build this society. This is not opposite of what we do today, it is in addition to what we do today. We've added the future to our data bank. All three of us are somehow able to tap in to both the past and future at will, much the way people can by 2020. But then this is the way it is with telepathy—time disappears. In other words, the present moment has expanded to include the past and future.

Please come along with me then, and I will share with you what I have learned both about 2020, and the process itself. If you wish, you can attempt to use my techniques. Or you can just read…and enjoy. You do not have to do anything but immerse yourself in your own experiences. For those wanting to know about my actual techniques for transcending time, please read the next section. For those wanting more on telepathy, there is a guide at the back of the book titled, "Telepathy: Communication of the Future."

My method of time travel and remote viewing

What did I do to bring this futuristic material into my mind? I was not in a trance but in a deeply alert state. I put the information into the computer while doing it so I guess that tells you something about the process, for me. I specifically directed my consciousness to go "there" (2020), and then I "read" the information which came in the form of light, a very fast moving subtle energy, sensing it with my chest area, largely, right in front of my thymus…outside of my body. As soon as I sensed the movement, about six inches in front of myself, in my aura, I knew what it meant, or what was happening in society in 2020. I just allowed information to pop into my mind after entraining with the light, or merging with it. I did not ask myself if it were true but allowed it to be. And the information itself did not all come at once, like a movie…but bit by bit. It took several years to ascertain this information, then after that, I surmised what society was like as a whole, categorizing it into areas of society I thought were important. The bulk of the book was written in 1993 and 1994. And when I speak of this society of 2020, I speak of generalities everywhere, aspects of life applicable to all people in varying degrees in all places, even to those who will have passed over by then. Of course all areas are not exactly the same. Some are less "aware." (See Reference Libraries of 2020 in back for specific world conditions)

When I first learned to go beyond time and space, I initiated the process of time travel with my senses, sensing textures, smelling aromas, tasting "thoughts" in my mouth. Paul taught me not to rely on my eyes, the way we perceive today, explaining that envisioning something in our minds at the expense of other senses keeps us from feeling subtle energy—or accessing those deeper ideas in the first place. But I do not go through this routine anymore; I tap in to a line of energy almost instantly. I believe that line of energy is a conduit from the unconscious to conscious mind. So how then is this different from plain old intuition? It comes with more details. And there is a definite sense of tapping into something that is already there. Then it is just feeling what's there. So in this initial sense one does not have to create the future but discover it—the ideas that are waiting to be unraveled, or energized by us, the thinkers. This is all done by just feeling energy, or the movement of it, contrasted to today's method of thinking things through to know truth. I also learned from Paul how to differentiate belief-based energy which is jerky and tight from my own natural flow, which is harmonious, rhythmic, and evenly paced. I am talking about using my body more instead of my head to know truth.

Some people refer to time travel as mind travel. There are also some scientists who refer to time travel as remote viewing, SRV (Scientific Remote Viewing), with the latter being the more evolved form of the former, which was a system of spying developed in the 1970s by our military for data-gathering purposes. The difference between the scientific community and me is both small and great. On the one hand, we are both talking about using intuition and direct knowing, gathering information with the unconscious without the conscious mind *deciding* its meaning by analyzing, intellectualizing, reasoning…The scientific remote viewers use another mind (another person) to then decode, interpret, and summarize the data that has been gathered, at which point truth is ascertained, some sort of alleged objectivity. I don't, I use my own mind for that, using feel, as they do in the future—the feeling of energy to determine "truth." Of course there is no such thing as one truth for all as we are all inputting our perceptions with our own slant. SRV emphasizes specific instruction, a strict set of protocols, one system for all as the only way to remote view, or gather information. I do not think there is one method for all, certainly not mine (as evidenced by the future, where individualistic learning styles and methods are not only emphasized but preferred). In the future, people have their own principles, which emerge in the context of the moment, as opposed to principles of say, science, today, which are passed on from the past. When I learned from spirit guides (and there were others besides Paul), the instruction was tailored to me, and my strengths. Remote viewers suggest fitting into a system of perception, theirs. It is rigid and controlled. Compared to remote viewing, my method of knowing is infinitely quicker, more fluid and practical for everyday living, as it is all processed in one fell swoop (by the same person), then used in the moment. There is always the question of interpretation, but this is something that must be learned from within. Knowing truth will never come from another person, although others can be helpful in ascertaining our own truths. SRV has strict controls, as in one system—and hence itself is very controlled—the opposite of what I advocate, which is allowing energy to flow for accurate data gathering and interpretation. Again, the merits of "adapting" to one's unique approach are well documented in the future.

The importance of doubt

The more we tap in to "nonexistent ideas," Paul's term for new ideas, the more we encounter our own doubt. It is extremely important to accept doubt in the pursuit of truth, especially when dealing with the unusual, otherwise we are just smack dab in the middle of our belief systems, which orient themselves around the past. But it is difficult and confusing since it is not clear cut.

I have interpreted Rebecca to be who she is, based on what she has told me, even though we have not met in person including the predicted encounter in Paris in 1995. (I will never know whether this encounter would have ever happened. I did have a chance to go to Paris in 1995. I didn't go. Might she have been there? I cannot say. The way we interpret things now is to close down when an aspect of the whole idea is not true, chucking the whole idea. What we will do in the future will be to resort more to our own inner knowing, allowing the idea to evolve.) Besides what she has told me, I strongly believe she is human based on her more confined energy, which would indicate to me unresolved emotional issues, distinguishing her from guides. It could be, however, that my awareness will expand to include other possibilities for her. I could be tapping in to her unconscious rather than her conscious mind. I could be tapping in to someone else's unconscious. I could be tapping in to my own future self—my unconscious—but experiencing it as a separate being. I could be tapping in to the collective unconscious or to universal intelligence. I could be tapping in to combinations of the above. To break new grounds, however, it is mandatory that we learn first and foremost to trust ourselves, which includes our own perceptions, even when different from others and not as clearly defined as we are used to.

So let us go then collectively into the future, utilizing all of our experiences. When we do that as a group, we see the bigger picture better. We expand our minds. We work as a team. We allow those "nonexistent ideas" to guide us. This concept has been around a long, long time—perceiving more when working in a group. How do I know this? It's backed up in the future!

Warning

If you choose to relate only to my words about the future—or my description of it—you will not jump to the future at all (the old way of reading). However, if you feel the energy of the future itself as a pulsating, magnetizing, nurturing being, beckoning you, then you will have a much fuller and truer experience of the future. Think of it this way: You are a baby learning to walk. The future is your mother with her outstretched arms. Walk to her, feel her. It is not her words that compel you so. It is she, and so it is with the future. There is an undeniable energy above and beyond any description of it, and that is what I encourage you to relate to.

Scenario

Concepts Of Consciousness

We need to use the future as a frame of reference for what we know, realizing it as a valuable source for how we view ourselves which will affect how we perceive the world in the present moment. Instead of believing the future hasn't happened, realize that an important part of ourselves is "there," waiting to be experienced. When we know the future, we can then converse with it telepathically to grasp the details. Experiencing ourselves in the future—or knowing our potentials—is an important step toward developing our loving natures and expanding our overall awareness. It is also a significant factor in learning how to communicate telepathically, which is "the communication of the future."

Philosophy Of the Book

If you feel safe in the future—or have a vision of it—you will live more fully now.

Protagonist Of the Book

The idea of the future as something unto itself.

Characters of the Book

Jenna: a human being, the author, yes, me, whose *past* includes lifetimes in Greece, Africa and Tibet, the latter with Paul, whose *present* includes living in Colorado and Pennsylvania, as a writer, and whose *future* includes working with Rebecca teaching telepathy and new ways of perceiving, with subsequent lifetimes in Spain, China, and "Terreland," a yet-to-be named place.

Paul: my consultant, a spirit guide, with whom I have communicated telepathically since 1987, whose *past* includes lifetimes in Rome, Japan, and Great Britain where he learned financial expertise, whose *present* includes being a spiritual advisor to me, as well as "duties" on the other side, and whose *future* includes assisting with the "emergence of Jupiter," with a subsequent human lifetime in Virginia.

Rebecca: a human being, my consultant, with whom I have communicated telepathically since 1991, whose *past* includes lifetimes in Guadeloupe and London, whose *present* includes communicating with me, working in Austria in a government job, and whose *future* includes more work with me, and a new profession, therapist, with subsequent lives in South Africa, Georgia, and Wales.

You, the readers: whose *past* includes a variety of lifetimes, whose *present* is varied and viable, and whose *future* is gaining momentum.

Place

Wherever anyone is in the universe.

Time

Now, enhanced by the future.

Preparing Yourself for the Year 2020

• Using self-doubt to guide you • Meeting the new you • An expanded identity that includes the future • Not having to decide if something is true • Allowing flow in your mind • Discovering the tunnel • Allowing voices in your heads, and getting to know them • Not having to put anything in specific order • Using the future as a reference for knowing in addition to the past • Incorporating the energy of others • Dealing with the skepticism of others • Allowing your imagination to go wild • Relating to everything with a sense of movement • Discerning self-love

One of the most amazing things you will discover about yourself is you are not who you think you are. You are not in one place and one time. You probably think of yourself right now as here, one body—just as you are in the moment.

Try a new concept. Try this one. You are all of your past and all of your future. That makes up you "now." But since we are specifically talking about a time period of now until 2020, you must think of yourself as this entire time period...all of the yous in it. Sound simple? If you believe so, you're well on your way to 2020, this society of which we speak. It is not as easy as you think, though...you are that big? If you took yourself in 2016 and 2010, and 2003, and 2017, my gosh...think how big you would be. Then throw in what you did...or what you're *doing* each day of those years, along with all the other days of the years leading up to 2020...you would have so much movement within you. Zip, zip, zipping around, doing this and that.

When you know yourself as a culmination not only of your past but all of this time in your future, imagine how your self-concept would change. You are many things then—a whir of energy—not just as you know yourself now, pretty much in one time and place in space. Feel the movement in your chest, in your heart, and in your head when you sense yourself—the *new you*, who is vastly more aware. You have an expanded identity that includes the future!

You don't have to think of everything you've ever done in the future. Just sense yourself as one being, using your chest, as they do in the future, then remember that "form"—that subtle movement—and carry it around with you always at a feeling level. That's you, in a more refined, less familiar form. Can you feel how static-less you are, how your energy is expanding rather than contracting? This is a key to expanding your awareness—an entirely *new you*, one that is "bigger," more fluid, and more energized. Besides knowing yourself, it is what allows you to bring into your mind *what else* is going on in those years—with others and throughout the universe. To know your future then you must feel yourself as a being of tremendous potential—*who is already using it in your own future.* As soon as you accept that, discovering yourself there is the easy part.

Well, not quite so easy. Let me tell you what happened to me while time traveling to just this period we are talking about, the years before 2020. I met a family member before I met myself. Sound strange? Prior to writing this book I had learned how to time travel from my spirit guide Paul. I often took trips to the future to check things out.

One day I met Allen. I asked him who he was. He said, "Your grandson," and laughed as if I should recognize him, but I didn't. (I have no grandchildren, only college-aged sons, neither of whom is married nor is a father.) So I was talking to a being who hadn't even been conceived yet. Now this is the hard part (not that that was easy). I was to communicate in terms of how you will know yourself in the future—with an identity that covers many years. Outside of time.

Allen was many Allens, all lumped together. I was to relate to him from a deeper level, not personality to personality but essence to essence in order to share deeper truths. We were perfectly able to carry on a conversation with his telling me about myself at a particular time in the future, the details of which I was hearing for the first time. I was so curious that I kept asking him what it was I was doing and he was able to tell me! I bring this up because when you start acknowledging that you have voices in your head with whom you can communicate, which are not yours—and you will if you are open—you may meet someone you know before you meet yourself. You see? You will need to be coming from the *new you* concept in order to connect with someone like this. That's the way it works with telepathy. A deeper knowing necessitates a deeper identity.

I didn't need to know how old he was in order to know him. I didn't have to place him in space someplace as we do today, in order to know. I just had to feel his essence (his inherent movement) in order to "talk." In fact, if I had zeroed in to his age, at one time in his life, I would have only known him in that limited time frame. That's how it works. When you begin to communicate telepathically, you will tap in to not only beings but ideas that are far more compelling—and alive—than the ones we share today, with *the future* being one of those ideas. Yes, there are "people" out there who want to talk to you who are loving and helpful.

Many have reported experiences with spirit guides, angels, extraterrestrials. I'm saying in addition to those, our fellow human beings long for deeper connections. There has been research to show that we all are communicating unconsciously with our bodies with one another, but I don't mean with just body language. I mean there is a *conversation* going on that can be tapped in to…by just increasing our awareness. During the time prior to 2020 you will discover that this unconscious communication will become conscious. You will also discover a grander plan, that you are not alone—a delicious discovery. Friends you will make, like I have with Paul and Rebecca—which will be a real treat. And whomever you meet will have a treat too because they will get to know you. But best of all, you will be bathed in love because it is ever-present during telepathy.

On a practical level you'll learn about love during this time period. In compiling my details about 2020, a society of love, I utilized my grandson Allen's energy, or information, along with that of his friends. You'll learn how love affects perception, when you love all ideas, for example—what it does for you. When I was unclear about certain details pertaining to this society, only having surmised the bigger, more easily attainable ideas, I would ask Allen what he had learned about something in school, whatever interested me. He would then tell me, from a perspective of many years, including his future, integrated very quickly—a simple idea or two.

Next I would say, what did your friends learn? And then I would repeat this question, asking about others' perspectives very quickly in order to expand my *own* awareness. With telepathy, it can be done very quickly. As an example, Allen and his friends would tell me what they learned about balance. Their combined viewpoints seemed to trigger in me more of my own wisdom, beyond what they told me. Each time I would hear another

3

viewpoint, and accept it—actually embracing it—it would enhance my own ability to see the bigger picture in 2020, and you will do this too about whatever you choose. You will learn to assimilate very quickly the ideas of others, putting them into a big pot—which will elevate you towards a more sophisticated perception…yes, getting glimpses of the Divine. What you will need to know will pop right into your mind very quickly if you do not resist. But you will first need to consider others' ideas as important as yours. Hmm…this may take a few years. Others' ideas as important as yours? It's the only way flow can occur in the mind. As you allow movement in your mind, you release an enormous amount of energy, which has been stuck due to your unresolved emotional issues. But you do not have to have all your emotional issues resolved to be telepathic or even grasp the concept of combining energies with others. I merely point out the merits of relating to ideas in new ways and the benefits ahead for you.

Much will happen to you during this time from now until 2020. Learning to truly love yourself will come about gradually as you eliminate many thoughts. An example would be not having to put anything into any specific order. Can you imagine the amount of free time you'll have just relinquishing those kinds of thoughts? You'll be able to focus on new things, more important things, like love. This will be because of your *new you* identity, which will also assist you in resolving your "emotional stuff." You'll feel more capable. With more flow in your mind, you will become much more aware of your own self-doubt but in a new way, using it to propel you and energize you, rather than reason for reprimand. Like a nurturing mother, self-doubt will accompany you as you explore the unknown.

Not having to decide truth will be the initial step for allowing your imagination to fly, which will also energize you. It will thrust you into greater knowing, including knowing yourself more in the moment instead of the way we do today which is to look for evidence of what we already believe about ourselves, which keeps us trapped in rigid identities. Then we get caught up in obsessively assessing as to how we're doing in these identities—being ourselves—which is not even an accurate reflection of who we are in the first place. When you realize the merits of being in the moment—like feelings of ecstasy—you will wonder why you ever insisted on being who you were in the past—and only that person, allowing yourself so little change. And finally, you will piece together that joy and self-love are synonymous. But it will not all come at once.

You will make amazing discoveries like discovering *the* tunnel. I don't want to give it all away…there's something to be said for the thrill of discovery…but you will come to know how to crawl inside of a light beam, and then ride it. This will come about because of the need to process information more quickly…yes, faster than a computer, but you will learn how to do it. You will demand it of yourself as you crave being yourself more. The future will *pull* you right into this craving. It will draw you right into your very own desire for yourself. You'll jump right into your own lap, hugging yourself. And you will fight this loving yourself, and you will love it…and you will fight it and you will love it.   But you will do it, with increasing fervor, eventually learning it.

You will learn to trust what you feel and be more willing to express yourself in spite of the skepticism of others, which will be plentiful. You will recognize that skepticism from others is their fear, not criticism of you.   And you will accept this, allowing it to transform into love—in your mind—for you are in the gradual process of learning that you must relate to everything with a sense of movement. *You are finally getting it. You must allow everything to move. You cannot control anything, beginning with your own thoughts.* You start to perceive the world as jiggling a lot, and you relinquish your absolute need to stabilize it in order to understand. It doesn't make you dizzy. It makes you delirious.

One day it occurs to you that people care about you, people you don't even know…you can feel it. Then it occurs to you that you care about them. You can feel that too. Then it reoccurs. Wow, you think. Then it begins to snowball. Love starts to infiltrate every cell of yours and you don't do anything to stop it. Why should you? You are well on your way now.

PAUL

Jenna: Hello, Paul. Do you have any advice for the readers upon entering the year 2020?

Paul: Notice that you are looking forward to getting there, that you can actually feel a magnetic pull as you anticipate a society that is loving, that there is something profoundly missing in you and the society in which you live. Consider the possibility that you long for a truer connection to yourself. You will feel a truer connection to yourself if you try to feel me, not my words but me. Many of you have never spoken to a spirit guide before. So be it, now you have.

5

Jenna: Paul, that was a little abrupt, don't you think? I was just telling them in the prologue how loving you are. Are you not up for this?

Paul: I take this assignment with dead seriousness, speaking of the dead. Advice for 2020? Believe it is you there. Don't worry about the society itself, feel the truth of yourself. That's where I would start.

Jenna: How would they do that, feel the truth of themselves?

Paul: Okay, most will go in assessing the truth of the society, whether you told them to or not. I am suggesting they take a truer form of themselves in "there" in the first place. I'll say it directly to them: When you start to read, notice how you feel. Notice your emotional response. The less you think, the better off you'll be. If you want to experience the glistening nature of 2020, more of a sense of being there, versus reading about it, I suggest you allow the ideas to take you. You are not in charge of them. Let them pull you. Instead of looking at them and thinking, "Hmmm, who are you?"... do your best to feel them attempt to dance with you. Let them seduce you! If you just read, it'll seem flat to you—the whole society, yourself, the words, everything. The ideas won't come out and play and neither will you. You'll just sit there, thinking. I'm saying knowing is not enough.

Jenna: Awareness is just the first step.

Paul: Look, it's imperative that each one of the readers jump inside of those ideas and do a serious rumba with them. No glancing at the words without feeling the heart of them—what's behind them, the bigger meaning. Meet those ideas head to head, like a do-si-do, and come away stronger for it.

Jenna: I see.

Paul: Going into the year 2020 is more like getting to know yourself than a whole new society, anyway.

Jenna: Could you explain that to the reader? Also, how does your advice relate to love?

Paul: How you relate to this society, including the ideas, is how you relate to yourself. Notice if you embrace this wonderful society with love— how you relate to it in other words—if it makes you happy to be there. Take a moment to realize that this emotional response is your own response to yourself. I suggest you remember that feeling because that feeling is love. When you read and feel happy, know that it is you that you love, not so much this society. It is easy to forget that sometimes.

Jenna: Anything else to take note of?

Paul: What do you notice that is different about yourself? Do you feel differently from how you feel in your life now? In the future do you feel your potential more than now? What is it that you are feeling there, and contrast that to now. Does it scare you, excite you? Entering into a different time zone is like entering into a different zone of yourself. Plant your feet and reintroduce yourself to yourself. I think you've been there before.

Jenna: What do you mean by that?

Paul: I am just talking about the sense of familiarity. There will be an absolute sense of familiarity when reading about how wonderful things can be, and I throw this out...what is this all about? I also throw this out. When dancing with those ideas, don't hold them too tightly, and don't insist on leading all the time...or being led all the time without reciprocating. What do you think love is? It is a dashing dance of colorful scarves swirling around all over the place, a give and take, an intermingling, a swishing in and out, a true mixing, a dramatic introduction of yourself to yourself, and others! And I throw one more thing out: Allow yourself to be known to this society. It is also looking at *you*. Few of you know this, as you are so wrapped up in what you think about something else, outside of yourself. But the truth is you will get your first dose of exposing yourself to others...well, maybe not your first, but it will be different for you if you allow it. But do not be surprised if you feel extremely open, as if people can "read" you— or know what you are thinking or feeling— your author, Rebecca, me, the people of 2020. I just warn you. It may make you feel uneasy. On the other hand, it may be a luscious kind of feeling. If you do not feel more in touch with your emotions than usual, well...I guess that is your choice, but notice you are being a wallflower.

Jenna: I know you mean that with love.

Paul: Of course. I am encouraging love. I am encouraging participation. Okay, if you just want to read and feel like a flat balloon with all the air gone...

Jenna: Paul.

Paul: *"Ve vant to get to know you!"*

Jenna: Yes, yes, thank you so much, my newly hired consultant. Ve vant to get to know you too.

Paul: Goodie. Let us proceed.

Jenna: Yes.

REBECCA

Jenna: Rebecca, do you have any advice about entering 2020?

Rebecca: Know that you are welcomed there. Many people today do not realize that when they go someplace new, they have enormous anxieties about it, even a mind place. Recognize that this is entirely your own doing. There is no one in this society who dislikes you. What you carry in is in you, not it.

Most are wondering...well, are there real people there? I'd like to know what people think about that, actually. Are there real people in 2020? Perhaps at sometime I will get some telepathic information from people about that. Are there real people or only real in the mind?

My advice...notice your response to the society because if you do not feel welcomed, it is something within you. There is something you expect when you go someplace new, in the real physical world or here. What is it you expect? Do you expect to feel loved and welcomed? I am talking about subtle feelings you may not be aware of, beneath your intellectual veneer. Some more things to consider: Where are you in relation to this society? Are you there? Are you definitely not there? Are there some aspects of the society that you find especially familiar? Or repugnant?

Does anyone feel in any way this society of 2020 is a past life of yours? I say that because if it feels familiar, you might conclude you've lived "there" before. I would like to offer another possibility. It feels familiar but you haven't been there before. It is a new kind of familiarity, one that is vaguely familiar but familiar. So do not rule out a new kind of experience, remembering the future, even if you do not have vivid impressions of having been there before yourself. Some people might even experience that they are looking back in time at 2020, from even a later date. I hope this hasn't been too much for openers. We do like to play in this book.

Jenna: Thanks, Rebecca. That was really interesting. Anything else?

Rebecca: See if you recognize anybody in this society, between the words, so to speak…between the words of description. Someone you know. Ah, yes, read slowly and feel. There is nothing unusual about getting to know yourself. It's about time for all of us. I look forward to hearing from you telepathically, and I am speaking to you, the readers.

Jenna: Me, too. Please communicate with me at any time telepathically, anyone! Just try it intuitively, then *listen*. You may be surprised at what happens.

Rebecca: Boy, is this going to be fun.

Jenna: We're on our way.

Rebecca: With open hearts.

Author's comments

My advice upon entering 2020 is to have fun, not to worry about anything, and to trust yourself. Your experiences are unequivocally real—whether you just "read," as you are used to, or whether you ride those ideas like bucking broncos. I encourage the latter, allowing the ideas to lead the way. However, if you prefer to stand back a bit, and just read the old-fashioned way, "thinking" about the words, that is okay, too. If you want to practice being "futuristic," by all means burrow right through my words and feel with your chest…sense what it is I am trying to say. You have the innate ability to do this, apart from my use of language. Allow your imagination to go wild, yes, again, a technique of the future! Whatever way you choose, come along, please—everyone is welcomed—I want to share my experience with you!

Mental Health in 2020

•Tremendous knowledge about love •Absence of laws •High degree of intuition •Awareness that goes beyond self, including knowing others' thoughts and feelings •Timelessness •Understanding of the role of emotions in physical and mental health •Growth, idea of the day •A craving for experiences •Mindcare clinics •Understanding of one's own impact on society •Extensive knowledge about learning and fear •Desire to contribute to the whole

Welcome to year 2020, a "time" when human beings have finally learned how to open their hearts. It is awesome, to witness how this simple act has affected life. Look around, people are nicer, happier, funnier, more giving, more intuitive, more sexual, less selfish, less threatened, less afraid, and better at giving and receiving love than today, resulting in more suitable friends, lovers and spouses. Since awareness has increased mucho—to the degree of actually taking on others' viewpoints—people are also vastly more forgiving, compassionate, and empathetic than today. This has all come about due to new ways of perceiving. Maybe you are one of these people. Look around, do you recognize anyone here? Although all are growing at different rates and are in different places in terms of awareness, everyone reaches out to others on a regular basis, not judging one another, grasping the idea that people's growth rates and needs are all very different. More aware of thoughts and feelings—both theirs and others'—people are more open, which means they are more accepting of everything and everyone. Because of this, the entire human experience has literally expanded into the cosmos, magnificently, like a flower opening…thrilling people. With joy a given, people have combined their hearts at last into one collected vision— which they treasure. But this doesn't mean they have no need for mental health care, for they do. By 2020, however, it is known as mindcare.

Mental Health Care to Mindcare

By 2020 the whole area of mental health care has been revolutionized. Instead of treating people for problems, an idea that implies an enduring state or one that cannot be easily remedied, mindcare technicians assist people with growth, the "idea" of the day. Because of this, there is absolutely no stigma attached to going to mindcare clinics; rather, it is "in," much like health clubs of today.

Amazing things are offered at the mindcare clinics. Because of the tremendous knowledge in both physics and metaphysics, as well as the availability of extremely sophisticated technology, technicians are able to offer their clients the opportunity to actually see—on a screen of sorts—how their ideas and emotions affect society. This is done by measuring the client's energy field, or the electromagnetic field around the body. In addition to being told how much energy flow is in their auras, which is discernible by energy patterns, people can learn very specific things, such as how each idea of theirs impacts other people. Individual ideas and emotions, or combinations of them, can be "lifted" right out of a person's energy field and plugged into other pertinent societal data such as what is going on elsewhere, to illustrate what effect they are having on others as the client sits there at the clinic! This information is very valuable to people, as they want to know which ideas need "modification" and which ones are to be nurtured, so that they can be contributing members of society, the world, and the universe. The idea of the greater whole has long since replaced the idea of self as one of the more prominent ideas of the day; that is, people have equal regard for others as they do for themselves, and see all as working together in the same interdependent, interactive system. This eliminates the need for laws in society

By 2020, mindcare, like almost everything in society, is highly self-regulated. There are in fact no rules, regulations, laws, or guidelines in society by 2020. People decide themselves if they want to go to the clinics; they are not diagnosed and sent there based on somebody else's standards of what is healthy. In 2020 people do not tell others what to do, or what to be. That would be much like turning to your dog today and saying, "Now *here's* how I want you to be!" People go to the clinics because they want to go. And they make their decisions intuitively, based on "feel," which is very much the *modus operandi* in 2020. People are experts at the use and feel of energy—or flow, as they would call it—especially their own. This means that when they don't feel "right," they're likely to do something about it. Many go to mind-care clinics for this reason.

Not everybody needs the services of the mindcare clinics, however. Those whose inner knowing is especially well developed, and who have very high degrees of trust, are the least likely to go to the facilities. They just *know*, for example, what is in the best interests of all, including themselves. For those needing emotional reassurance, though, mindcare clinics are the place to go. Some just crave experiences, which is another highly valued idea of the day. People crave all kinds of experiences, including those that cause emotional pain. It's not that they're masochistic, but by 2020 pain is considered just another experience—with great inherent learning value. And of course people now have an expanded data base for learning—the future—so they are not so limited by their past. This experience, alone, sensing from a more evolved self, then bringing that experience into the moment, has totally taken the cap off of old ways of looking at things, making people not only more insightful but also aware of more in their environment. The "thrill" of the day is definitely learning, much as the pursuit of pleasure is predominant today. It's insatiable, this desire to learn, starting first with learning about themselves.

Amazing Technological Equipment

One of the most amazing pieces of equipment at the clinics is a machine that measures love. This is an apparatus that literally measures the presence of love. People are fascinated by it, aspiring, of course, to have a high degree of it within their own energy fields. In addition to the present, they can measure love in their "pasts" and their "futures," which is actually the case for all the measuring devices at the clinics. By this time people live in an atmosphere of timelessness, which simply means that the present is comprised of all time frames, not just the present, as would be the case today; that is, people are aware of their past and future as much as their present. So by 2020 then, not only is love highly understood and valued, it is also measurable.

Also available at mindcare clinics are "idea facilitators." These high tech devices assist people in forming ideas and understanding perception, through the use of sound, color, motion, light, taste, smell, and flowing water. Knowledge about ideas is extremely important as a way to both grasp and enhance intuition, which by 2020 is understood as inner knowing.

Classes in idea-forming are some of the best attended at mindcare clinics. By 2020 the processes for forming ideas are well understood—and taught! In fact, clients get a real kick out of seeing their own ideas form as they happen, again on a high-tech screen of sorts.

Classes in interpretation can also be taken. Although people are very adept at ascertaining information, they are not nearly so adept at interpreting it, being limited by their belief systems. There are classes to help with this. How to tell which old ideas are having undue influence on new material and how to balance what is in the mind are taught. In addition, there are many, many methods of learning taught because there are so many methods. People are encouraged to supplement their own preferred methods with the methods of others not only because it increases what's in their own conscious minds but also because it increases the chances of relating intimately with others.

Classes in relaxation are also offered, in which people study emotional flow by observing animals because they flow so beautifully, in a totally natural way. They just *are*. One is instructed to merely emulate the animals—and to do it by feel. Children are particularly good at grasping this, but they are also often the least needful of the classes because they have not learned to restrict their "flow."

Subtle Effects of Fear

Fear-detectors or devices to help people identify the ramifications of the fears they hold are also available at the clinics. Although people can almost always tell when they are afraid and often what they are afraid of, the detectors enable them to determine the likely effects of their fears on themselves and others. The detectors are very helpful in this regard. There's usually a line for these machines, as people come to understand the extensive, highly corrosive effects of fears. They also become aware that fear is the number one reason for closed awarenesses, a condition they want to avoid. Fear itself, however, is not nearly so prevalent as today.

Regarding emotional expression, people can come into the clinics and see where their "blocks" are. Clients can also see the flow of their emotions in their own physical bodies—or what is manifesting in the moment—if they choose, again through the use of technology. Charts are available to show the likely manifestation of physical disease from blocked emotional flow, although the word disease itself is no longer used. Fear-based words like disease have been allowed to die a natural death, the absence of which has influenced people's health in a positive way, both mentally and physically.

14

Expressing Emotion

By 2020 the whole area of emotional expression has changed so much that everything is experienced with more depth. People can actually feel others' feelings in *the same way they do*, not as removed observers. They also experience all emotions much more quickly and with much more harmony than now. Anger, for example, is spontaneous, rhythmic, and flowing. People light up! Some can see this. Rather than turning people off, for many this is an attraction. In the process of expressing anger, not only is insight experienced, but there is also a connection at the heart level for both the person expressing the emotion and those around him or her. This feels good to people. Anger, like all emotions, even the so-called negative ones of the nineties—jealousy, sadness, hate, and so forth—feel good to be around, and to express. As is the case today, people in 2020 like and need emotional flow within themselves and others. It's just that by 2020 people are more willing to be involved in such activity, which by this time includes a vastly wider range of emotions which are not only accepted but encouraged.

The relationship between mental and physical health is also well understood by 2020 and is the reason that physical health care is completely integrated into the mindcare clinics. By this time, though, there aren't many physical health "problems," just the ebb and flow of growth. Emphasis is on preventative measures or what is going on in the mind…and the mind itself, due to new spatial understandings, is known to be everywhere, not just limited to one's own energy field, but also includes others'. By 2020 everybody's thoughts and feelings, or the group mind, has the same kind of reverence that is reserved for individual minds today. Good mindcare then—in 2020, and to some degree in the years preceding—has allowed people to view and treat others as they would themselves.

PAUL

Jenna: Paul, this is not the way society is today. What will it take to create a loving society like this?

Paul: First of all, a lot of caring. Is that not why you are asking me questions, because you care?

Jenna: Absolutely, yes; it got me to thinking a lot about love. Is love really just intent?

Paul: Now that is an interesting way to perceive love, but I would have to agree with you totally, yes...if you meant that from out of love comes more love.

Jenna: Yes, that caring must precede any change, really.

Paul: What do you mean by that, exactly? I like that.

Jenna: I guess that it needs to be there; it's the energy for everything: thought, feelings, behavior...

Paul: Remember that because that is a big one.

Jenna: Paul, regarding the frames of mind of people in 2020, their mental health, actually, I have mentioned many prominent ideas: tremendous knowledge about love; a high degree of intuition; awareness that goes beyond self, including knowing others' thoughts and feelings; timelessness; understanding of the role of emotions in physical and mental health; absence of laws; idea of growth as a driving force; a craving for experiences, mindcare clinics, understanding of one's own impact on society; extensive knowledge about learning and fear; and a desire to contribute to the whole. What else can you tell us that will help carve the path to 2020? What will it take to "get there?"

Paul: Probably the first thing to keep in mind is that nothing you have mentioned is impossible. People will say it is impossible to accomplish all that by 2020, but nothing is impossible. Starting with the idea of the absence of laws, why do you think they exist now? Because people do not take the responsibility for themselves. Once they get this idea, laws will fall by the wayside, like layers of an onion. Also, the fact people care so much more about others and things outside of themselves, as you mentioned, gives them even more reason for the absence of laws. Not only do they feel more responsibility for themselves, but they also feel responsible *to* others. Now that's a big change from today.

Jenna: Speaking of a change from today, what about individual rights? Don't strong individuals make a strong society?

Paul: Ah, ha! You ought to be a lawyer! That was pretty good. But the truth is...you want to know how to get there. I am trying to think of one idea, one that will help you. Individual rights? What do individual rights do in your society? Isn't the intent to protect? Well, what are you protecting *from*? If you start out with the idea of enemy, I can

16

assure you, that is exactly what you will create. Do you see? So what you have to do is start out with a new idea. What is that idea? Well, that is for you to figure out, but for openers, maybe you should take a look at your idea of always having to protect yourself from enemies.

Jenna: Yes, often starting with seeing ourselves as enemies.

Paul: That observation will be paramount before laws are eliminated. How you view yourself is how you view others.

Jenna: Well, what *does* it take to feel responsibility for both one's self and others?

Paul: It takes learning that responsibility is not a dead weight but a ticket to freedom. Since humans are so control-oriented, it means taking the control from "out there" where you have no control, to "in there" or inside of you, where you have a great deal of control. Think of it this way: responsibility *is* control.

Jenna: What about this vast knowledge of love everyone seems to have? How do we learn that?

Paul: You learn it by experience, just as you learn everything else. Think of all the different ways people experience love; in some homes, unfortunately, a good whack in the face or on the behind means love. There will never be one way to experience love, but there are ways which promote the growth of others. That is the love that will need to be learned. When "love" doesn't promote growth, it is not love. "True love" promotes growth for everything and everybody everywhere.

Jenna: So once we experience love, we automatically start caring about others? How do we make this leap to be so caring about everything and everyone in addition to ourselves?

Paul: Well, first of all, at some level, you need to learn that what you feel has validity, even if it contradicts everything you have learned. This is tricky, because your society reinforces the prevailing ideas. It is not easy for a person to learn that what he feels is just as valid—or more nearly valid—than what society professes to be true. And certainly loving all things, and all beings everywhere, is *not* reinforced in your society. What is taught is *you* first. You must somehow learn that reaching out to others is in your best interest. Each person must learn this. Each person must have direct experience of growing because of loving what is outside of himself. How do you think people grow? Do you not think that love—or the connection with someone else or some

17

thing—is not growth? Your ideas of self-help are quite convoluted. Self-help has much more to do with others than self!

Jenna: Can you tell me what concepts people will have to grasp to eventually experience this timelessness?

Paul: As soon as people start *feeling* time, rather than thinking it, they will have taken their first step to eliminating it. And I don't mean feeling stressed out by the lack of time; I mean feeling it within the context of anything and everything they experience. I'll give you a little hint. Time does not move. We will talk about this a great deal more as "time" goes on. I could spend a "century" on this one!

Jenna: By 2020 everyone is extremely intuitive. What exactly is intuition, and how do we develop it?

Paul: When you are who you are, that is intuition. And knowing who you are first of all takes learning to feel. If you learn who you are from others' opinions, you will largely know yourself as others do. If you learn by feel, you will access the real you. It is at this point that you can begin to share yourself, as you know yourself. Do you see any connection to love here? In order to love, you must know who you are, and knowingness is ascertained intuitively.

Jenna: What do humans have to learn to develop such a high degree of technology, those love machines, for example, in the mindcare clinics?

Paul: They have to learn about love. Now let me explain that, because I'm sure you are thinking there is a great deal of high-tech today, changing at an ever-faster pace, that has been developed in a society that does not have a high degree of love. There is some…don't get me wrong. But to develop the technology to monitor love, as you say, you must know love. It is really as simple as that. So, if you're in the high-tech field and you want to contribute to a better society, study love—and study it by experiencing it. How am I doing as a career advisor?

Jenna: You're doing great; I'd hire you in a minute. Are you saying then that all careers by 2020 will be love-oriented?

Paul: Of course.

Jenna: Wow, now *that*'s something to think about.

Paul: Something to get ecstatic about. We can talk more about it later because I know now you want to talk specifically about mental health and mental health care in 2020.

Jenna: Yes...Paul, what about this vast awareness people have of others, including taking on their viewpoints? How do we learn that?

Paul: To take on another's viewpoint, you must identify with him or her. This takes the realization that people have similarities, certainly much more so than differences. People will need to learn to focus on the similarities they have with others rather than the differences. When people focus on differences, it has to do with fear. As fear dissipates, so will differences.

Jenna: Can you tell me how people learn to focus?

Paul: Focus has to do with the clarity of ideas, which has to do with greater awareness. The more you learn to open your awareness, the more you learn to focus. So I would tell people if they want to learn focus to allow as much as possible into the conscious mind. Believe me, they will learn it fast if they truly learn how to open their awarenesses.

Jenna: Okay, thanks, Paul. By 2020 people have learned that to be mentally healthy, they need to have their emotions flowing. How do people learn this? Today, the mentally unhealthy people don't even know there's anything wrong with them, or that lack of emotional flow is involved.

Paul: Well, I'll answer that for the so-called mentally unhealthy, then the more aware. Clearly, that's all we are talking about. Today, in the nineties, people do not know there is anything wrong if they do not know what's "right." This would be especially true for those who have not grown so, or who are mentally ill, as your society labels it. They are in a double bind. They do not know what is "right" because they never learned, and even if they did, they would not know when they were experiencing it because their feelings are largely absent. For those ill ones who are in touch with their feelings, their perceptual processes are in error. I will not go into how this came to be, but what they need to learn now. They need to learn who they are. You cannot have a perspective or meaning if you do not know who you are. I cannot tell you exactly how you will do this. This is for you to experience, and learn. Knowing who you are comes through the experience of being itself.

Regarding the ones who are "healthier," they will need to learn that emotional flow has to do with a wider perception, and wider perception means enjoyment! Wider perception, of course, is just greater awareness. They will learn this through the repeated experience of emotional pain. One day it will dawn on them that when they are truly happy, feel contentment and inner peace, that their emotions are flowing. They will notice this pattern, then they will realize that they are in charge of this pattern. From then on it's smooth sailing. And the same holds true for those who have grown less, the "mentally unhealthy." Once they recognize the joy of knowing themselves, they will be just as highly motivated as the others.

Jenna: I can hardly wait. Paul, the idea of growth is highly revered in 2020. What key ideas do we need to learn here?

Paul: That growth is very joyous. Do you remember the mentally impaired humans about whom I just spoke? Well, not only will they feel joyous as they grow, but others will share their pleasure. Had you even thought about that—and the ramifications?

Jenna: Yes, I am aware of that, people experiencing others' feelings.

Paul: But I am wondering if you are aware of what this means for society. As people become aware of others' feelings, including sharing the joy of their growth, do you see how this will accelerate and how truly interactive it will be? Each person sharing the others' growth and the joy of it? Think about that.

Jenna: Yes, I think it sounds wonderful. How do we know when others are growing, though?

Paul: You will need to redefine "growth." The process of becoming who you are is growth, not who your government wants you to be, your family wants you to be, or anyone else wants you to be. The judgment will have to be taken out of growth; it's as simple as that. No one person's growth is any more important than another's. When this is learned, largely what anyone does is growth. But more specifically, I will answer you by saying that you will feel their growth because you will feel their joy.

Jenna: I am not surprised that people in 2020 actually crave experiences since that's how they grow. But what can you tell us about experiences?

Paul: That fear will have to be diminished greatly before people crave experiences. I think I will just begin with one idea; it is such a grandiose concept! What is your next question?

Jenna: Okay, thanks…What kind of feedback will people need in the upcoming years in order for them to recognize the vast impact they have on society?

Paul: It will have to be personal. For many, it will be painful. People already get the idea that their behavior affects others, also that it comes back to them; this is what I mean by painful. What they don't get, is that their thoughts and feelings also affect others. I presume this is what you are talking about, largely.

Jenna: Yes.

Paul: In order for people to get that message, first they'll have to be able to experience their own thoughts and feelings. Many people aren't even at that point yet today and have only begun to experience them on a very superficial level. They can see that what they say about others or feel about them might come back to them, but what they don't understand is how the thoughts and the feelings affect, say, more than the direct object of them. I am talking about others being affected as well, even though those thoughts and feelings weren't specifically about them. Also not understood is that physical manifestation is the result of thoughts and feelings. All of this will be in steps, starting with the personal. A person will make the connection, say, with what he has, to what he thought and felt previously. I am talking about physical manifestation. "All my life I wanted to be a carpenter and build my own house, and so I did it, and here is my house." Much learning will be done in retrospect, where cause and effect can be seen—after the fact.

Jenna: What about this extensive knowledge about learning and fear? How is that learned?

Paul: Learning has to do with increasing awareness. Eventually, humans will just *know*. But in order to get to that point, you have to experience some knowing, where you say to yourself, "I just *know* that; I have no reason, I just *know*." Then the correlation will be made between that and the state of your awareness—open! People will notice patterns, and they will also come to the realization that they are in charge of the patterns.

In regard to fear, in order for there to be extensive knowledge about fear in 2020, there will have to be extensive experience with fear prior to that. *And lesson number one will be that fear of fear keeps one from experiencing fear.* At some point, too, people will have to recognize that there is more good than bad to this experience of fear. It will come through something like this, thought-wise, "There's something in this for me," then they will be more willing to fear.

Jenna: Do you think that people's desire to contribute to the whole is largely the desire for purpose, or recognition of one's own purpose? And if so, why is this experience so compelling?

Paul: Purpose is like a magnet. When people *know*, they know their purpose. But what is purpose? Today it is still largely purpose of self; in 2020, it has more to do with purpose of all. Do you see the difference? You want to know how that leap will be made. They will learn that doing for others brings joy; then they will seek more joy. After that, they will realize that what they do brings joy to others, too. So, then they seek it for them, too. Eventually they will realize that joy can be shared, or that one person's joy is another's. What a day that'll be. Of course, it won't all happen at once for everybody.

Jenna: Paul, do you have anything else you want to comment on about 2020? Perhaps something about economics or money, since that is your "main" expertise, after all?

Paul: Yes, to have any of what you mentioned—or all of it—you must first have the intent. I want to thank you for visualizing what you have about 2020. It's the beginning of intent, on the conscious level, is it not? Or perhaps I should say the next step after your caring. There will be others who will envision other things, but the important thing is to envision, or to let the possibility of your mind wandering into the "future" become a reality. In your scenario of 2020, you don't mention money, but perhaps this has something to do with you. We will see. As for investments, perhaps you should look into those love machines, the ones that measure love.

Jenna: Thank you, Paul.

Paul: You are very welcome.

REBECCA

Jenna: Hi, Rebecca. I suspect you were in on this. Were you aware of what Paul just said?

Rebecca: I was aware of the main ideas, yes.

Jenna: Okay, I would like to ask you how you think we might get to this highly evolved, loving society in 2020. Would you be willing to chat?

Rebecca: Of course.

Jenna: What do you think we will have to learn in years ahead in order to incorporate the idea of having no laws?

Rebecca: My approach would be a little more detailed. For example, Paul commented on what we might learn, an idea or two. At least in some instances, I would like to comment about learning itself. Regarding laws, people will need to recognize that laws are more restrictive than anything else. Now there are many who for years have decried governmental interference—laws. Unfortunately, some of the people yelling loudest are the most motivated by self. What will it take to bring the selfless, more loving ones into this camp? Will it take new kinds of laws? Laws that protect others as much as self? Will the next trend be family rights, or some kind of group rights? Does the society wean itself off individual rights? The point I want to make here is that we have to learn a great deal more about learning.

Jenna: What do we have to learn about learning?

Rebecca: Well, there is something amiss. How can we go all these years, centuries upon centuries, in fact, and make so little progress in terms of creating loving beings and a more loving society? There would be some who would say we haven't made progress, that we are going backwards. I think it is most helpful if I give you, like Paul, just one or two things to think about. Here is one: Learning is individualistic, and if we want to progress in our learning, we need to know who we are and how we learn. Think of all that each person has missed because he has no clues as to where his learning ability is? It's just kind of random—one's learning—although I'll admit, there's something to be said for intuitively leaning in the direction of one's natural ability. The point I am trying to make is we need to know much more about individualized styles of learning. Do we really want some psychologist telling us how we learn? I would like to pose this to the psychologists, how do they know? It is guesswork and not even very good at that.

Only the person can tell you how he learns. My second point is that learning is impacted by emotional flow. If we don't understand this, we will not understand more about learning, nor will we be able to learn more. And both of those things are necessary if we are to create the kind of society you so envision.

Jenna: Do you have any insights into how each of us learns love? I mean, is there anything you can expand on, besides experience?

Rebecca: Well, let me tell you how I learned about love. First of all I learned that I was not using my physical senses properly or fully. I was just using them superficially. This came about quite by accident. What happened was, I did not see the whole picture; I misinterpreted, in lay language. I only saw through my beliefs, and beliefs block information! Once I learned how to use my physical senses better, my perception changed completely. When your perception changes, so do your experiences of love.

Jenna: Well, how did you realize you had misinterpreted?

Rebecca: Someone told me! She said "No, wait...that is not what I was feeling." Because I couldn't assess what she was feeling, which is what the physical senses help with, I deduced based on my beliefs—and I was quite wrong.

Jenna: I see. Well, is there anything else you can tell us about how we might know when we aren't using our physical senses fully?

Rebecca: When love isn't working. Now I recognize that sounds like Paul, but it's true! Also, when there is a tremendous yearning in your life, but little joy in it. My advice is this, if you want to learn more about love, start with your physical senses, one at a time, and learn to develop them because they have everything to do with how you perceive the world. This will be discussed later; I would prefer to take something as large as this one step at a time.

Jenna: I'm not surprised at your answer about physical senses because I discovered this myself when I "visited" 2020—that people's physical senses were just pulsating with energy! But what I don't understand is, how come we've heard so little of this before?...I mean, about our underdeveloped physical senses in terms of perception?

Rebecca: Because it is "human nature," or maybe I should say habit, to view things to the extreme, at least at this point, based on beliefs. First, humans view things one way, then they swing back to the other side. At this time in history we are very much into the non-physical—there is a gush toward the metaphysical—but you wait…then we'll swing right on back to the physical, suddenly reexamining the importance of that again. It's the old either-or kind of thinking. And here is another point. Scientists know that physical senses bring us information, and so do a lot of lay people, for that matter; the problem is we are just not using our senses well enough.

Jenna: What about learning to love more than self?

Rebecca: I think I should be very realistic with you here. In my opinion, people learn to love others, I mean, with great momentum and sincerity, when they learn how to deal with loss. I am talking about all losses: death, relationships, family, dreams. When people can experience the pain of loss, then they will learn to love others—and in abundance. So many hold back from loving others, for fear of the emotional pain of loss. This is not always conscious, of course, but I think when people learn that loss is tolerable and that something can actually be learned from it, then there will be more loving of others.

Jenna: That was really nice, thank you, Rebecca. How will this come about, this willingness to tolerate more emotional pain?

Rebecca: It will come about from direct knowledge of others' energy. When people really start to feel the flow of energy in themselves and others, they will get the idea of interconnectedness. Also, they will need to be able to recognize that what they do *does* impact others. It will probably be learned first from their own emotional pain from the actions of others—or at least that is the way it will be perceived. Of course, people have felt emotional pain for thousands of years, but somehow what others do to them is perceived as much graver than what they do to others. Why is this? Because they have not learned full emotional expression. When they learn this, they will have much greater insight into their effect on others. Today very few understand the correlation between perception and emotional flow. When one is feeling like a victim, he is not too concerned about the victimization of others. But this will change, and the change will come about from learning better emotional flow. A good sign, although it may be confusing, is when people start to get mixed up over whose feelings they're feeling. This is actually progress.

Jenna: How does someone know whose feeling is whose? I mean, is there a particular insight for something like this?

Rebecca: It has to do with the perception of movement. People will first feel lack of movement, then movement. Lack of movement is painful, movement is joyful. I am talking about the movement of energy. This is where individualized learning methods come in. I cannot say that all have the same insights, because they don't. This is precisely the kinds of questions that will be addressed before long in therapists' offices. Yes, the patient will be asked to describe how he knows what he knows, and it will be highly related to feelings, and the origin of them. I am talking about therapy later in this decade, actually, when I am a therapist! As you know, I am able to talk from the perspective of many time frames. In the late 1990s I am a therapist working with people on things just like this, helping them discern who they are!

Jenna: Yes…and speaking of timelessness, what can you tell us about "time" in the future? Do you recall, say, the first idea you grasped which helped you ultimately understand and experience the timelessness that is experienced by everyone in 2020?

Rebecca: I turned the corner when I realized that time has been given much too much power. When people spoke of it, they revered it, as if there was no way to control it. This gave me a lot of insight into how people related to ideas. I knew I had no desire to control time. As soon as I accepted that that was okay, I stopped thinking about it for the most part; or if I did, I didn't think about it as something I was competing with. Practically, I am saying, to think of time as a part of you, then you won't be so apt to compete with it. When you feel frenzied, just say to yourself, "Wait a minute, time is just me," then go on with your life. You'd be surprised how much better you feel.

Jenna: Do you have any thoughts on how to develop intuition?

Rebecca: You are asking me essentially how to learn to trust yourself. Again, let me see if I can access something from my own experience. I would say that being aware of others' feelings is very important. People learn from interaction with others. If they cannot feel what others are feeling, they are not going to get adequate feedback to learn about the effectiveness of their own feelings. Trust has to do with tapping into information in feelings, both yours and others'. When people are having trouble trusting, it is not just an inability to feel their own feelings; it also has to do with not being able to feel others' feelings. Feeling is a two-way street, or maybe I should say highly interactive. When one person feels, it encourages others to. So what I am saying to those who are good "feelers," is to keep up the good work because you may be helping others to learn to trust. Learning to trust does not just emanate from one's self.

Jenna: Is there a specific way people will be aware of others' thoughts and feelings? How did you, for example, learn to empathize with others?

Rebecca: I learned by studying light first of all. Once I realized that light was a part of all beings, I tried to hone in on the feel of it, each person's light. I did this by trying to feel the meaning of what they were saying, for example, as opposed to deducing meaning; then empathy came naturally.

Jenna: What does light feel like?

Rebecca: Light feels like something moving, with an even rhythm—and within that rhythm is meaning.

Jenna: Could you amplify that a bit, please?

Rebecca: I recognized I was dealing with light when I learned about emotional flow—my own. Once I got beyond fear, I experienced the light within my own emotions. What I am saying is, much came into my awareness during my own emotional flow, and I learned it was light.

Jenna: Are you talking about visual perception?

Rebecca: No, I am talking about feeling light, not seeing it.

Jenna: Did you say, Oh, this is light!…or how did you make the actual discovery? Did you later read about what you had experienced?

Rebecca: Somebody else asked me if what I was feeling was light, and I said yes. I just said it; I don't know how I knew. This was after the fact. I don't know what you call that, certainly not reading, but it took the question from someone else to bring it into my conscious mind. I'm sorry I can't define it better; you'll just have to feel it. It's a kind of an aliveness that you sense.

Jenna: Are you saying that you had to first experience your own emotional flow in order to truly experience others' thoughts and feelings?

Rebecca: I am saying it happened in that order, or I was aware in that order, and that the more one experiences the light in one's own emotions, the better one is able to detect light in others', which is the key to knowing their thoughts and feelings.

Jenna: Were there any specific observations you recall you made when you recognized the correlation between you emotional flow and your mental health, or what can you tell the readers that might be helpful in terms of learning the importance of emotional flow to good mental health?

Rebecca: It will be something simple, like recognizing that when you are angry, or stuck in your anger, that is, that you are not happy. I know that sounds ridiculous, but it's these kinds of insights that start one off into greater awareness. Many people do not recognize, for example, that they are causing their own anger; they actually perceive it as being caused by an outside force. Little ideas come into the awareness like, "Gee, I don't want to feel this way, I want to enjoy life more; I am sick of feeling like this all the time." Anger, in fact, will have to be redefined, so that it can be experienced in new ways.

Jenna: More on that, please.

Rebecca: People act ridiculous when they are angry. Of course they don't all act the same, but it should be a learning process, this experience of anger. Today the way people experience anger teaches them nothing, except to reinforce old beliefs that are nonloving. You show me an extremely angry person who has great insights. As of this time in history, the expression of anger, as is the case with other emotions, closes the awareness. This is backward. The expression of emotions is supposed to open the awareness. This will take much new learning in the years between now and 2020.

Jenna: I can't believe you said that. It gives me chills, because I have already seen this same thing in 2020, that all emotional expressions—even "negative" ones—are joyous, and filled with insight. This made me realize that we are *not* experiencing our emotions fully now, rather only the "beginnings" of them.

Rebecca: You mean today.

Jenna: Yes. I didn't realize this until I actually saw people in 2020 "feeling" in different ways from us today.

Rebecca: You are using the same methods then as I am to *know*, going to the "future" to get information.

Jenna: Yes, as you mentioned earlier, I, too, at times, am operating from more than one time frame.

Rebecca: Do you think you would have known we were only experiencing the "beginnings" of emotions now if you hadn't seen what you saw in 2020?

Jenna: I think it brought it into my conscious mind.

Rebecca: Similar to the time I said 'yes' when someone asked me if what I was experiencing was light.

Jenna: I am getting kind of lost here, what is your point?

Rebecca: That you are bringing in material from outside of the usual way of experiencing time which affects how you perceive the "present." Don't you realize how unusual this is? It's revolutionary, especially pertaining to the future! This is great; let's keep going. My point is that we can pull this thing off, this 2020 scenario! You and I, and others!

Jenna: Are you saying that because you and I are able to grasp some things in the future, we are on our way to creating it?

Rebecca: Absolutely, I am saying that. But I am not saying to those who can't—or who *think* they can't—that they will be of no help. I am truly excited. Tell me, is there anything else I can answer for you? This is fun.

Jenna: How does one learn the value of growth, which is truly revered in 2020?

Rebecca: By little experiences like this. When one senses that great things are around the corner and realizes that one has to grow to get there!

Jenna: But what if one doesn't sense these great things ahead?

Rebecca: The first step to recognizing great things—or anything —is to recognize the possibility of all things. I am saying that the idea that anything is possible is essential for changes of the magnitude of which we speak. For those not sharing that viewpoint, I ask them to open their hearts.

Jenna: I would love more on that one.

Rebecca: Opening the heart is the beginning. So if they don't believe in all possibilities, I would have to say the problem is no, not their hearts, but their connections to them. How do I say this? The answers lie in the heart. Those who say whatever is impossible are not speaking from their hearts, they speak from their intellects. Nothing is impossible from the heart's viewpoint.

Jenna: That is terrific. I love that....

Rebecca: And that craving for experiences in 2020 about which you have written, this is what I am talking about. Craving means an extreme desire for, and this is what opens the heart!

Jenna: Rebecca, people are very knowledgeable about both fear and learning in 2020. Is there anything specific you can say about that?

Rebecca: First of all, people will learn more and more how to benefit from the experiences of others. In addition, there will be an increased desire to experience things differently. This is a part of growing, of learning who you are. Experience is highly individualistic. More and more will recognize that how to think, feel, and be is not something that comes from others, rules of society, whatever, even tradition—and they will find themselves compelled to experience *everything* in their own unique way. Even fear will seem inviting. Can you imagine that? It will become clear that there are better ways to experience than the way we are currently experiencing. This will not have to be taught so much, that there are better ways. It will be obvious. However, what will be taught will be skills for enhancing experience, starting with better emotional expression.

Jenna: Who's going to do this teaching?

Rebecca: I am, and you are, and many others. Perhaps we are even helping some now, with this book.

Jenna: I hope so...Rebecca, that love machine in the mindcare clinics slays me. In your opinion, what will it take to develop it?

Rebecca: Besides having to know themselves, people will need to know others. In addition, they will have to discover that there are ways to have meaning outside of the realm of ideas.

Jenna: Are you talking about in the conscious mind? Don't tell me you are going to get into physics.

Rebecca: Physics itself will be turned on its ear by 2020.

Jenna: You're kidding. Give me an example.

30

Rebecca: People will perceive what's not there.

Jenna: They're doing that now.

Rebecca: No, no, I mean what's not there in a category apart from the physical world and the nonphysical world.

Jenna: There's another category?

Rebecca: This is the part I love so much about you. *You* are instrumental in this finding.

Jenna: I can't stand this! You are always getting into my future, and I still don't know what to make of it.

Rebecca: Do you want to get into it right now? I sense you really don't want to talk about it right now.

Jenna: Well, I'm wondering if we are getting off track. I'm not sure how important my actual near-term future is right now. I'm just trying to steer us in the right direction.

Rebecca: Here's my point. How we find meaning will also evolve, and you have a lot to do with it. There will be new ways to perceive energy. Energy is evolving. Do you follow this?

Jenna: Barely.

Rebecca: I don't think you don't understand on a conscious level yet...maybe we should just go on.

Jenna: I think I should explain something to the readers because this might seem confusing, that you are able to read my intent, so to speak, which is not conscious to me. You're able to read my mind, I guess you'd call it. Rebecca, wow, this is massive...I think we should go on.

Rebecca: Well, I'm not the only one; you're doing it too, with me.

Jenna: But I'm not telling you about your future.

Rebecca: That's because you're not focused on it. You *could* if you had to.

Jenna: Oh, no, here we go again, the little carrot on the string, luring me into greater awareness. I'm wondering if it would be all right with you if we just finish our agenda here about 2020.

Rebecca: Oh, sure, sorry.

Jenna: Rebecca, do you have anything else you want to comment on regarding 2020?

Rebecca: I would like to ask the readers to take a moment to assess how your ideas about 2020 hit them, feeling-wise, not so much for your credibility, sorry, but to give them some idea of what it will take to have a loving society like this. If they felt something in their gut, a sensation of excitement while reading, then this is exactly the kind of feeling they need to keep trying to create, because this is what it will take to "get there." This sensation *is* intuition; it *is* the very person who is doing the reading; it *is* truth, it is a small but sure indication of which way to turn. So readers, *please* remember this feeling, if you have it, because it will take you a long, long way...Sorry to get on my high horse.

Jenna: That's quite all right.

Rebecca: I just wanted them to know how important this feeling is.

Jenna: Yes, I can understand, the one those psychologists today would never be aware of, in terms of how somebody *else* learns.

Rebecca: Yes, you are absolutely correct. How did you know that? That was very good.

Jenna: You and Paul have taught me a lot through the years. And I want to thank you, too, Rebecca, for answering my questions on how to "get there."

Rebecca: You are most welcome.

Jenna: It's starting to feel like a team, Rebecca.

Rebecca: Yes, and remember *that* feeling, too!

Author's comments

Some of the things that strike me, having heard what both Paul and Rebecca had to say: how little we know right now about love; how little we know about ourselves; how deeply entrenched fear is in all of us, especially our fear of emotional pain. It also makes me wonder what humankind has been doing all this time and how frightened we've been all along to be ourselves. Another thing that comes into my mind is how casual people are today about their own existences. Not that they have to be deadly serious, but there is this *assumption* that things will just go on—for humans, whether we are responsible or not. Will they? If we don't grow?

Also, I am very touched by my relationships with both Paul and Rebecca. I like the fact we are close emotionally, working for the good of humankind, carving this path together toward a more loving society. What am I trying to say? That I hope you will join us, truly join us? After all, the more love we have the better our chances are! If you need to first feel our love, that is wonderful, as it is probably our best hope in getting you enlisted! Please feel free to experience Paul and Rebecca any way you want—and that is best done by feeling their love. And I send mine as well, as this is truly a project of love.

Families and Communities in 2020

•Group awareness •Synchronization of body movements •Giving up control •Relating to everything equally, even objects •Heightened sexual energy •Increased knowledge of purpose, need and intent •New respect for birth, death and the moon •New ways of experiencing memory •Emotional flow and the physical body •Experiences with food

Today we have an awareness that is tantamount to, "What's in it for me?" Twenty some years from now it's more like, "What's in it for us?" What has brought about this change? Pure and simple: energy flow. And since people's energy is flowing so much more by 2020, it's affected the groups of which they are a part. This means families and communities are very highly energized. It also means that group awareness is "where it's at," for by this time people have gone beyond thinking of themselves first and foremost and now cherish being active and loving members of groups. By 2020 there are groups of people working together everywhere, with families and communities exemplifying a degree of loving unimaginable today. Families and communities *feel* good to people. They ought to; they are the manifestations of the love of the people themselves.

How did all this awareness and love come about by 2020? People learned about the flow of their own energy—by being. They also learned about the flow of others. This of course was only possible when they gave up trying to control everything. Today people control themselves, others, and virtually everything with which they come in contact, through rigid beliefs, which they also control. Giving up control was the only way true energy flow could occur. Not only that, in the years between now and 2020, people in our loving society specifically learned that if they allowed the flow of one person, it actually enhanced the flow of others, as well as the flow of society. In addition, they learned that all things needed to flow, or be—ideas, people, physical objects, the physical senses, emotions, everything! So, what taking on another's viewpoint means by 2020, is just allowing all that is to be, taking on its point of view,—merging with it—then honoring that perspective. The result of this? Everything radiates from within its own unique brilliance. Literally everything "does its own thing" in 2020.

On a practical level what I am saying is that when people are encouraged to be who they are, they are better people; when anything is encouraged to be, it is better, because authenticity fosters the flow of love…and this is what has happened by 2020. Being aware of other people's energy—or group awareness—is exciting for people; it's like being a part of the love that bonds them. From a behavioral point of view, what group awareness means is that people do things intuitively to enhance a group's energy. By 2020 people not only do things to keep themselves in balance, but they also do things to keep their groups in balance, which is just another way of saying that people are highly skilled at moving both their own energy and that of a group. The moves they make, the way they wiggle…even the sounds they utter, are all geared at an unconscious level to synchronize and bring harmony to groups. For example, it would not be at all unusual to see group members frequently changing their body positions, moving various parts of their bodies, or even making a wide range of sounds, particularly harmonious ones, relative to the movements and sounds of other members in their groups. By 2020 people are so sensitive to the movement of energy around them, the rhythms and patterns of it, including a group's own pattern and frequency, that they do whatever it takes to enhance the flow of the group. In fact, they are so sensitive to this energy that they can actually feel one unifying, giant rhythm within the group, pulsating, escalating, connecting them all, which feels ever-abundant and eternal. To say that this is vastly different from today is the understatement. Today people are barely aware of their own energy, let alone that of a group.

In addition to synchronizing with the group as a whole, people in 2020 also synchronize with individuals within groups, since group awareness also involves harmony with its parts. In other words, people are just as aware of the parts as they are of the whole. As an example, let's say one person in the group drops an object. At the same time another person in the group steps back from the person he is talking to; still another, in a different locale, grimaces. These are all instantaneous behaviors that happen spontaneously, in conjunction with the person who dropped the object; they are not responses to, but simultaneous, empathic moves made by the human body, which is a far deeper version of compassion than we have today. Today people are focused on how they compare to others, not on how to enhance love within a group. By 2020 people unite with their fellow beings on such a deep emotional level that it is discernible in their physical bodies. And in the case of families, or lovers, where the degree of love and awareness is at its very highest, people's actual body movements are sometimes exactly the same…for moments upon moments upon moments. People go in and out of extremely aware states in 2020, which is also the case today, but when they are truly "in touch" in our loving society, their bodies intuitively mimic their loved ones. Imagine watching a mirrored version of yourself, for say, several minutes! This is what happens when people are acutely aware of others: their thoughts, feelings, needs, and intentions: their bodies intuitively synchronize with one another!

The movement of energy also shows up in another way in these energized bodies of 2020. Emotional flow is so great by this time that it can often be seen on the outside of the body, so much in fact, that people's whole bodies appear to bend, looking like big "S's" at times! And the movement of the body itself is more fluid, with each moving part of the body flowing into the next, like a series of waves that just keep coming. When people don't feel love, which is common today, movements are jerky and disjointed from the rest of the body, with rigid bodies not being uncommon. By 2020, however, people don't resist love, and their bodies reflect it.

Family and Community Dynamics and Locales

As one might expect, families and communities themselves are more fluid and dynamic. By today's standards, family and community activity would be considered extremely chaotic, since people are so much more active physically and vocally in 2020. But for these futuristic people, this same activity is perceived and experienced quite differently,—it's calm, soothing, relaxing,—for by this time people are able to cut right through that which doesn't produce harmony for them and zero in to what does. This means that people in this society are better able to go right through others' defensiveness and connect at deeper heart levels. Today we think of strong families and communities as being highly defined, having definite power structures, highly organized, controlled, stable, anything that favors the status quo. This is exactly the opposite from 2020 since it is the antithesis of flow. There are no such things as typical anything, by 2020, as there are restrictions, laws, rules, ordinances. (So families and communities, and other groups too, with people coming together, go where purpose leads them, not where tradition dictates.) Today people are more likely to move into a community because that's where the jobs are. When they marry, they are often doing it to impress another, or to prove something to themselves; but, it's frequently externally based, or fear-based. By 2020 people are more internally motivated, or love-based, coming together with others more for reasons of spiritual growth, just *knowing* where they are supposed to be, for example, and having a much better sense of with whom. Spatially, this means that families and communities are everywhere, as now much more of the earth is being utilized and appreciated from "its own point of view." People don't travel as much, people don't move as much. And when they do physically move themselves, they're apt to walk. Some people have the ability to teleport themselves to wherever they want, but more often choose to just be "at home" with family and community. By 2020 world populace is considerably smaller, with people in smaller, more intimate communities, with the populous being more widespread, no longer clustered, as it is now, in crowded cities.

How this came about is of note. The population became smaller not because there was one main event that killed people off, or even a series of events, but more because there weren't as many pregnancies for conscious and unconscious reasons. In the case of conscious reasons, many families chose to have smaller families, while other people chose not to replicate themselves, feeling more worthy than we do today, instead truly self-actualizing. In the case of unconscious reasons, there seemed to be a natural attrition that occurred that was not alarming to people but welcomed. Scientists did not go around trying to figure out what was wrong, for example. People just seemed to know it was right, having fewer people. Indeed it was one of the first times in history that nongrowth was considered growth, so to speak, and accepted by the masses.

In regard to scarce food, this was never the case. It was a perceptual error and one that compounded itself. There were periods of time during these years leading up to 2020 when people's fears of not having enough food were so intense that the impression was created that there was not enough food. But this was never true. People were also not able to factor in their own needs for less food. Add a third factor of new kinds of food not being accepted and a panicky populace resulted. The good news is that out of this came a renewed sense of appreciation and reverence for reality—the food and people who were there.

Well, back to the year 2020…. In terms of families themselves, they are more likely to be extended than today, with members living with their families for much longer periods of time in order to gain wisdom from them. After all, by this time people recognize they have chosen their families to learn from, so they have grasped the meaning of spending time with them. There is also more integration among families, per se. In a word: they share more in 2020. All sorts of activities, knowledge, and meals are shared on a regular basis. People's homes are considered places of respite, although they are no longer "owned." Yet there is privacy. Others honor homes as the specific creations of particular families. One of the reasons homes are given such respect and "privacy" is to accommodate sleeping people, who are ever-present. Although people generally sleep shorter periods of time in 2020, they sleep whenever they want. Night and day blend right into each other…and although people are very much aware of the world and universe at large, on a day-to-day basis they are much more focused on and highly immersed in their own families and communities.

Relationships

People do marry in 2020, although it is more often thought of as forming bonds. Not pledging allegiance to the people they marry, they commit to the person's beingness—not only as they are, but have been, and will be! Anyone can marry, aside from relatives, and the marriages last much longer…and like friendships, there is a sense of eternity to them. However, this is a positive eternity, unlike today's "eternity," which for some, carries the sensation of being "trapped." By 2020 eternity means freedom, not a constraint on one's liberties, carrying with it a sense of security, not a heaviness. In 2020 people do a better job with their relationships, which they have more of, and the relationships themselves are not as apt to be destroyed by new bonds, rather enhanced by them. There isn't that sense, for example, of people being threatened by their spouses' friendships, either; instead their spouses welcome them. There is also not a sense of pitting one gender against another; nor is there an obsession with one's own gender, as there is today. People speak of the strengths of female energy and male energy in males and females, and they focus on combining *with* other people, not competing against them. Today people focus on other people's weaknesses; by 2020 they're more apt to focus on their strengths.

In terms of the size of families, this depends on people's intentions and purposes, but generally biological families are in the size range of 2-4 children in families that choose to have children. By 2020 parents communicate telepathically with the spiritual energy of their unborn baby's soul prior to conception to see if it wants to come into this world! If both parents are in favor of this—and the soul, on the other side, too—conception happens! If not, there is no conception. Obviously, there is no abortion "problem" in 2020.

Sexual Experiences

What we would consider a peak sexual experience today would be like the blink of an eye to someone in 2020, with sexual experiences not being limited to just one's "spouse," nor to "intimate" times. All of life is intimate in 2020, with people relating sexually all the time with others. That is not to say they have sexual intercourse with them. What it is to say is that the flow of energy which is shared among people is highly sexual, as we would know it today. Day-to-day life is highly erotic; it's like breathing, a part of being—and it is not frowned upon but encouraged. People are sexually aroused much of the time, feeling energized by it. And there is no way to describe orgasm. "You'd have to be there." Think of it this way: if people are sharing all of their emotions at the cellular level, which is what they are doing, they are also sharing all of their joy. Multiple orgasms? The term has new meaning by 2020...There is much more of a sense of people uniting with all people during orgasm—loving all people, that is—with people experiencing orgasms more frequently and more intensely—and in every cell of their bodies, for in the years leading up to 2020, they learned about orgasms of the sense organs, then it was of other organs, then other organs...then other body parts until finally it was the whole body shimmering in ecstasy. It is a way of being in this highly loving, highly erotic society. And there is nothing considered wrong about it, or shameful. It is also true that orgasm itself is no big deal, nor is it a goal for people but just exemplifies how people feel in 2020—due to increased energy flow—which is slightly more "up" than we feel today! Sensuality is a way of life, not the exception in 2020, and it would not be an exaggeration to say that by this time people experience orgasm 100 times more intensely than even the most adventuresome today.

Again, I ask you. Look around, who are these people? Are you one of these beings in 2020? Is the sensual, fluid, erotic and relaxed body you have in your mind yours? Perhaps it is one of your children's, or a young person in your neighborhood who ended up teaching you something through the years about intuitively allowing your body to *just move*. You have learned to move your body differently by 2020, you know…and you are enjoying it.

Children

Children are naturally encouraged to love their bodies. Sexuality is not so in check, as it is today. This has eliminated "inappropriate" touching among all people, as everyone can sense what is desired and not desired, by others, and that is honored. Adults, flowing sexually themselves, have no desire or need to impose on others, such as children. Child care has been "redefined" by 2020. Children care for parents, and parents care for children, but there's more of a nurturing quality to it, with no one being of a lesser value, or helpless. Caring is much more interactive, with each learning from the other. Nurturing is also more prominent in families and communities. There is a kind of rotating system, in fact, which people sense, providing nurturing for everyone—and the experience is joyful, not dutiful. Familial and communal "duties" are gone, with people doing things for reasons of love. People just seem to *know* when they need nurturing or to be nurturing, so it happens naturally. Nurturing is in fact part of the group dynamics inherent in group awareness.

In 2020 children do not make so much "noise," but beautiful harmonious sounds. Rather than telling kids to be quiet, parents encourage sound, which the children emit instinctively. Children know their own sounds the way children know their names today. In fact, they soothe themselves with their sounds, both audibly and silently. The same is also true for others of different ages, but it is particularly true for children. Children today scream a great deal because they are frightened, with their screams being an attempt to quell anxiety; whereas in 2020 their harmonious sounds are reflections of their feelings of peace. Now children panic at the loss of feeling love, often screaming, at their mothers usually, demanding their attention, i.e. Look at me! Look at me! This is because they have lost the sense of who they are. By 2020 children have a much better sense of this, hence eternal love, and are better able to slide into a larger hum, which is the sound of many uniting. As a result both adults and children are not so preoccupied with getting something from outside of themselves, always trying to attain something more, as in "peace of mind," which is so common today for many. This has come about largely due to better entrainment with the rhythms of sound—or expanded use of hearing. By 2020 children have become some of the greatest teachers in this regard in communities, having an exceptional ability to feel the rhythms of love through sound.

Tremendous Exchange of Ideas

One of the nicest aspects about society in 2020 is that there is a huge array of opinion, differing opinions. People are not at all threatened by a diversity of views, in fact encourage them, as they know from them emerge even better ideas. This means that in addition to the exchange of love, there is also a tremendous exchange of ideas—within families and communities. Today power tactics often accompany the "best" ideas, with individual egos on the line. In 2020 people would find that comical, railroading certain ideas based on the source of them. Even "dumb" ideas, as we would see them today, are honored for what they are—someone's expression. A true flow of energy means everything is allowed to be, so there is much to consider in 2020. By this time no one hides anything, which has resulted in both healthier people and healthier ideas.

Flow in People's Homes

Flow also affects homes in which people live in 2020; they are built, for example, to serve the needs of the people, not the builders', as is so often the case today. Where people live, what they live in, is fueled by intent, not circumstance. In addition, there is much community help in building homes, again not so common today. Designed with more appeal to the physical senses, texture has become particularly important to people. How a home feels, for example, is more important than, say, durability, or (horrors) its likelihood to appreciate in value! All that is in the home excites or calms them, depending upon their needs, energizing them, stimulating all of their senses. They can taste, smell, hear, see, and feel with their bodies that which surrounds them so much better than we can today.

People like to integrate with their homes, meaning that the contents of the house have taken on new status. Their furniture, for example, has new respect, with people relating to it, as equals. A chair has the same respect as a human! That is, there is equal energy flow between a person and a chair, not the way it is today, where we "use" chairs. In 2020 they love them, honoring them once again, from the chair's point of view. As silly as this sounds, this kind of attitude has revolutionized society. And there is also a great deal of increased awareness about household objects, besides furniture, with people having a sense of who made them, as well as a sense of the history of the material from which they're made. People also have an intuitive sense for a higher use of materials, so in regard to their homes, they don't use things in short supply. The interiors of their homes are not as organized, or as defined as today. People don't, for example, put everything "in its place," but are more likely to consider the needs of the object! Where does it want to go? Again, as strange as it sounds, this is what makes society work in 2020, a deep awareness of others' beingness, even objects.

Since people are no longer into control, they are not into habits or routines, the way we are today. In fact, habits and routines are considered "defense mechanisms" of the day, obstructing flow! Regarding lost items (the bane of our lives today), people don't spend inordinate amounts of time looking for things because, again, of a much better ability to feel where they are…and yes, this has to do with the flow of physical objects, themselves. People are able to beam right into them, being able to feel the flow of all things. Of course the more one feels the flow of something, the more he is able to know about it, like where it is! So in addition to knowing where objects are, people also have psychometric experiences with the physical objects of their homes, meaning they know a great deal about them, just as they would people. And pets, as well, have equal status to everything and everyone else, as do plants, who often live together in one harmonious setting. Homes in 2020 are alive with small animals, birds, and other animate and inanimate objects, collected from "outside." But the truth is, there is no longer an outside as we know it today, with a kind of natural flow from outside to inside, making many homes like arboretums. Like day blending into night, outside has blended into inside. People can feel this natural flow, by 2020. Change is not so abrupt. It's smooooooth….

What does this have to do with perception? In 2020 people move their eyes more smoothly too, sensing more of a continuum. Today we think of things so separately that we do not give equal value to the space between them, or the link that connects them. It is no wonder our eyes dart back and forth, rather than seeing all that is truly there, and it is no wonder that our sense organs don't work very well, with our eyes in particular being so dysfunctional that practically every adult wears glasses. Could it be that our idea of separateness is one of the biggest causes for our contorted eyes?

Birthdays, Weddings and Gifts

Birthdays and weddings are both celebrated in 2020, but the focus is more on the bonds among the friends than on the people themselves. People in 2020 orient themselves around the interaction among people, not so much on specific people, which means revering certain people is no longer fashionable. Respecting them is another story. In the same light, birthday gifts and wedding gifts are not so much for certain people, as they are in honor of the friendships those people hold. Today people often do what's easiest for them in terms of gifts, grabbing something at the last minute, or buying things ahead of time, for potential gifts. By 2020 they're more likely to actually make something for the person, instilled with feelings of love, or at least acquire it with great feelings of love for that person, honoring the bond. Not that this is unheard of today, but it is much more common in 2020 as it was in the past. In our society of love, the intention of the gift is likely to *be* the gift. Today, the truth is, we do almost everything in terms of our own needs first. In 2020 people are much more aware of others, and it shows up in their heartfelt, often personally crafted gifts.

Experiencing Food

By 2020 eating has become a totally new experience. Not only are people aware of their own perspectives when eating, but they are also aware of the food's perspective—or what it's like to be eaten. And the food has a say-so too, if it wants to be bought, cooked, or eaten! Those who honor the food the most are those who are the most loving, being able to sense the integrated whole, or the totality of the eating experience. Where there is a melding of energies of the eater and the food, a higher viewpoint is accessed. Today we see food as prey! Incidentally, food gained a great deal of respect prior to 2020 when it appeared to be in short supply. One of the reasons many of us throughout the world are so disrespectful of everything we have today is due to the fact of a worldwide oversupply of everything, including food, especially in the developed countries, which has contributed to our narcissistic like entitlement, instead of R-E-S-P-E-C-T for all that we have.

Birth and Death

Both birth and death have gained new respect by 2020, as by this time there is quite a sense of accomplishment with both. There are people who attend funerals who help ease the pain for relatives and friends, by describing what the deceased is experiencing—before, during and after death—allowing them to share in the actual death experience. Mostly, what is described is sensory material carried around, then released at death, which was never articulated—thoughts and feelings which for whatever reasons weren't shared; maybe they weren't conscious. It is not considered an invasion of privacy but "welcomed" by the person passing over, who "feels" this exposure as a gentle, nurturing boost to the other side. Today, unfortunately, people have a tendency to shut down and focus primarily on their own grief and unresolved areas associated with the deceased one, often manifesting in thoughts such as, "Why didn't I tell her I loved her more," rather than staying attached to and being aware of the one who is "dying." By 2020, because of the "reader" at funerals, there is a truer love connection at the time of death—a real one, not a false one forced to the surface by guilt. Although almost all communicate telepathically on a regular basis with those who have passed over, it is actually easier after death than it is to communicate telepathically at the time of death due to the living one's unresolved emotional matters, and to a smaller degree, the unresolved issues of the deceased. The reader at the funeral serves as a unifier, not just a comforter for people. This does not mean that people do not fully resolve their emotional matters with the deceased. It just means that funerals are far more joyous than today, and are more like celebrations.

There are also readers at births, sharing the fetus' views—before, during and after "birth,"—but this is somewhat less common, as mothers are much more apt to know "all" and willing to share with those attending the birth; in other words, readers aren't necessary. Births are still fairly "private," attended only by family members and close friends. Births are not as likely to occur in unexpected places but are prepared for and planned ahead of time in conjunction with the fetus—consciously communicated with the fetus—which allows for pleasant birthing circumstances.

Moonlight and Memory

Like birth and death, the moon has also gained new respect by 2020, as by this time people recognize there is an actual physical need for it, which would be comparable to the physical need we have today for water. What they have discovered is that moonlight helps them access memory and that there is also a real physical need for that, too, much the way we think of humans' today having a real physical need for dreams. People actually feel the magnetic pull of the moon in 2020. As a result, children love to play in the moonlight and their mothers encourage it, saying to them, "Have fun! Go out and play in the moonlight!" Playing under the moon is as common as playing under the sun—for both adults and children. As for memories themselves in 2020, they are experienced much more as they originally happened. That is, they do not flash through the mind as they do today in an abbreviated version but reoccur more authentically, with a sense of a curtain opening—and *being* there. Today people magnify certain aspects of an experience, then carry around that distorted version sometimes for a lifetime. In this loving society, because they are not stuck in their emotions, people are more willing to allow the memory to move, or evolve, actually having a relationship with it, not being imprisoned by it, like today. That's because they are better able to process their emotions, learning from their experiences more quickly. Then the memory itself is allowed to shift, or realign on its own, being elastic, and keeping its vibrancy. It then physically manifests. When people think or remember in 2020, they experience it more the way we experience physical reality today, as being there right in front of them; it is not just a mental process anymore. Thought manifests so quickly it takes on a dense form, the speed of which depends on factors like clarity, awareness, and intention. So memories and/or thoughts can be viewed, smelled, tasted, heard, and touched. In addition, by 2020, people experience their environment (which now includes memories/thoughts) from many different angles, not just one place in space. In the case of a memory then, not only is it physical, as we would know it today, but people experience it from the front, the sides, the rear, whatever they choose. This skill was learned in the years prior to 2020 when people learned how to be truly empathetic with others. So in the presence then of moonlight… people find extremely lifelike memories entering into their awarenesses, which they welcome.

Religion, Stories, and Art

There is no longer religion in 2020, as we know it today. Instead, there is just a natural flow of ideas, since this represents a more natural flow of energy. In the years previous to 2020, religion died, because it favored some ideas over others, some people over others, and some time frames over others, namely, the past. It was not a true energy flow and died a natural death. With the giving up of control came the giving up of unhealthy ideas or those discriminating against other equally important ideas. In our society of love, all is allowed to be, which means no one set of ideologies presupposes another. Also gone are stories, as we know them today, since they are told from a singular point of view. Stories told from many points of view, however, are around, as they are more fluid and better depict reality. Common in families and communities are stories creating themselves in the moment, begun first by one person, then continued by many others, with no particular pattern to be followed.

Artwork flourishes, having energy of its own and flowing in its own right, and is comprised of anything that does not trap energy, as is the case today with photos, drawings, paintings, or sculptures. Although some of these items are still around, it is for the sake of nostalgia. New materials and new ways of perceiving allow artwork to have more of its own identity in the current moment. Dreams are considered some of the most sophisticated and vibrant of all artwork and are available to all. In some cases, "highly aware" dreams are on display in art galleries of sorts. Nature as it sees itself in all time frames is also commonly displayed. Nothing remains in 2020 that is comprised of untruths or "lies," or where the intent was not loving by the craftsman. All untruthful objects and ideas...or those permeated with fear...have actually disintegrated by 2020. What remains in society is only that which flows...in everything everywhere,...in families, communities...and so it is in 2020...everything is flowing and *alive, alive, alive* —and people absolutely love it.

PAUL

Jenna: Hello, Paul. I can't believe how buoyant everyone is in 2020.

Paul: Isn't that what love is all about?

Jenna: Absolutely, but what I'm wondering is, how do people today learn about this overall love energy—or harmonious energy—in a group? We have talked a lot about love in general. Is there something specific you can tell me about how people tap in to the rhythms of love in their families, communities, and other groups?

Paul: There are some big ideas here that are important. First of all, ideas of self will have to be upgraded in order for people to tap into the minds and hearts of others.

Jenna: What do you mean?

Paul: People are going to have to learn to love themselves first before loving others.

Jenna: In order to feel group energy?

Paul: Yes. When they feel that rhythm in a group, the rhythm you wrote about, it is love they are feeling. But my point is they won't feel it unless they are loving toward themselves.

Jenna: Could I have more on that, please?

Paul: It is important that people tune in more to their own behavior, including perceptions, which often signify less than loving feelings about themselves. They truly need to know that what they perceive is filtered through their own judgmental eyes, namely, that what they see in others is themselves. As it is now, what people don't like about themselves, seems to be ever-present in their judgments about others. As soon as they love various aspects of themselves, they will learn to see *those* aspects in others. This is why in 2020 people are so focused on strengths people have rather than weaknesses, because they are in touch with those same loving qualities within themselves.

Jenna: Oh, I liked that, Paul, thanks…. Do you have any advice on how people can learn to love themselves more?

Paul: Learn to know the feeling of love. If I were a teacher in your school system or a parent, the first thing I would teach would be love. This is not just a subject for poets. It is at the heart of all of evolution. I would turn to my children and say things like, "Did you feel love today? Tell me about it…. how did it feel?" and so forth, engaging them in regular conversations about love, using examples from their own lives, including instances of fear and hate, which are certainly related to love because they are so contrasted to it. Although love is best learned through experience,—just by emulating it—perhaps it's about time humans learn to first focus on it! Who knows, maybe that takes conversations.

Jenna: Are you saying in context with self-images that people need to start talking about love?

Paul: Absolutely, for it is true in all learning, that intent and focus are very important; that is, to be loving, which starts with self-love, one needs to have that intention, and focus, too. Society is in such disarray now that both of those issues need to be addressed—and fast.

Jenna: Intent and focus.

Paul: Yes, in regard to whatever, including the intent to be more loving, including toward one's self. I am saying that people need to learn something about intent and focus, if they're going to be more loving. What is it you talk about? Do you talk about love? What are your intentions? Does your behavior exemplify it? You have to go backwards in a way. Study yourselves!

Jenna: I get your point. You are saying we are focused on the wrong things— and therefore not creating love.

Paul: Exactly. You need for your intentions and focus to be on love.

Jenna: Well, that leads me right into another question. People are very aware in 2020 of their intentions—all their intentions—unlike people today, and they realize the power of them, too. How do we learn that between now and 2020?

Paul: It starts with a responsibility for one's self. This can only happen when blame stops, when people truly realize no one else is forcing anything on them, that what is, is set forth by thought. They get what they intend. I think people will actually realize this when they get things they *don't* want; this will be the changing point which will thrust people into greater awareness. It also applies to who they are. They will have the conscious thought that they don't like what they have and/ or who they are—a common combination!—and realize they caused it. It is only then they will recognize and change the kinds of thoughts they carry, realizing the power of them.

Jenna: Okay, thanks, Paul. Any insights on how people stop blaming?

Paul: They will learn from repeated instances of emotional pain, the pain of isolation. People will not want to be around them if they are always blamed for something, so they will leave. Eventually, they will actually get to the point where they will dig deeper and deeper, finally making some sort of realization that they have the power to create what they want—and I don't just mean relationships, I mean everything.

Jenna: What kinds of insights will that entail?

Paul: They will make the connection that who they are—how they are flowing!—is actually the key to manifesting their intentions.

Jenna: You are not talking about humankind's wanting to be rich, beautiful or other superficial values.

Paul: They will not want those things when they are truly themselves, or at least they won't be the most important things. Those things may *happen* but it is because they are being who they are.

Jenna: You are saying, too, that people aren't as likely to flow, if they don't love themselves.

Paul: Absolutely, yes. I am also saying that's what it takes to synchronize in those groups of which you speak—love—notably in families and communities.

Jenna: Are you also saying that love is the key to sensing balance in one's self and others, and if so, could you elaborate?

Paul: Sensing balance *is* sensing flow. They are the same. To sense balance in others, or in a group, it is just a matter of sensing flow.

Jenna: What about knowing others' intentions? In 2020 people are also very clear on the intentions of others, including knowing whether or not a new soul wants to enter the earth plane! This is clearly hard to grasp. Communicating with a baby before conception?

Paul: Do you remember how often I have talked to you about "before, during and after," our exercises in timelessness, or what is in your mind before and after you are conscious of it?

Jenna: Yes.

Paul: Well, this is the way people live in 2020. They are aware of something before it is, as you would see it today. As for the baby, it can feel its energy prior to physical manifestation. This is really very much the same as your feeling the future. Do you not honor the future's input into its own beingness? It is not that you have created the future, rather it is creating itself and you are "in" on it. Knowing another's energy is what society is all about in 2020, as is knowing the energy of all things. All of these things go hand in hand, knowing one's own flow, tapping in to feelings of self, loving one's self, allowing for the flow of all things. Within the interaction of flow of all things come great insights, including the intentions of others. Let me ask you this. Because you can communicate with me telepathically like this, don't you know my intentions? How do you know them?

Jenna: It happens so fast, I have no idea.

Paul: What do you feel like during these conversations, where questions and answers are derived so quickly?

Jenna: There is certainly the movement of energy, flow, that is going on within me.

Paul: So, do you think that has something to do with knowing another's intentions?

Jenna: Definitely.

Paul: Would you say I am able to read what's in your unconscious?

Jenna: Absolutely. I have already written down what you are responding *to* sometimes before I'm even aware what I'm saying to you, myself! I wouldn't know my intent, actually, if it weren't for you.

Paul: Well, that's debatable; you know it at a deeper level, you are just not aware of it. But my point is we learn from experience, and you know something about intent because of how you feel when you communicate. You feel flowing. If you want to know more about intent, then notice what's in your awareness, how your body feels. Tell me everything you are aware of when we communicate, because this entire conversation is being fueled by both of our intentions. And I say the same to others, if they want to know about their intent, to study what's in their awarenesses, their bodies, and so forth, for what they do is also fueled by their intent.

Jenna: You are saying that intent then can be felt very clearly.

Paul: Of course, that is the way *all* things will be surmised as "time goes on," just as you have alluded to yourself, in your observations about 2020. Inner knowing will be "where it's at," to use your lingo.

Jenna: Cool it.

Paul: I'm just teasing.

Jenna: I know, I'm just teasing you.... Paul, by 2020 people are feeling others' emotions so deeply that emotional flow can be seen on the outside of the body, like rolling waves. What will have to happen for this to occur?

Paul: People will first have to experience their own emotions, which will necessitate a willingness to feel one's own sadness, fears, anxieties, the entire range of emotions. As of now, people are not willing or knowledgeable about their own emotional expression. When they learn this, their bodies will reflect it with tremendously fluid motion, so much in fact that the body will appear as one—one unit—that is, working very cohesively.

Jenna: Well, what about people's sense of privacy? Don't people feel that their emotions are their own personal stuff? What will thrust them forward into revealing themselves, instead of hiding, the way they do today?

Paul: At first they might be sensitive to revealing themselves, but as they learn to express their emotions more fully, they will realize there is more to gain—insight, health, love—than there is to lose. Not only that, they will learn what they thought was loss, the reasons for it, were just illusory.

Jenna: Illusory?

Paul: Well, I don't want to give away all the secrets, but perhaps people should think right now about the kinds of reasons they fear loss. Could it be possible that fear of having others know who they are has more to do with the lack of love for one's self than anything else? Also, there are other equally unsophisticated ideas humans carry around.

Jenna: That was lovingly put, Paul; I can feel your trying to be nice!

Paul: My point is there will be much more sharing of one's self, and tapping in to others, when the fear of what one has to lose has been reined back in to an area of reason, as opposed to the hysteria attached to loss today.

Jenna: Are you suggesting there will be increased panic when learning about loss in this upcoming decade?

Paul: There will be increased panic in learning about all things, in this decade and beyond, but that's all a part of humans' getting back in balance—and it's worth the price.

Jenna: You are talking about how people will feel when they give up control.

Paul: Yes. They will panic, no doubt about it.

Jenna: By the way, how do people learn to give up control? We're probably the most controlling beings in the universe, universes?...well, anywhere.

52

Paul: By trying it. By experiencing all that comes with giving it up and finding that there is more good than bad when allowing a natural flow of energy. Giving up control is allowing flow, and it affects all that is, not to mention creating all that is.

Jenna: It all seems so natural.

Paul: It is, and the irony is, you'll have to reacquaint yourself with what's natural!

Jenna: Boy, have humans gotten off track.

Paul: That's just where you're at.

Jenna: Paul, how do we learn to focus on bonds among people, the way they do in 2020, as opposed to the people themselves, or their personalities?

Paul: Learning to focus on love; that is all you are talking about. People will become as familiar with focusing on movement by 2020 as they are today focusing on stagnant energy, or anything highly defined.

Jenna: This is hard for me.

Paul: You're trying too hard to understand every little detail. Feel what I'm saying.

Jenna: I don't seem to feel comfortable until I understand.

Paul: You and everybody else.

Jenna: I guess what I'm wondering is, how do we learn to focus on movement in the first place if we're so used to highly defined form?

Paul: Maybe you should stop wondering. Has it ever occurred to you in itself is a form of control? In 2020 people allow what is to come to them, within the context of its own energy. When you wonder about something, you filter everything else out!...and that is when you don't feel movement. When you truly are feeling, movement is what you feel. But to answer your question about discerning flowing energy, that will come about by learning the energy of love. Are you noticing a pattern here? There is movement in love, a special kind of movement. People have to learn the value of love. It's so simple, and that takes feeling it, which is a harmonious, rhythmic, fluid, moving feeling that one feels when one is flowing one's self.

Jenna: Okay, thanks, yes, I see a pattern! I'm almost done with my questions.

Paul: Sometime tomorrow, probably.

Jenna: Very funny.... Paul, by 2020 people view everything as separate, with its own will, needs, and so forth—and equal. Things like couches and food! This seems a bit way out there. How will we ever get to this point?

Paul: It is not all that way out there, just hard to conceive, especially with the human ego so intact, as it is today. As of now humans do not have in their intent that food is an equal to them, or a couch...so they aren't. You want to experience your food more intimately, then get to know it. You'd do that with a lover, wouldn't you?

Jenna: Of course.

Paul: If it seems way out there, that objects have a beingness to them, think of it as energy, that way you won't lose the readership of the physicists. What is hard for you is the whole concept of equality. Well, that is the only way direct experience with anything can occur, when both are flowing, without judgment.

Jenna: Well, how does this new way of remembering fit in here? In 2020 it's as if a curtain opens and people actually reexperience everything all over again, unlike today where we remember selectively.

Paul: People will have to learn that the way they remember now—in the 1990s—is very controlled, that they themselves are the ones controlling their memories. Allowing memory to flow—with its own energy—will allow more into the conscious mind, as it was, actually. So why are they controlling memory? Because they are controlling who they are, their own identities. When they get the fact they are not who they believe they are—but who they feel they are—then it will all fall into place, and that will include memories that are more authentic.

Jenna: Is there anything we need to learn to have more fluid movements in our bodies? By 2020 everybody's body movements are so integrated.

Paul: Again, there is nothing you need to learn, other than the nature of flow—then flow yourselves. Be your flowing selves, and I can assure you your bodily movements will be just as fluid as "you" are! It's kind of like letting your body "do its own thing," as you have already referred to in regard to physical senses and emotions in 2020. Well, guess what? Your body knows what to do, too—when it is energized!

54

Jenna: This is really just a matter of our egos backing off of controlling everything, isn't it?

Paul: You've got it…and perceiving food from its own point of view, as you would say it.

Jenna: What do you mean?

Paul: Well, the downside is someone has to be the first to experience, maybe even talk about it.

Jenna: Look, I'm already writing about it; I'm not going to go around talking about it.

Paul: Don't worry about it. It's years away. Just keep doing your research.

Jenna: I am also wondering about new respect for birth, death, and the moon.

Paul: What about all those things?

Jenna: Well, how will we learn all this?

Paul: By entraining with energy. You, my dear, are an expert already. Why don't you teach it?

Jenna: Increasing awareness?

Paul: Yes, and being and intuition, and telepathy; you know, everything we've been talking about.

Jenna: Paul, you are my consultant.

Paul: Yes, darling, but you are the one already doing it, don't you see?…sometimes you are so naive; it kills us spirit guides.

Jenna: Paul, you're already dead. Besides, I don't know how to respond to this.

Paul: You are getting your information about 2020 by the exact method people use to live by in 2020, don't you get that?

Jenna: Well, yes, but I'm not totally clear on how I'm doing it, let alone teaching it. I'm sounding a little wimpy, aren't I?

Paul: Well, not completely confident, but that's good. You are being truthful. You are feeling! And we want you to know one other thing. It is the process here, which is so intriguing, not the facts. You are getting your information about the future from the flow of energy itself; it is not trapped, again, to use your term. You just pull out of that moving, harmonious, rhythmic energy the facts of love—which is to say, what is! Ah hum, do you see a pattern here? And we spirit guides think you'd be just great on the lecture tour, talking all about this! In fact, we're already giving some consideration as to what you should wear.

Jenna: Sometimes you are too much.

Paul: Look, I'll tell you something. Rebecca and I can respond to all these questions, but people will have to learn for themselves—and the only way they can do that is by jumping right in and flowing themselves, for only in that instance will they learn about love. And they can also learn from others. That is all I am saying. Your experiences are valuable to others. We just want you to know that you already know a lot, and you need not grasp every detail in order to help others, even speak to them.

Jenna: I get that, and thank you, Paul. I'm complimented. You are just talking about the importance of being myself, aren't you?

Paul: To know yourself is to love yourself, so why don't we just end with that?…unless of course you'd like me to book the auditorium.

Jenna: Help.

Paul: We send you love and encouragement, and that is our message to you, sweet Jenna. We wouldn't push you so if we didn't think you wanted to help create a more loving world. Deep in your heart, from its point of view…

REBECCA

Jenna: Hi, Rebecca.

Rebecca: Are you a little upset with Paul's needling you all the time?

Jenna: I know it's done with love, but it's starting to get to me. I think I'm scared.

Rebecca: That you might have a big part in teaching new ways of perceiving, and so forth?

Jenna: Yes. Also that there's so much change ahead; my stomach is in knots. Most people have no idea. I would like to talk about the energy of fear, since I am dealing with it now, and because others will be dealing with it more as time goes on. What can you tell people about the energy of fear?

Rebecca: That it affects perception, including how love is perceived. I suspect you are not experiencing fear fully right now. Not only does unexpressed fear prevent you from feeling the true energy of love, but it also distorts everything else you perceive. This is the way people basically perceive today, through the eyes of fear.

Jenna: Could I have more on that, please?

Rebecca: Fear affects how you experience your life: whether you are happy, sad, angry, afraid, silly, joyous, kind, funny, aware, unaware, diseased, healthy…

Jenna: Okay, I get your point. It is the key to you, right?

Rebecca: That is absolutely right. How you experience love is the key to you.

Jenna: Well, how do ideas of self fit in here? Paul talked a lot about that.

Rebecca: Your perception of love affects your ideas of who you are.

Jenna: Including how much you love yourself.

Rebecca: Exactly.

Jenna: So what are you suggesting?

Rebecca: That people know the energy of fear better. As it stands, people don't know when they are distorting. If people can detect the energy of fear, knowing when it is affecting their perceptions, they will have a better idea of love…a better idea of everything, for that matter!

Jenna: Could you apply this to what we have to learn, starting right with this very day?

Rebecca: To get in touch with yourself, you need to know when your perceptions are good ones. This is what people are able to do in 2020. We don't do that now. We don't recognize when there is a lack of flow within ourselves, hence inaccurate perceptions. We do not realize how often we are reacting to something today, when we should be more centered on who we are. We are more into our reactions and other people's reactions. This is very different from the highly interactive society you have depicted in 2020 where buoyancy is a factor, and each moment is a creative one. The reactive state today is characterized by getting stuck, which is not a creative state at all. There is a slowdown of energy, in fact, and one of the big reasons for this is humans' inability to express emotions, which is due to fear—so we're right back at fear!

Jenna: Are you saying that people in 2020 allow fear to run its course, while people today try to direct it?

Rebecca: That would be one way to look at it.

Jenna: Well, what else are you saying?

Rebecca: That inner knowing is the best way to know when one's perceptions are accurate, and this entails allowing all to flow, even fear! Because when fear doesn't flow, neither do your emotions, which in fact act as a barrier to inner knowing. I am talking about your own intuitive self.

Jenna: Well, more on inner knowing, please. Or better yet, how about some insight on things we do which are not inner knowing?

Rebecca: My guess is that you orient yourself around a belief—attach yourself to it in a way—then run that belief through your mind over and over, or similar ones, so that your ego is soothed, and so that you are "in control." The only problem with this is, when you do that, you yourself are not in touch with who you are, which means you certainly won't be tapping into inner knowing, and hence your barometer for good perceptions is thrown out the window. You are in fact focused on your beliefs and others' beliefs, which is a far cry from that deeper part of yourselves and others.

Jenna: And in 2020?

Rebecca: Suffice it to say, just as you have said, everything is allowed to flow: beliefs, ideas, thoughts, you know, everything. What I don't want you to do now is start to think well, what are beliefs, and what are ideas? How do beliefs differ from thoughts, and so forth, because that is what people do. At this time in history most people literally turn on this switch and start to define. Yes, they define to know, and this is just what they don't do in 2020. They feel to know. So my point is this, when all is allowed to flow, perceptions are great. You need not worry about what it is you are allowing to flow, just do it! Get the feeling of it. Whatever comes into your mind, just let it flow. When you define, you constrict.

Jenna: Well, how do we learn this feeling?

Rebecca: It is harder than you think because we have gotten used to certain kinds of perceptions, which feel natural to us but are in fact controlled. We have learned fear-based perceptions. We are literally used to seeing through the eyes of fear. I am saying that humans do not know the difference between constricted energy flow and a natural energy flow. They don't know how to feel the difference.

Jenna: Well, what will that take?

Rebecca: More sophisticated perception.

Jenna: You mentioned earlier that you teach your clients in the future how to magnify their own emotions. Is this the kind of thing you mean? And if so, please tell us more.

Rebecca: Well, in regard to fear, they learn to feel the energy of it, just as we have been talking about here. They actually feel it in my office, and since they feel safe there, they allow it to flow. It is quite a meeting between clients—and fear!

Jenna: Do they separate fear, so to speak, from themselves?

Rebecca: Yes, they do, and I also teach them to feel their mother's love at the same time they meet fear!

Jenna: Rebecca, sometimes this moves a little fast for me. Are you saying that this is your method to help people actually experience emotional pain more fully?

Rebecca: That, and to perceive everything, as it's a more accurate view of reality. But actually I prefer not to talk about method but principles. The idea of a mother's love is an important one.

Jenna: Are you saying your clients feel love from the point of view of the fetus, child, young adult, or what?

Rebecca: The earlier the better. The point is that when my clients can feel their mothers' love—and they all have memories of it—they have direct experience with whatever they are dealing. The more they can feel it, the more they meld with the energies of their lives, which translates into intensified emotions. This happens right here in my office. For some, this direct experience is a first, being very dramatic, very magnetic, and very touching for both the client and me, the therapist.

Jenna: That is fascinating. You are saying that if they can get in touch with themselves which can be brought into their conscious minds by "remembering" feelings of their mother's love, that their perceptions will be more accurate because fear is allowed to flow, making their experiences more intensified.

Rebecca: Well, I must say one thing; you are excellent at reiterating what I am saying, but let me be the first to say something else...I am sorry if I embarrass you; I trust you understand...but that is not the way they know in 2020.

Jenna: You are right.

Rebecca: I am not knocking you.

Jenna: I know.

Rebecca: Yes, you know what I am saying, you understand it, but if you had experienced it differently...let me see, how do I say this?...if you had had direct experience grasping that, not just an intellectual one, you would remember as they do in 2020, too. I am amplifying what you said about how memory in 2020, how it has changed. Do you follow me?

Jenna: Yes, you are suggesting I won't remember very well because I am just repeating what you are telling me, not really experiencing it.

Rebecca: Yes!

Jenna: Hmm...that leads me right into my next question, and no, I don't mind being a guinea pig! Rebecca, what do we have to learn between now and 2020 in order to experience memory more authentically?

Rebecca: In order to remember more authentically—or more—you need to experience something more than intellectually. I agree with Paul that people now control memory. In order for people to make this leap, or to allow into their minds what actually happened, it will have to be perceived as nonthreatening to the ideas and beliefs they already hold. For example, today people believe that some ideas are superior to others—or right—while others are wrong. On this basis alone, certain ideas are allowed into their awarenesses, and others not. Judgment of ideas will have to stop, in order to allow for the flow of all of them, which is what it will take to allow memory to flow freely—or as it originally was, and is!

Jenna: Rebecca, what are your thoughts about perceiving from a physical object's point of view and relating to it as an equal?

Rebecca: That you will be able to feel an object only when you let go of your beliefs about the object and yourself. My feeling is that equality just happens when people can actually feel others, or in this case, objects. Now if people are still carrying around beliefs that they are superior to something else—or I might add inferior, as it is not always superiority that gets in the way—then of course they haven't let go of all of their beliefs. The idea of equality *is* a belief. Have you ever thought of it that way? True equality will only come about when all beliefs are gone. Eventually beliefs of their own accord will just dissipate.

Jenna: I came across that in regard to objects themselves, that certain objects have actually disintegrated by 2020.

Rebecca: Yes, and so will beliefs.

Jenna: Can you elaborate, please, on objects?

Rebecca: They lose their ability to be elastic. A certain ebb and flow is necessary for life. Have you ever seen a brittle pine needle? As of now, it just breaks with the wind, or the paw of a dog. Later, everything happens so much faster.

Jenna: Could you describe what happens to the object?

Rebecca: Ping! a glass shatters due to just the right pitch... I know, it doesn't disappear, the pieces of glass are still there. This concept of disappearance will not occur until people can accept themselves disappearing. Does that make sense?

Jenna: Absolutely, accept their own death.

Rebecca: Yes, or at least not be so fearful of it. That will be the first step.

Jenna: This is amazing to me, makes me a little anxious, I think. It scares me that things will just start disappearing.

Rebecca: They won't just start disappearing. Your thoughts will have to create that, remember? You need not worry about the particulars or that your things will suddenly be missing, or that you will be missing, okay? The things that disappear will "will" it upon themselves. No one will be in charge of disappearing things. Think of it this way; they will choose to die. It will not be loss but transformation. What do you think the objects think about people dying?

61

Jenna: Are you serious?

Rebecca: I am trying to get you beyond your own point of view, as this is where fear emanates. But that is too big to tackle here. My main point is not to worry about objects disappearing, but if you can imagine this, please do. It will be pleasant.

Jenna: Yes, we're always worrying about loss. That is really something, allowing all of these new ideas into my mind! Well, do you have anything to say about heightened sexual energy in 2020?

Rebecca: That in order for this to happen, beliefs will need to flow, then go away. Sexual energy will be inversely proportional to the beliefs imbedded in us. Although this will seem like a catch 22 again, the answers as to how to increase one's own sexual energy will come through the experience of sexuality itself. What I mean by this is, I don't really teach anything like heightened sexual experience or response or whatever you want to call it, even energy flow. What I teach is more an accurate perception.

Jenna: People have more respect for birth, death and the moon in 2020. What kinds of new insights will that entail?

Rebecca: That all of those things, just like objects, have their own beliefs about you!

Jenna: You don't really mean that.

Rebecca: I use that to illustrate their own beingness. What I am talking about is getting away from defined concepts of whatever it is we already know, such as birth, death and the moon. Because if people can feel movement when I say that, about the moon, birth and death, then it's a start. Getting away from how we know now, of course, is what I'm talking about. We simply do not feel movement when we know by belief because beliefs are highly defined.

Jenna: Thanks, Rebecca. Any particular thoughts on relating to food more intimately?

Rebecca: Well, it is just the same as relating to anything else more intimately. When you can feel love for something and its love for you, then you're home free. I'm sounding like Paul, aren't I? But you can't feel love for something if you have all sorts of preconceived ideas about something, like how it's going to taste, how it will affect your body, or whatever, because that is what you are focusing on—what you already know about something. You are not taking your information from current data, and are in fact in the past.

Jenna: Are you suggesting people don't think when they eat?

Rebecca: Well, if they want to experience their food, yes. As of now the main data people take in about food comes from their beliefs. Their senses are barely taking in anything.

Jenna: Oh, I've been wanting to ask you more about that, more about the role of the physical senses. Many say that love is experienced by the heart, but you say physical senses are a big factor in experiencing love. Tell me more about that.

Rebecca: Well, the physical senses have a lot to do with love because they have a lot to do with perception. And the way we experience love has to do with the way we perceive it. Believe it or not, the physical senses have hardly started to experience love. When they are used more fully—and together, in a more balanced way—there will be all sorts of new dimensions to love, believe me. The heart is the impetus for perception, that is for sure, but the physical senses make our experiences more colorful, and I mean that as a general term, not just applicable to sight.

Jenna: Wow, this has got my head spinning. Okay, here is one last question. What do we need to experience to know fluid body movements, and do you teach anything later in this regard?

Rebecca: What I teach are the fears of the body from the point of view of the body.

Jenna: Not the ego.

Rebecca: That is exactly right, from the cells' perspective…which means the body itself starts to flow more. Now this might sound kind of corny, but when you take on the point of view of that which you experience, you encourage its flow; it is like acknowledging it, loving it; it is very much the same as interrelating with another human. Here we are talking about acknowledging cells in the body. When that happens, there is flow and inner knowing—from the perspective of the cells! I help people perceive more, from more points of view, essentially.

Jenna: Could you sum up briefly—if that's possible!—how you help people increase their awarenesses?

Rebecca: I teach a sort of rotating perception, where people learn to take on many points of view, expanding upon their own. First, they learn to see from one point of view, then they gradually add more; after a while it comes naturally. People today who are the most loving already do this to a great degree. It is largely a matter of teaching their method.

Jenna: But aren't there different ways of perceiving?

Rebecca: Yes, and we will get into those later. All methods necessitate the idea of flow, though, so the principle remains intact, that when you incorporate more points of view, a greater reality is represented. The more viewpoints, the more motion, the more buoyancy. It is a spiraling upward to increasingly finer energies.

Jenna: But sometimes I can't put this all together.

Rebecca: It will come. Allow it to flow!

Jenna: Okay, thanks, Rebecca.

Rebecca: You are very welcome.

Author's comments

If you feel as though you are emotionally uncomfortable after reading this chapter, don't feel like the Lone Ranger! When I was communicating with Paul and Rebecca, I did too. There were so many ideas, my head was spinning. We are in the process of learning new ways of knowing, whether it's reading or communicating telepathically. The more we feel to know, as opposed to think to know, the more we might feel anxious, maybe even panicky because we feel such a loss of control, something we are very much used to. As we increase our awareness, we allow more and more ideas into our conscious minds but at times are uncomfortable with this. We can't put them all into the bigger picture, how one idea affects another, and so forth, the way Paul and Rebecca can—or the people in 2020. One of the hardest parts about letting go of control is giving up the idea that we are in charge of arranging the ideas in our minds the way we want, so everything makes sense to us. Oh, we can if we want…but it won't give us a very good idea about reality—and we need that if we are going to create the path to 2020. So relax, and allow all these ideas to do their own thing. Why not let them meander around in your head a bit? Trust me. They *know* what to do!

Humor and Entertainment in 2020

•Joy and humor through energy flow •Intimate entertainment in small groups •Humor on the cellular level •Expanded use of the physical senses •Laughter and the physical body •Sharing emotional flow •Abstract humor •Age of the physical body •Laughter as a learning tool, a source of joy

By 2020 people are totally infatuated with the state of joy—or being-ness—and have chosen to consciously live this way moment to moment, finding it painful, actually, to stop their energy from flowing. They've also learned that humor is as natural to them as telepathy, when they're open, honest, and loving. In addition to being extremely humorous themselves, there is also an abundance of humor elsewhere—everywhere, in fact. Since people are highly aware of others' perspectives, not only do they have their own experiential bases as sources for humor, but they also have everybody else's!

Sharing Emotions

Probably the biggest difference in society in 2020 from today is that people have much broader perspectives, hence broader experiences, which means everything is intensified a great deal more. This would pertain to humor. Emotional expression itself is vastly different by 2020. Unlike today, where people's emotions get stuck due to fear of emotional pain, by 2020 they're flowing much more fluidly. Emotions themselves are experienced more broadly. Take joy, for example. Rather than experiencing it just from their own hearts, it would be more like experiencing it from everybody's hearts! Talk about a broader perspective. This is what life is like in 2020, interconnectedness at its most intimate level—and people welcome sharing their emotions, which is also true for other emotions, although the so called

65

negative ones, as we know them today, are apt to be experienced more quickly, being transformed very fast to a higher vibratory state. Today emotional expression is like the dripping of water; in 2020 it's more like the rush of water.

A specific example of a broader experience in the field of entertainment in 2020 could be illustrated by the following. In 2020 someone in the audience of a "live" or on-stage performer would perceive very differently from someone watching the same material now. A performer in 2020 jokes about something, an embarrassing situation, say, he finds himself in. Today a person would view it as such: she would laugh, with thoughts something like, "Oh, how funny. That is so embarrassing; I've been there myself," but that would probably be the degree of her awareness. A person in 2020 would be aware of much more. For example, in addition to identifying with the embarrassing situation, she might be aware of the true motivation of the performer (not just that he wants to get laughs), perhaps something about his purpose in life, something about the performer's past, including emotional experiences, his current feelings, maybe even his feelings in the future. She would know instantly and intuitively—as is the case with all of these observations—the effects the performer is having on herself, as well as on others in the audience. In other words, people are not just aware of what is happening in the current moment to themselves and others in the audience but also something about the entertainer's "past" and "future," bringing it into the now, as they view him.

In addition to the audience member, this same broad perspective also applies to the entertainer himself, in 2020. He too sees the world through many eyes, and many time frames. In fact, if he is a highly skilled entertainer, his perspective is probably even broader than that of his audience members. Today on-stage entertainers definitely prepare ahead of time but also rely on just "winging it." In 2020 they really wing it. Since they are highly aware of their audiences' perspectives, they are able to use that energy—well, for their acts. They integrate the thoughts and feelings of their audience members right into their routines—and on the spot. In some ways, the audience becomes the entertainment. But I am not just saying they are highly skilled improvisational performers, I am saying they are vastly more aware than the same kinds of entertainers today. The same would also apply to the audience members, who are much more interactive than audiences today. Today, blurting out laughter uproariously whenever one feels like it during a performance might be considered rude. Not so in 2020...a person laughs, another laughs, then another. It's all very spontaneous, even raucous at times. Though not experienced like "waves" in a football stadium (groups are much smaller in 2020, allowing for more intimacy) waves of sorts are experienced. Not distracting but soothing, people in the audience feel the building of a rhythmic, harmonious sound wave while remaining totally focused on the performer...not only focused—but at one with him. So, by 2020, it's not as if they have no respect for the entertainer, it's just that they know they have a part in the totality of the act. In fact, it would not be unusual for the members of the audience to join the performer on stage, turning it into a dynamic group experience. So much is done by intuition in 2020, which is fueled by this vast awareness on both the parts of the audience and entertainer, who feed each other. Today, although there is an interaction between audience and entertainer, it is nothing compared to the interplay in 2020.

Expanded Use Of The Physical Senses

The actual preparation of entertainers in 2020 also differs radically from today. This would be particularly applicable to those performing "live," which makes up the majority of "entertainment" in 2020. I will elaborate more on this in a moment. Because they truly do use energy from all around them, entertainers must make preparations to be open to it. What they do, before walking on stage, is to exercise all of their five physical senses, by smelling, tasting, touching, hearing, and seeing. Starting with one at a time, they exercise each to its fullest, then add the next, then the next, and so forth, until all five senses are "open." This allows them to be more aware when they walk on the stage. By 2020 people not only understand the correlation between the five physical senses and perception—one of clarity—but they use it, and there's no more obvious place than in the "entertainment industry," although by 2020 there is hardly an "entertainment industry." By then, it's just a bunch of people doing a bunch of things spontaneously—and with love...whenever and wherever. Everything is less organized by 2020. After all, people have given up control.

In addition to enjoying live performances, people are also able to tap into entertainment telepathically, without actually being there, and the experience is truly authentic and intense; however, being there, even in 2020, is still a bit more encompassing and heartfelt. This kind of difference of actually being with someone as opposed to communicating with them from a distance is referred to as "depth of feel" by 2020, which is influenced among other things, by the physical senses. In other words, being there taps into much greater sensations of feeling. Although memory of the "past, present, and future" has evolved a great deal by 2020—which is just another way of saying awareness has increased—people still prefer others' physical presences, which is why entertainment most often tends to be in small groups. This way there is more intimacy, and intimacy is what people crave in 2020.

Humor On The Cellular Level

Humor itself is more physical in 2020. It can be felt on a cellular level, which is indeed at a very deep, visceral level. What this means is that when people feel humor, they feel a certain physical "fullness" to it, or to be more accurate, pertaining to themselves. The closest to what we know today would be the sensation of a liquid flowing through the human body. Overall, it is extremely pleasant. Feeling their cells literally saturated with humor, it is much more of a whole body experience than we are used to today. This is because by 2020 people have a much better connection to and with their physical bodies. Some even refer to this time as "The Age of the Physical Body," since there is renewed interest in it as a vehicle for spiritual growth. But back to the physical body, what actually happens during humor—or joy—is a stretching of the cells a bit beyond what they normally are, an actual physical response that is elastic, and particularly noticeable during laughter. When people laugh, their cells get exercise—or therapy—releasing what they don't need, ideas that don't work for them anymore, essentially. This release is important for the cells in order for them to be in good health. What it feels like to both the cells and the people themselves in 2020, is that all of the cells are joining hands, loving one another, which they need to do from time to time, in order to remind them that they are all working together as a single unit. This is one way to look at humor in 2020, from the point of view of the cells, and people do this regularly in 2020; for by this time they have come to realize they *are* their cells.

Laughter And The Physical Body

Laughter itself has changed dramatically by 2020, being more guttural, involving more of the body, and not surprisingly, having greater depth and flow to it. Like humor, laughter is fuller. Today it is not uncommon for laughter to be experienced by grabbing one's stomach or by lurching forward; a certain jerkiness presides, characterized by a kind of stop and go action. What people don't realize now is that this clutching gesture is actually an unconscious attempt to stop the laughter! This is what we are doing today, trying to stop our own laughter and joy. In 2020 people experience the whole laugh, which begins in the stomach, then moves from head to toe, in "waves," much like the movements of a swimming dolphin. Of course the waves aren't as big, but the flow is just as smooth. Joy then, just as the case is with all other emotions, has flow to it—energy flow, which can be seen on the outside of the body in 2020. In other words, people do not grab their stomachs or lurch forward as we do today to stop joy; they just let'er rip.

The physical senses are working with more depth by 2020, and in unity with one another, allowing these broader experiences. It doesn't just feel as if the ears are hearing, for example, for they aren't; the eyes are also seeing, the tongues are tasting, the skin is responding, and so forth, with the experience being "cell deep," which means people are better able to sense from all over their bodies, not just knowing with their heads. In addition, they are able to gather information from all of their senses at once, experiencing them with much greater clarity and balance, unlike what we do today, which is to focus on one or two of the senses at a time, actually favoring one or two of our sensory organs. In terms of experiencing the laugh, today there is a relaxed feeling and release of energy, but people do not experience their bodies enjoying the laugh, thinking of it more as an experience of their heads! In 2020 it feels more as if all of their cells are laughing—each one of them! And there is an awareness of the interconnectedness of the cells, not only within their physical bodies, but also to a bigger whole—to other people and the universe. And the same would be true for sadness, or any other emotion. In the case of sadness, the cells themselves would be feeling sad, and in the case of empathy, it would be each cell itself that would feel empathic, magnifying the emotional experience many times over from what we know today. People call this riding their senses in 2020, and since people really crave these full sensory experiences, it is not surprising that entertainment reflects it.

There is also more awareness and embracing of sound by 2020, particularly harmonious sound. And people's range of hearing has vastly expanded, hearing a great deal more than we do today. Specifically, they hear more sounds and also more within a single sound, which they do both with their ears and other sense organs, feeling sound more than we do today. Now, for the most part, people hear only the initial echoing of a sound. By 2020 they have developed "inner hearing," which has more to do with focusing on sound within one's self, than hearing sounds outside of one's self.

Do people howl in 2020? You bet they do. They also think it's one of the funniest sounds they've ever heard, the actual sound of an uproarious laugh, which by this time contains a wide assortment of rhythms, tones and overtones, facets of sound, unfamiliar to most of us today.

Amazingly, because people can hear so well, many can hear smiles! In fact, the gesture of appreciation in audiences is no longer the clap. People wave the air. Some do this with thought, while others push it with a physical gesture, such as a hand. Still others smile while breathing out very hard through their noses! By contrast, laughter can be quite loud, but it is not interruptive, as it often is today; it blends better. And when somebody laughs, it rolls—which others can hear long after the actual physical utterance has stopped, as we would describe it today. Not only can people see the flow of the laugh on the outside of the body, they can also hear the flow of the laugh, *even* after it "stops." The same holds true for all the physical senses, actually. People can see, taste, sense textures, and smell things that are no longer there, if you will, after they have "disappeared," which gives an eternal sense to all of their experiences. Whereas we often use sensory data to trigger past memories today—taking us out of the moment-—people in 2020 carry sensory data around with them moment to moment, keeping them in the present.

Intimate Entertainment In Small Groups

What is the actual entertainment in 2020? Besides the live, preplanned kind of event described earlier, most of it is quite different from today. The vast amount is very spontaneous, more intimate, and with people most likely to attend what is in their own community. Often, it just happens among friends. In the case of scheduled events, performers are often leaders who encourage others to join in with them, stimulating them to become more of who they are. Today people relax and distance themselves from who they are, when they attend, say, films, watch television, or watch anything, recorded or live. It's not that they can't identify with the performer, it's just that they choose to be entertained, not entering into the process; it's almost as if they have given themselves permission to kick back and not be, which they feel they "deserve." Well, by 2020 people are champing at the bit to enter into new experiences, largely consisting of getting to know themselves and others better. Because of this, the majority of entertainment is live, since this lends itself best to true intimacy. In addition, there is much colorful dancing, singing, and improvisational kinds of plays available to people…but it's not as if they need outside entertainment in order to express themselves this way, for it is very common for people to sing and dance themselves, alone or in groups of friends. And people love kites! Even Mother Earth has taken on more of a role as entertainer in 2020, having become far more than a dumping ground. The oceans, in particular, are now a maze of activity—deep down—both in sports and exploratory adventures. There are no longer films, television programs, video games, CDs, or recordings of any kind around—any copies—as they constrain energy and create barriers among people. In terms of entertainment in families, there is much spontaneous laughter and joy, with children often "entertaining" their parents with demonstrations of, among other things, physical manifestations of paper airplanes. Yes, they pull them right out of the air. It would be akin today to parents showing their children how to cut out paper snowflakes, only by 2020, it's children leading the way, "teaching" their parents.

What is Funny

What actually makes people laugh in 2020? Whatever makes them feel good! People laugh not so much at other things or people, as with something, when there is a feeling of interconnectedness which feels joyful to them. The most common time people laugh is during times of true enjoyment and pleasure, with the laugh itself being an expression of joy, not one of power. It would not feel right to them to laugh at others, for example, for reasons of individual differences. From an intellectual standpoint, people in 2020 laugh when they identify with ideas that fuel growth, or when they identify with what is valued, with truths of the day showing up in humor: growth, equality, naturalness, love, change. Truth is joy for people in 2020. In terms of actual jokes, the most popular ones are those that create, not take away. What adds to one's worth, or another's, is what's "funny," or enjoyable. By 2020 people are so oriented around growth, and know so much about it, that they actually crave change; whereas people today are more comfortable feeling what they are used to, which means today humor often reflects the status quo, while in 2020 it reflects change.

Not surprisingly, surprise is often comical in 2020. It is often comical today, too, but more often it instills fear in people because their identities are so fragile. This is not the case in 2020. People expect change, they process it very well, and within it they frequently find humor. One of the biggest reasons for this in 2020 is that when people experience something unexpectedly, it makes them realize how narrow their own perspectives are, which is very funny to them, spurring them on to more open-mindedness. Today people are more likely to be threatened by opposing views and ideas, or those differing from their own. By 2020 people have a tremendous ability to deal with change, which they consider a challenge, fueling growth.

What is Not Funny

What don't people laugh at? In addition to not laughing at other people, they don't laugh at things that don't work, which would include, among other things, ideas! Today people laugh at others' ideas, labeling them ridiculous. Not so, in 2020. All have a right to be, even ideas. Laughing at something is a way of distancing. Well, by 2020 people relate totally differently to both ideas and people, relating to ideas just like people. They don't judge ideas, for example, allowing them to flow, honoring them for what they are. Because of this, although it might appear they are giggling at something at times, they are not. One thing they do not appreciate in 2020 is someone's claiming his ideas are better than another's. This way of thinking, and being, is about as dated as stuck emotions and aborted laughs. As a result, this kind of claim—that one idea is better than another—is seldom heard in our society of love.

Laughter as a Learning Tool, a Source of Joy

When people laugh in 2020, it is because they are actually identifying with something much deeper. Their laughs are fueling more advanced ideas, if you will, for within laughter is insight, a potent evolutionary force, which people can feel. After laughing, it is not the least bit unusual for a person to comment on his insights. True laughter is very enlightening, joyful, and a wonderful way to connect with other people. So, in addition to being a great healing tool in 2020, laughter is also a great learning tool.

Abstract Humor

Another example of something people would laugh at in 2020: everything going wrong on a honeymoon. Now this might be funny to many today, but in 2020 people would laugh for entirely different reasons. Now people would probably laugh because "whatever can go wrong will go wrong," but in 2020 they'd go one step further, realizing that the true flow of the idea is often not what one expects. People in 2020 realize that when you carry around a lot of expectations, you are narrowing your perspective—or limiting the flow of an idea. In other words, they see how they are limiting both themselves and the ideas with their expectations. So when they laugh at everything going wrong on a honeymoon, it would be very much like giving power back to the idea, which they fully believe has its own rights. They are not laughing at the nature of love but rather enjoying knowing it. They love it when an idea exerts itself! Shaping an idea to be what you want is a "no, no" in our loving society, just as shaping other people to be what you want them to be, is a "no, no." Flow is flow—and in 2020 flow shapes itself!

As can be seen by the above example, humor has also become more abstract, with people being able to identify literally with everything, not just with what has individual meaning for themselves on a very personal level; in other words, truth has more to do with the truth of ideas than whether or not a particular idea applies to them. Truth is truth, which spells joy for all, in 2020. Today people find little humor, or joy, in that which does not affect them directly. Oh, they might grasp it intellectually, but today people are a long, long way from feeling humor at an abstract level; it's hard enough for them to feel it at a highly personal level, preferring instead to unconsciously or semiconsciously distance themselves from joy.

Because people do look at ideas differently in 2020, it is very hard to define anything. Ideas interrelate so, they affect one another like infectious laughter! Then before you know it they have a whole new look to them. But looking at humor from the perspective of people in 2020, I would "define" it as such: Humor is everywhere; it is not just what makes people laugh. It is the laugh, too. It is the person who espouses the humor, it is the listener. It is the mother who influenced the child in what he knows and feels, the joke teller, so to speak. It is the resultant behavior because of the humor. It is everything humor touches; it is everything it doesn't touch. It is not just the joke. It includes all time frames, before, during, and after the immediacy of the humor. Humor is the combined laughs of many; it is the fuel for the jokes or the truths that make up the jokes. It is life itself because life makes up the humor.

PAUL

Jenna: Paul, hi. Well, at least people are laughing a lot in 2020.

Paul: That they are.

Jenna: Tell me, what do people need to learn right now in order to have broader experiences, so that they see humor everywhere? It sounds terrific, but I would like to know more about seeing through another's eyes.

Paul: Seeing through another's eyes first of all takes empathy for another person. This means more than anything one has to feel his pain. We have discussed the importance of feeling our own pain. The ability to feel humor is related to this ability to feel pain. One has much more ability to detect what is humorous for another if he can detect what is painful for him. These will be learned in tandem. And of course, before one can learn others' pain and joy, one must know one's own.

Jenna: Why is that?

Paul: I do not think that people are likely to know what is humorous for others if they do not love those people first.

Jenna: More on this, please.

Paul: Well, what is humor? You have amply described it as the experience of joy. To know another's joy, it is necessary to know what that feeling is. I can assure you your experience of joy has been enhanced due to your experience of emotional pain. All I am saying is that to know another's joy, it is necessary to know his pain. Do you not have to contrast feelings to know them? This is how humans know what they know at this time in history.

Jenna: Yes. But this is not the way you know, correct?

Paul: That is correct, and it is not the way you will always know, either. But you asked me how to know another's humor or joy, and what I am trying to get across is that you will need first of all to be able to distinguish joy from other feelings; pain is quite contrasted, don't you think? And you start with yourself, knowing first what joy/humor is, then you can know another's; second what pain is, your own, then you can know another's. I am talking about some of the very first steps of learning to get to this joyous society of which you speak. There are many who do not know joy. I have spoken about this in reference to love. People barely know what their feelings are. They can barely distinguish between "good" and "bad" sometimes, meaning what is preferable; sometimes they can't even tell a thought from a feeling. This is the state of affairs for humanity, I'm afraid, at this time. I am not saying in any way that people all experience joy or pain similarly; that is certainly not the case. I am saying that first humans must learn to feel joy, so that you will know to what you aspire! Let us start there. You know pain better, in many cases, not that you feel it, but you are quite adept at when it's about to appear—so that you can avoid it! How can you bring about this great joyous society if you do not feel this fine feeling yourself? Well, I'll tell you something, you can't. So, my advice to each and every one of you is to start feeling joy/humor, whatever you want to call it, right now because, trust me, it is worth it now, tomorrow, and yesterday. Yes, in all time frames, it is mighty worth it. And I add this. You want a good investment? Try joy, try laughs, try love, try laughing cells and all that you have written about. You can't "get there" intellectually. That is my point. What do you think manifestation of an idea is? It is you. You want a society of joyous beings? Then be one.

Jenna: Thanks, Paul. I've never heard you so forceful. You're not angry, are you?

Paul: And let this be a lesson to you, too. No, I am not angry. I know that you do not mean that, even though it feels that way to you. Here is the lesson. The next time you feel someone whom you perceive to be angry, think of it as love. It is my love you feel. Now that you are becoming increasingly more aware, you will feel more. This force that you feel is love; it is desire; it is my concern for the human race. Yes, I like that. When you feel someone's anger, think of it this way—it is just love—and the problem lies in the perception, okay? Do you think you could actually do that? This is just a follow-up in a way to Rebecca's saying you'll need to redefine anger and experience it differently. Because you truly will.

Jenna: Yes, I guess it was just my own perception, my own discomfort with anger, if you will. Your point is well taken about humans and anger. When perceiving anger, it just may be a perceptual problem; I like that, too, Paul. Thanks. Are you ready for the next question?

Paul: You bet. You understand that I am not saying people will suddenly not be angry anymore. I am saying that when they are angry, it is important to feel their underlying love. Do you see?

Jenna: Yes, instead of getting angry or whatever yourself, focus on their love.

Paul: Yes. It is a start.

Jenna: Paul, how about this great emotional flow in society in 2020? Any ideas on how we might arrive at that?

Paul: You will learn once again, in reverse. No flow produces pain. I am talking about emotional pain. At first it will be experiences in how to endure pain, then it will be the desire to experience joy. There is quite a difference there. Do you think that the knowledge of joy, or anticipation of joy, might be helpful in getting through pain? Just thought I'd throw that one out.

Jenna: You are suggesting that a greater awareness, or anticipation of something better, is an actual ingredient for experiencing emotional pain.

Paul: Well, maybe it is. I am just giving you little hints at how to experience emotional pain, so it doesn't seem so overwhelming. You could try it, you know. We guides will try anything to get humans to stick their little toes into the lake of emotional pain! The important thing is to get your toes wet. Maybe you don't even know what emotional pain is yet—or what it could be, that is better put. It may be that it is not at all what you expect. Have you thought about that? How do you know what something is until you experience it? Well, I'll tell you something, you don't.

Jenna: I like it when you're so emphatic.

Paul: That's because you feel my love.

Jenna: I do…and thanks.

Paul: You're welcome.

Jenna: Paul, there was much said about humor on the cellular level in 2020. Do you have any specific comments in this regard?

Paul: Before you start sensing others' laughing cells, you will have to start sensing your own. How do you do that? You will have to be truly alert. You will have to feel energy in your body; you will have to be aware of what your thoughts and feelings are; you will have to recognize when the signs of your body tell you, yes, this is funny, or this is joy. You will have to notice patterns, so that you know the signs of joy, both in body and mind. But most of all you will need to listen to your heart, for your heart knows. Yes, even what's funny—or joyous, as you would put it. Let me try to give you one thing to remember; I recognize how expansive this is. How will you learn humor on the cellular level? *You will need to get to know your cells first, and the way to do this is to first of all get to know that they are there.* When is the last time you thought about that—or felt the presence of your cells?

Jenna: You have made a good point. Be your cells.

Paul: Yes. You know that point you are starting to make over and over about taking on others' viewpoints in 2020? Well, take on the viewpoint of your cells. Put your eyes, ears, nose, tongue, fingers, and heart right inside of all your little old cells. How's that?

Jenna: Paul, you are making your points so well that once again I am feeling my shoulders sink. The weight that is on each one of our shoulders is enormous. Can you tell me something light here, before I sink right into the floor?

Paul: Yes. You know that weight that you feel in regard to your own responsibility?

Jenna: Yes.

Paul: Well, put it into joy. Do not think of it as a task, think of it as contributing to the overall perspective of joy. Just think if everyone did this, how joyous joy would be! Now that was novel, don't you think? When you think of something as a task or heavy responsibility, just turn it around so that the end product, joy, is your most predominant feeling.

Jenna: Not bad, you ought to be a therapist.

Paul: Let me ask you this. Why does it feel like such responsibility? Rather, what are you feeling?

Jenna: It doesn't sound very easy; it sounds like a lot of emotional pain. It sounds like work to get to this joyous state!

Paul: You are going to have to redefine work, so that you can experience it more broadly. I'm serious. Let's go on to the next question. And I can hardly wait until fear drops dead. Sorry for my brevity. Let's move on.

Jenna: Paul, there has been much mention of expanded use of the physical senses, even reference to 2020 being "The Age of the Physical Body." What can you tell us about that, in terms of learning?

Paul: That you will need to get to know all of your senses in the same way you are getting to know all of your cells. Is anybody having any fun yet? Okay, okay, I can feel your shoulders. Let me see here. If I told you that you were on the horizons of one of the greatest exploratory adventures for humans in all of time and beyond time, how would you feel about that?

Jenna: Better.

Paul: Okay. Look at it this way. All we are talking about is human perception. We are not even talking about work. We are talking about releasing…poof!…not taking on more weight, do you see? We are merely talking about letting go of what you have learned, so there is room for the heart. Yes, the heart wants to exert itself. Think of it that way. We are talking about making room for you, the real you—with the heart leading the way…. I have a question for you.

Jenna: What?

Paul: What is it you are experiencing when I tell you that you have to reacquaint yourself with this and that, and get to know this and that? Are you thinking about all that you must do?

Jenna: Yes.

Paul: And it feels heavy. Well, let me be the first to point out that you have to do nothing. When I say get to know your body, or your mind, or your behavior, all I am saying is be. This is a most important point. In order to get to 2020 as you have so envisioned, you need do nothing but be.

Jenna: Why do I always forget that?

Paul: Because you are like all humans, constantly thinking about what you must do. I would like to change that word do to be.

Jenna: And marry it off to fear.

Paul: Now I've got you going. What is your next question?

Jenna: I am not clear on the physical senses entraining with the cells. I thought we had been overdoing it with our physical senses, out of balance in that regard.

Paul: Yes, when you use them to only look outward. I am talking about the physical senses being used to perceive who you are, or as you would see it, looking inward. You might want to ask Rebecca to clarify this, as this is more of her bag.

Jenna: Okay. How is it that laughing is a learning tool? What about these insights during laughter?

Paul: Do you think you could be the laugh without doing anything? Next time you laugh, don't think of it as your laugh, think of it as you. As you learn to do this, you will be amazed at the insights that will come to you. Your laugh is not something you do, it is something you are.

Jenna: I had never thought about the eternal nature of the laugh until right then, Paul.

Paul: Yes, the eternal nature of the laugh. Remember that one. In fact, remember the eternal nature of everything!

Jenna: I'll try, but that eludes me at times, too. Speaking of eternity, how does one gradually take on that perspective? We seem so short sighted, all of us, in our perspectives.

Paul: When you define something, you limit it. It is that control you are talking about…and the flow of ideas. When you have expectations of ideas—or how something will turn out—you are immediately shutting yourself down. You know that example of allowing the honeymoon to be, allowing the flow of love? Well, you have to do that with everything. That *is* allowing flow. So, when you don't know the outcome and allow for different possibilities, you have a sense of eternity. And that applies to the simplest perception, as in experiencing a chair, one of your favorite examples. If you view a chair as just something to sit in, you have defined it; you have put it into a box, deemphasizing its past and its future. You do that with yourselves and you do that with others. And when you do that, you do not feel joy. How can you when you are so focused on rigidly controlling it? Perhaps this is something to think about. Could it be that a component of joy is eternity?

Jenna: Are you saying that when one starts to experience joy more—or flow—that one will automatically view things more eternally?

Paul: Yes, I am saying that, and also that the reverse is true. When one experiences eternity more, it increases one's joy.

Jenna: Okay, thanks, Paul. Is there something you can tell us about abstract humor? I find it interesting that people don't even have to relate to something personally in 2020 to find it funny. This seems like a long way off.

Paul: Abstract humor has to do with abstract thinking. In order to get there, you need to get beyond focusing on self. Ironically, that takes first doing that. So if you haven't done that, begin with that. Get to know yourself. It all starts from a perspective, that's for sure—even appreciating humor. As for making that leap to where you can enjoy something impersonal, hmmm…this will come when there is more respect and interest given to ideas themselves. I know this sounds odd, but abstract humor will be in vogue when people can view from the perspective of the idea. Okay, okay…I know that is a big leap. Think of it this way, you know those cells and physical senses you are starting to get to know? Well, after that, it will be ideas. Oh, forget it; it's too abstract. Ha! ha!

Jenna: Paul, you really make me smile a lot. Actually what you are saying is that perceiving from another's point of view, even an idea's—and defining are inversely proportional.

Paul: Yes, when you're defining, I can assure you that you are not feeling or even coming close to another's perspective.

Jenna: I want to know more about the laugh, though. Can you give us some insight on what we have to learn in order to incorporate this great flowing laugh of 2020? It sounds terrific.

Paul: Notice how you are not doing that now, if that is indeed the case. Notice how you short-change yourself when you laugh. What is it you do exactly when you laugh? Does it feel good? What is it that is in your awareness? What is involved here in terms of your body? Is your laugh rhythmic? Is it jerky? Notice what you "do" now.

Jenna: Laughter itself is a source of joy in 2020. Can you give us any particulars on that?

Paul: You are wondering if the laugh itself could possibly be the beginning to incorporating more humor in your life, which would mean more joy, more learning for you now. Are you not asking me if you could start with the laugh itself, maybe even change it if it is not as you like—in order to start this growth?

Jenna: I guess I am wondering if the laugh is reflective of joy or possibly a cause for it.

Paul: Let me tell you something, by 2020 you will be in love with all laughs; everything will be so intermingled and simultaneous that cause and effect will be viewed as one, if it is viewed at all. As for now, notice how you feel when you laugh, truly experience it, mesh with yourself, mesh with others, get to know your laugh, get to know their laughs.

Learn how to enjoy! I do not tell you to critique your laugh—or others; I tell you to get to know your laughs. Get to know yourselves. The point here is to enjoy, and to do that you need to know what enjoyment is. Start with the laugh! For heaven's sakes, be your laugh if you have to.

Jenna: Paul, I just had the oddest experience. I felt you as a laugh.

Paul: As much as I hate to admit it, I think you are getting it. I tease.

Jenna: I know. I didn't mean that literally, that you were a laugh. I just felt all sorts of love for you when you were talking about laughs, and knowing yourself, and enjoyment, and all that stuff.

Paul: And I didn't mean what I said literally, either. I am glad you are getting it. Do you think this says something for humor? Are you laughing? Are you smiling? Are you feeling love? Well, what a coincidence, and it all seems to be simultaneous. And you are noticing it, that's the important part. Patterns, patterns…all wrapped up in love, and that's no joke.

Jenna: Thanks, Paul.

Paul: You are most welcome…. Isn't what you just experienced the same as what you wrote about in 2020? That humor is a real love connection, that it is the ultimate joy, in so many words?

Jenna: Yes.

Paul: Well, how about that? Now that is what I am talking about—the importance of direct experience of humor as love. Hey, I've got an idea. Forget all that stuff about the cells and the physical senses and the heart. I am serious. Next time you want to connect with someone lovingly, you just think of them as a laugh.

Jenna: Paul, I was just kidding.

Paul: Well, I am not. If that's what it takes for you to feel that very special connection, then by all means do it.

Jenna: Paul, now you're a giggle.

Paul: Keep doing it, if you have to. Sense all the world as a cosmic giggle!

Jenna: Now I am really smiling.

Paul: Good, just keep doing it.

REBECCA

Jenna: Hi, Rebecca. It looks as though 2020 looks like a pretty joyous place. I can't believe how much has changed. Would it be all right if I ask you some questions about humor?

Rebecca: Of course.

Jenna: I am fascinated by the fact people have such broad experiences in 2020. Of course, it has everything to do with their broad perspectives, but can you tell us how we're going to pull this off?

Rebecca: Broad perspectives first of all have to do with the ability to feel. I have spoken to you about light; well, this is what we all must do—feel light. As of now, people see light. In order for this wonderful change to take place, where people's perspectives incorporate the views of others, learning how to feel a higher vibratory light is essential.

Jenna: You mentioned before that you feel what people are saying, rather than deducing meaning. Is there anything else you can tell us in regard to light?

Rebecca: You are asking if there are any particular human experiences, I think, that may be anticipated.

Jenna: Yes.

Rebecca: Well, here is the point I'd like to make in that regard. It is important to know the light of one's own experiences. This is a little abstract compared to feeling meaning from what another is saying, because light itself is so abstract for humans today. What I am talking about is the importance of experiencing light in all of one's experiences. This will come about from experiencing through one's own eyes first of all. So much has been said about how to grasp another's view. Well, hold the phone. First of all, it is important to grasp the light created by one's own unique experiences, in other words, truly experiencing what one is experiencing. As for unique experiences to be anticipated, many will begin to see things totally differently from how they have seen them before, with the following thought common: "I have never noticed that before." People will be amazed how different things will begin to look to them and at a very rapid pace, starting now, this very day, if they haven't already noticed it. It will throw them for a loop initially, confusing them, but then they will get used to it, this persistent change, actually welcoming it.

Jenna: Yes, I am noticing that myself…just the other day, in fact, I found myself noticing several "new" objects in a friend's house, which turned out to have been there all along.

Rebecca: Yes, and there will be more of this…and other things as well. More will filter into your mind, literally, and you will find yourself allowing ideas to do their own thing, as you mentioned earlier. When you do that, new insights pop into your mind.

Jenna: Sometimes it sounds so simple.

Rebecca: It is but first you need to learn how to feel the movement of ideas, apart from how you would like to define them.

Jenna: Rebecca, you have referred to the kinds of methods you use with your clients later this decade to teach emotional flow in order to enhance perception. Is this what you are talking about when you refer to knowing one's own energy?

Rebecca: Yes, I am talking about how humans will need to learn emotional flow—or how to move their energy. And yes, I am already doing this with clients in the future, even though I think of it as in the now. I understand how odd this might seem to some readers, my knowing my own future, to a degree. But this will happen to others, too, as "time" goes on.

Jenna: They will have more and more awareness of the "future."

Rebecca: Yes.

Jenna: Perhaps you could tell us briefly what some of the main principles are you use to teach emotional flow, as this will apply to everyone, not just those in "therapy."

Rebecca: I will be happy to comment on my approach. One of the biggest problems for humans has always been the inability to discern their own energy. As of now, when they feel energy, they cannot tell from whom it emanates: it feels either "good" or "bad" to them, and they choose the good. In other words, they orient themselves around what they are used to. You have written about this yourself in regard to humor today, saying it generally reinforces the status quo which is the same thing as saying people prefer what is familiar. What I do with my clients is help them discern their own energy by interacting with them in such a way that they cannot feel my energy. This puts them in the position of having to magnify their own. Since they are used to feeling some energy, they intuitively create an environment of energy. I am talking about energy movement which they intuitively turn to in order to know who they are. I am not saying there is no pain, or no confusion for them. I am saying that because they are used to feeling energy, they are forced to interact with their own. I am introducing them to their own energy! And for some, it is a true revelation.

Jenna: You are saying they are forced to find meaning through their own energy.

Rebecca: Part of learning about your own energy has to do with distinguishing it from others. What I am talking about here in the office with my clients is the experience of truly focusing on one's own energy and feeling good within that context, not having to bring in "outside" energy to feel okay. I am not suggesting in any way that people not interact with others. I am talking about knowing your own energy and how to move it, as I said earlier.

Jenna: Well, how is that different from contemporary therapy?

Rebecca: Therapists today don't know how to put their clients in the position to magnify their feelings. They go on the theory the client will recreate what he is used to right there in the office, which he usually does. Old behavior, in other words. Then they look at that and see where that behavior has led. What I do is make the client create something new, something he's never experienced before, in most cases. The value of this is insurmountable, in the sense that herein lie the answers for growth. One can only grow when one understands how to interact with energy, starting with one's own. Do you remember all the stuff you and Paul talked about regarding cells?

Jenna: How could I forget?

Rebecca: Well, what do you think I am talking about? I am talking about the process of getting to know your own energy, the movement within your cells, if you will. I help clients with this in therapy in the future.

Jenna: What else do you do in therapy that's different from today?

Rebecca: I use memory in the future.

Jenna: Would you be willing to expand?

Rebecca: You know what we are doing here? Well, I teach this.

Jenna: Telepathy?

Rebecca: No, not communication, per se, methods of increasing awareness. I virtually teach people how to feel. Then with proper emotional expression, it's amazing what they can see! I am talking about their broadened perspectives, of course. Regarding how I teach people to feel, I take much information out of the future, actually.

Jenna: This sounds like what we are doing right here.

Rebecca: It is! In the same sense that you and I are dealing with other ways to experience, namely, the kinds of things you have written about in 2020, I do the same for my clients, but I use their scenarios of the future.

Jenna: Are you saying you teach them to feel in some ways experiences they haven't experienced yet consciously, but at some level are aware of?

Rebecca: That is absolutely correct.

Jenna: I am speechless.

Rebecca: It is all fitting into place, isn't it? And I have another shocker.

Jenna: What?

Rebecca: You are helping me with these methods in the future.

Jenna: I knew you were going to say that. Here we go again. I really don't want to get into my future here. I need to clarify to the reader, if I haven't already, that I am not consciously aware of this interaction with you later, yet you have brought it up over and over again.

Rebecca: And at some level, you know it's true.

Jenna: I can't even respond.

Rebecca: Well, let this be a lesson to the reader—and a first hand one, that's for sure. What you are doing right now with this book and me is intent for what you are doing in the future. It's a funny feeling when an idea hits you at a very deep emotional level, isn't it, rather than just intellectually? But let us change the subject, so to speak, if you are uncomfortable. There is such a thing as semi-awareness, you know. Why don't you ask me some more questions about humor?

Jenna: Do you yourself use humor in your therapy?

Rebecca: I use humor in the sense that I help them access joy.

Jenna: You are not talking about cracking jokes then.

Rebecca: Well, I will say this. There is not that deadly serious atmosphere that penetrates some therapy of today. I encourage joy in my office, not reverence toward me—or any theory. Excuse me, if I seem to be a little hard on contemporary therapists…Also, my growth is considered as important as theirs. This is a given in therapy not too long from now. So therapy in 2020 is more interactive, with an equal flow of energy between the therapist and client, not the way it is today where therapists feel "above" their clients.

Jenna: I don't think most therapists are actually aware of that though, do you? I mean that they are coming from a position of superiority, hence the flow of energy is not equal.

Rebecca: No, that's why they're not very good therapists. And for those who are aware, they seem to think it's perfectly all right, but it isn't, because it is patronizing. Many are totally unaware at a feeling level because they are so sure they are healthier than their own "patients." They justify their superior intellects as "helpful," but this is not just true for therapists. It is everywhere in society. People everywhere think of themselves as superior to others. I do, even you do.

Jenna: Yes. I have been noticing it in the feel of my own blocked energy, which is how I feel when I feel superior to someone. Communication totally breaks down when there isn't equal energy flow between equals. People are just not open and so they are not insightful when someone else is giving them advice, or implies it's needed, which is just as bad, sometimes worse. And the same is true for the advisor. It's like bam, the doors are shut to each.

Rebecca: A point well made.

Jenna: I am amazed sometimes how subtle it is, feeling superior to another, not that we don't have skills or talents more developed in some areas.

Rebecca: Well, it's an area that people are going to have to notice everywhere, not just therapists. When people are feeling superior to others, they are blocking their own joy. How's that?

Jenna: Terrific! Rebecca, do you have one idea you could pass on which might help people feel joy, either from how you encourage it in your office—or just in general?

Rebecca: Ironically, I help people step out of their bodies a bit, teaching them about the ideas themselves, so they don't feel so attached to them.

Sometimes people feel the weight of the idea as if it is their own weight. Let me give you an example. You spoke earlier of feeling the weight of your own responsibility. I have my clients look first a bit more abstractly at the issues. If they want to feel hopeful, we look at hope itself. It does not work to look at a depressed person and say, "Feel hopeful." The first step is to help them understand the existence of hope, separate from them. So my approach is more like this, "Would you agree that hope exists for some, although you are not feeling it right now?" This for one, removes the element of fear, helping with their perception. So, to answer your question about joy, I would say to the readers, "Although you are not feeling as joyful as you would like, would you agree that joy exists for some?" And then we would go from there.

Jenna: You are teaching a much broader perspective, in essence.

Rebecca: I am talking about removing their own preconceived ideas about an idea and introducing them to the idea itself.

Jenna: I can see how it all relates to what we will need to learn ahead. Rebecca, what about humor on the cellular level, what can you tell us about that in terms of what we have to learn?

Rebecca: I am trying to think of some of my early experiences with humor. Give me a moment. Bees. Humor has to do with experiencing pain differently, fear differently. Well, I wouldn't say it is very humorous to get stung by a bee, but one time I did, and it was during this time that I had an insight into humor. The bee stung me, and for some reason I laughed! I think that was when my perspective of humor began to broaden.

Jenna: I'm having trouble following this.

Rebecca: I am merely saying that it was an unusual time to laugh, and I noticed it. To this day, I don't know why I laughed, but what I do know is my focus was on my laugh, not the fear or pain normally associated with a bee sting. It was the first time I noticed humor had a flow to it, its own flow. Prior to that I think I always tried to shape humor, control it a bit. I think that was the insight that I had, that I couldn't control humor and that it was in charge of itself. All I am saying to people is not to be surprised if sometime they laugh at something totally inappropriate. Rather than thinking they're going crazy, it just may mean growth.

Jenna: Are you saying you experienced this bee sting on the cellular level?

Rebecca: I am just talking about these little steps that one takes to get to the point of where he can feel tremendous joy. I am not experiencing joy as do the people in 2020, that is for sure. But I am telling you that my awareness has opened in this area of humor—and continues to do so.

Jenna: Okay, thank you very much. Rebecca, regarding the physical senses, I keep reading that we are over-relying on our physical senses—using them too much—yet you speak of them as if they are the key to getting to know who we are. Could I have more on that, please?

Rebecca: Those unique new experiences where people perceive differently, where they say, "Wow, I never noticed that before," will come about largely because of increased flow within the physical senses, perceiving both inward and outward, thanks to fluid emotions. Look, here is something that perhaps needs to be stressed. The physical senses work better when people are emotional. When they aren't, the senses are actually deprived of energy which they need to work. We do not need to get beyond our physical senses, just get them flowing. As you know, yourself, the physical senses carry a great deal of fear within them, distorting what humans perceive. When fear is reduced, the physical senses will flow, allowing more to come into the conscious mind, which will also be more accurate.

Jenna: Okay, thanks, Rebecca. Anything else you can tell us about the actual expansion of the physical senses in years to come?

Rebecca: That it will not all happen at once. And not only will people be using their senses more, and integrating with one another, but they will also be using them in different ways. I am already doing it now. Do you remember when I was telling you about feeling light? Well, what do you think about smelling it some day?

Jenna: I can follow this intellectually, but when I try to actually imagine that experience, I just draw a blank. Do you actually smell light now?

Rebecca: Yes, but I cannot begin to explain what that is like. But I think I'll try anyway. Smelling light is like eating burnt rubber. Sorry, that is the best I can do, and it wasn't even close. Let me tell you something, the expanded use of the physical senses will be a lot of fun; it'll be exciting. It'll be like a small child learning to read. Wide-eyed adults learning about learning, and they will be excited about it.

Jenna: But won't this learning be forced, so to speak? This is something I have been wondering about for a long time. Are we really not talking about people groping with tremendous fear at the same time that they are confronted with learning in order to grow? I guess what I am asking is what motivates people to do all this growth?

Rebecca: Well, let me ask you something. Do you go to this computer when you are in pain? Do you communicate with Paul and me because you are afraid? What brings you back here day after day? What compels you to work toward this idealized society?

Jenna: It's not pain, there may be some fear; I would say it's largely love.

Rebecca: But you are not just talking about love for Paul and me. What compels you to do what you do? And I would like to ask the same of the readers. What compels them to read another line in this book? What compels them to want a better society? Not all motivation is fear-based. This is the exciting part, and we are starting to tap in to it now. Think of that child learning to read. It need not be unique to children.

Jenna: Okay, I get your point and it is a great one. Very true, and exciting, too…Rebecca, I have noticed that by 2020 the laugh itself is a true source of joy. How does one learn this laugh?

Rebecca: One does not learn how to laugh. What one learns is how to feel joy. This is done by learning to open one's awareness. When this happens, the body just reacts.

Jenna: And how do we learn to enjoy the impersonal?

Rebecca: When you can appreciate the impersonal, you are broadening your perspective of love. You ask about how to enjoy more, in essence. Share your humor, yes. You want to broaden your perspective of love? Then share your joy. I am not talking about joke telling, although that is fine, too; I am talking about sharing what you feel with others when you feel it. When you feel joy, share it. This is one way to broaden your perspective of joy. Do you not feel others' joy when they share with you? Well, now it's your turn. When you feel happy, share it with others. It is good for you, it is good for them.

Jenna: Thank you, Rebecca. I am truly enjoying this, and I love your therapy of the future.

Rebecca: You are most welcome.

Author's comments

What I noticed in communicating with Paul is how much we both use humor as a vehicle of love. All that teasing. It also made me think about my use of humor with people on this earthly plane. I had given very little thought to it until this particular conversation with Paul, and what I discovered was that I am often humorless with people I care little about and full of humor with those I care a great deal about. I even thought about my use of humor when flirting with people! My, my, but I can be funny when I am romantically interested in somebody, and desirous of getting to know them. Granted, it's an indirect way of saying I care, but my point is I am more conscious now than ever about the presence of humor in both myself and others. Paul's point about feeling love in another's anger was great. Clearly, his point is to feel love in everything, for it is, indeed, there. Because of this, I am trying my best to feel love in others' sarcasm or twisted statements directed at others which they claim to be "just a joke." And I am noticing when I employ such behavior—it's a start. It's mind-boggling to think we could actually see love everywhere, as the ramifications of it are enormous. And it's such a simple concept. Notice love—and feel it! Is it possible we are truly misinterpreting others' behavior? Just think if we could feel love in everything. Even in someone's threats, rages, and moods of emotional distance, for example. It is something to think about. We may, indeed, be in a perceptual crisis in all that we experience.

In regard to what Rebecca had to say, I cannot believe the exciting changes around the corner in the area of therapy. I have always thought contemporary therapy was lacking the way clients walk into an office, are categorized, then both the therapist and client are bound by that diagnosis. Both are constrained by preconceived theories, which seem to me to be extremely limiting in terms of growth for both the client and the therapist. And why is contemporary therapy oriented around just the growth of the client? Let's open this whole thing up! The human mind and heart, I'm talking about! Anybody else sick and tired of humans being seduced by fear—and for centuries? Well, I am! It's about time for a more suitable suitor—*love*! But as much as love is exciting it is also scary! Anybody else agree with me on that one?…Maybe we're afraid of love.

The Media and Communication in 2020

•Direct experience with ideas •More love-based ideas, fewer fear-based ones •Truth as perceived from many viewpoints •Meaning from light •Manifestation of ideas •Multiangular thinking •Physical body and highly interactive communication •Death of language •Light machines • A high degree of telepathy

The flow can be described as a sea of energies in which everyone on the planet is bathed. In fact, the entire cosmos is energy. Sometimes it is described as a spiral, evolving upward, capable of taking us with it if we don't buck it. Learning to "go with the flow" is one of the most valuable accomplishments we can imagine, and it is available to everyone. The key is intuitive sensing of the subtle movement of energy, and the method of accessing it is practice. When fatigue, disorientation, restlessness are in control of us, and nothing seems to "go right," we are bucking and resisting the flow of this universal energy. When we are peaceful, productive, in rhythm with our environment, we are aligned with the flow. It is a choice we make constantly, to be aligned with the flow, or to resist it, and the only way to do this is to be flowing ourselves. By 2020 people have this concept down pat, living it moment to moment, realizing that to flow within themselves also means synchronizing with and loving all that passes through their minds—even the "negative" ideas. In fact, in 2020 people realize that the way they relate to ideas, which is much the way they relate to people—harmoniously and equally—is one of the keys to their openness and loving natures.

Today humans relate to ideas in a remote, standoffish way, analyzing, controlling and judging ideas, as if they were superior to them, with some people actually believing they own ideas. As an example, note a conversation typical of today: "Now just listen to my idea about this `New Age' baloney. I can tell you one thing…" While at other times, people go to the opposite extreme of allowing an idea to completely take them over, which is also true for how many people relate to people today: either at too great a distance, or totally engulfed by them. Neither of these extremes keeps people in touch with who they are, for they are unable to maintain a sense of self, which is necessary for an accurate assessment of reality. It also does not allow the idea itself to unfold naturally. Being too close or too far has to do with fear of who one is. Fortunately, by 2020, all this has changed, with people knowing and accepting who they are and therefore not needing to stop their own stream of energy; that is, they are no longer interested in controlling ideas or being controlled by them but rather have learned firsthand the merits of merging with them, for each has a transformative effect on the other.

Beliefs about Themselves

Remarkably, in the years leading up to 2020, as people became increasingly aware of their most personal ideas, beliefs about themselves, they realized that they had the same emotional reactions to them as they did toward people with similar characteristics. They learned, for example, that just as people can be domineering, so can beliefs! As a result, people felt fearful, helpless, and angry at their own beliefs, which they came to realize as largely obsessive in terms of their own self-concepts—and inaccurate. As seen through their own eyes, a simple concept was learned: "Beliefs affect us on an emotional level the same way people do when the relationship is unequal, or when we do not relate to them equally." When they didn't do this, relate to ideas as friends to be loved, they felt the emotional pain associated with interrupted, unequal energy flow. The solution then was to learn to meet their own beliefs about themselves on equal terms, changing them from fear-based to love-based—or allowing them to evolve more freely so they could be released—which is to say they had to learn how to love themselves more. Unfortunately today people are slaves to beliefs, especially the ones about themselves, not realizing that this is the number one reason for blockage of energy, which hurts both the people and the beliefs. It is the *nature* of the beliefs—filled with fear—and how people relate to them now—either too closely or at too much a distance—that is the problem. It distorts reality! So in the years leading up to 2020, when people learned to love themselves more, it affected everything else: All beliefs and ideas everywhere began to transform, becoming more loving themselves. And so it is in 2020 that only healthy, flowing people remain, along with healthy, flowing ideas of all kinds, including beliefs. For by this time, just as objects filled with stagnant energy have died, so have unhealthy ideas.

Multiangular Thinking

What does merging with an idea mean? When one merges with an idea, not only is there a sense of oneness but also of eternity—for both the person and the idea. We are not doing this today. Ideas come and go. The truth is they are there always, have been always, and always will be. In our loving society, people interrelate with these eternal ideas, feeling the energy of them, not just understanding them in a removed way, with the whole experience elevating well beyond the intellectual linear way of experiencing ideas today. By 2020 people have direct experience with ideas, not battling with them on an emotional level so common today. Now many ideas offend people. That is because people are not clear on who they are. If they were, there would be no such encounter at all. By 2020 no longer do ideas just make sense, but feel complete and full, including a connection with all the human physical senses. For example, "thinking" about the idea of horse—one that is not physically present—means experiencing a horse as if it were there: smelling it, tasting it, seeing it, touching it, perhaps even hearing the swish of a tail to remove a fly! This is what people experience when they think! It is the way we experience a real live horse.

Perception has changed so much by 2020 that what is not there by today's standards is there. Both imagining and remembering are in the now, in the truest sense of the word, with the use of all physical senses, not a selective representation of "scenes" dictated by the ego. Not only that, instead of perceiving in linear planes, as we do today, i.e. seeing something in front of us, people perceive and think from many angles, as would be the case in perceiving inward from the perspective of many points of a circle. More expansive thought means being able to take the perspective of that which you experience, then riding that energy outward in evenly paced concentric circles, so that endlessness is the only possibility. Multidimensional selves, or the ability to transcend the physical, has allowed for a more extended view of the imagined horse, a broader view of it: from under, from over, from its sides, with the experience being more like surrounding the horse; while at other times, it seems as though the energy fields of the horse surround one's self! Actually, what happens is that when the two energy fields mix, an even greater awareness is created than the two combined viewpoints. In addition to perceiving the nonphysically present horse like this, when "thinking" about it, the same holds true for perceiving a physically present horse in 2020. Only in this case, the horse's radiant energy, as well as one's own, sparkle even more so, in an atmosphere of magnificent color. To say that people in 2020 experience ideas more fully than we do today is the understatement. (Use your own experience of this last statement, as you read it, and how you experienced it, somewhat removed, versus how people experience "thinking" about a horse in 2020: with all their physical senses highly involved and enormously expanded energy fields) Thinking by 2020 is multiangular, literally, or taking the perspective of many angles first before flowing outward in concentric circles, and it has a sense of extremely rapid movement to it, that defies boundaries, like frames of a never ending movie. It is more fluid and flowing, just like everything else in 2020. Whereas today when we think of something, it's more defined: one frame here, one frame there—and it's largely stop action with no sense of eternity at all. No flow, little movement. This is because we do not know ourselves as eternal. When we learn to know ourselves in this manner—as fluid energy—then the ideas we hold, and how we relate to them, will also be fluid.

Manifestation of Ideas

This new way of relating to ideas—or feeling the flow of them—has allowed the process of manifestation to speed up. In 2020 people themselves embody the ideas of the day, which are, to name some of the more prominent ones: love, growth, equality, naturalness, and change, meaning people are loving, growing, natural, changing, and treating others equally. This is what is meant by an idea manifesting. It doesn't mean viewing an idea from afar; it means taking on the energy of the idea within one's self and living it in the moment. Today people talk ideas, not understanding that they are a process, just as they themselves are, or that they have stuck emotions in them, dying themselves to flow. Still in the theoretical state, only the beginnings of the ideas are being experienced today; whereas in 2020 ideas are more mature, evolved, and in fact flowing with great vibrancy.

Telepathy

In our society of love, there are no newspapers, magazines, televisions, radios, telephones, faxes, wire services and so forth—language is all but gone—for by this time people have gotten used to and expect a fuller, more immediate, direct communication. The days of superficiality are gone, with people going right to the heart of the matter, communicating soul-to-soul, in whole ideas, which is to say telepathy is the main mode of communication. This is, after all, a natural occurrence when people are who they are, with their energy fields melding, allowing them to know intuitively what others are thinking and feeling, even when they are not in their presence.

Technology for a Different Purpose—light Machines

There is technology in 2020, but unlike today, it is used to help people perceive better, not provide "answers" for them. Today data ad infinitum can be accessed technologically, "invaluable information," of course; by 2020 people go within themselves for that information. An example of technology that is around in 2020, pertaining to communication, would be the light machines found in many homes. Although not all people use them, many find them helpful as aids. These apparatuses magnify light waves for people, helping them with focus, or honing in on light. The machines magnify light beams, which people walk through, getting reflected back to them increased movement of all that is, essentially, including themselves. The machines are not misused, keeping people from doing their inner work, just available to assist in learning. In no way whatsoever do the machines lend or impose any kind of interpretation to life, as the media do today. So in fact these light machines, which are cylindrically shaped and beam down on people, are just a magnification of what is going on; they're light waves filled with ideas, such as people's thoughts and feelings, reflected back exactly as they are, which could be considered the televisions of the day, bringing the "news" of 2020!

Interaction with Technology

Whether people are using the light machines or not, they're in a constant state of interaction with light in 2020. How they find meaning in life is to allow this very high vibratory light to form "a certain pattern" to make sense for them—what they need to know, based on their purpose in this world. This pattern is not what somebody else has decided they need to know, which is to say they pick right out of light beams—by feel—"valuable information." Unlike today, where the media often encourage people to shut down due to high fear content being presented, the light machines of 2020 encourage the opposite: openness on the part of people, resulting in increased energy flow and a closer look at truth, which they can feel deeply within their own resonating cells. When there is resonance, each cell shivers as if meeting an old friend; this is how people know their perceptions are accurate. In 2020 the light machines themselves are like friends, nurturing people. Contrast this to today where people rely on external factors for truth rather than their own resonating cells: analyses, opinions and surveys by others, which are ideas, presented intellectually, by removed people employed by the media, who themselves relate to the ideas in removed ways. What this has produced then today is a lack of love in society, little nurturing from technology, and very little ability to feel one's own internal truth.

Language

There have been enormous changes in language by 2020. Words are shorter, less ambiguous, and when people do use the spoken language, they use fewer words. People do not use their names so much anymore either, preferring instead to connect with people on a pure energy exchange. Nor do they define with words everything they have experienced when communicating. Why should they? That's not the way they experienced it in the first place. Although telepathy is the main mode for communicating, people still do use language at times for clarification. The word "you," for example, is clear and defined, as it is almost always used when talking face-to-face, therefore it is common in 2020. While more ambiguous words, such as "they" or "green," ones having many applications, have disappeared, since they remain in the mind too long, blocking light—or meaning. While people today get meaning largely from the definition of words when they communicate, people in 2020 get it almost solely from the movement inherent in light.

Although the written word is still around in 2020, it too has diminished considerably. Of course this doesn't mean there isn't anything at all to read or that nothing is ever written down. It just means that it tends to be used more often for formalities, as would be the case for weddings, birth and death announcements. People have kept family mementos, and in some cases, classics—but generally, the written word is not very common. The role of the written language is one of saving and definition and not very important to people anymore, as most people can access whatever they want, whenever they want, instantly from within themselves.

In regard to the spoken language and the voice itself, there have been many changes: the range of people's voices, for example, is wider; the sound of the voice is more pleasant and harmonious; and sound itself is more refined. Both sound and light are used in communicating in 2020. They are actually inseparable, but people don't care how things happen—they just communicate! And throughout society, there is much, much music, always…even in conversations! That is to say, not only do people sing more when communicating, or with themselves, but the sounds they make are also much more melodious and harmonious than today.

The Physical Body and Interactive Communication

Not surprisingly, the physical body is much more involved in communication in 2020 than it is today. Today we tend to look for something, listen for something, reach out for something to touch, expecting certain things to happen to us…limiting what comes into our awareness. By 2020 people use their senses in such a way as to allow much more to come to them, increasing tremendously what enters into the conscious mind. They experience much more with their eyes, for example. In 2020 people are so sensitive to subtle changes in air that they can feel changes in vibrations caused by eye movement! Earlier it was mentioned that ambiguous words are no longer in the language; well, often ambiguity is cleared up with body movements, especially eye movements. In fact, this is one of the main ways people ascertain how others feel, not by watching the eyes, although they do that too, but by sensing the vibrations of light as moved by others' eyes. In fact all of the sense organs have increased movement within them by 2020, which has improved perception. So with better flow then, in addition to the eyes knowing more, the ears know more, the nose knows more, the mouth and tongue know more, and the skin knows more! With more light entering the sense organs and more emanating from them, there is an abundance of memories to be shared among people in our loving society, both from the past and the future, which have been locked up in the physical senses for lifetimes. Knowing people's pasts and futures has to do with enlightened senses, literally.

In 2020 people notice more of the body, not being so focused on smiles, or the head. Those smiling cells throughout the body are "visible," because they can be sensed, with people relating much more to the whole body. Although they can feel a great deal more than we can today, they are still very "touchy, feely," choosing to be physically closer to others more often than most of us are today. People not only are aware of their own bodies but others' too. Body parts, in fact, can talk! As an example, people might respond to others, "Your knee is telling me something," or "Your toe has something to say!" Various parts of the body are often more expressive than other parts, which people notice and honor. Of course learning to communicate with one's own body parts preceded this kind of awareness. Often this is in context with the release of beliefs. So when people are releasing beliefs, there is movement in certain areas of the body, which means there is more whole body communication during these times. Increased awareness then manifests in more self-disclosure through body parts.

What does communication feel like in 2020? Not as tight, not as forced, not as contrived, more natural. Today communication is often constrained and blocked, just like the two people who are communicating. Not so in buoyant 2020! When two people are communicating, there is a flow of energy that has allowed for a continuous loop of energy between them, with communication being a *joint* process, whose success depends upon both people, with a "meeting in the middle." And when there are more people communicating, all contribute equally to its flow. Awareness is so great by 2020 that one person can be communicating with another person, and yet be very much aware of many other "conversations" going on at the same time, either in the physical dimension or other dimensions. People just know what's going on with others, no matter "where" they are (they could be deceased) or what anybody's doing since there are so many levels of awareness operating simultaneously. This has only come about because of the natural flow of energy, when people stopped trying to control everything...with one level of awareness helping people tap into the next. When people are flowing, they reveal who they are.

So it's an ongoing process then of self-disclosure in 2020. Today it is not unusual for people to push their energy onto others, imposing their points of view as if they were more accurate, rather than melding with another's equally important perspective. This is not an example of a person whose energy is flowing; it is in fact a person who is shut down: to himself and others. By 2020 people understand that all people are on different paths, meaning they have different views of the world, and so they honor all of these views. This concept in itself—allowing for others' opinions—has eliminated virtually all "misunderstandings" by 2020, the most common cause for breakdown of communication today.

In our futuristic, loving society, the ideas that have manifested are love-based ideas, reflecting in essence what people are. Love-based ideas are ideas that are saturated with love, emanating from loving people. The fear-based ones have transformed by 2020, joining the loved-based ones! As a result, what shows up in 2020 is vastly different from today. To know what people are like now, in the nineties, just look at society, as would be the case with the media, which reflect what people are today. The media today are fearful, competitive, selfish, demanding, pushy, omniscient, and condescending toward the "average human in Iowa" (their label, I believe), while the institutions in 2020—namely, the people—are loving, naturally flowing, interactive, balanced, nurturing, changing, honest, and growing. Even the light machines are nurturing! This is not to say that there are no loving people in society now; of course there are—many, many of them—but if one were to look around at the ideas highly valued today—money, control, the status quo, dominance—and the reflections of them in everyday life, it would be clear that people today are just beginning the process of self-discovery, with even less knowledge about the nature and importance of ideas.

PAUL

Jenna: Hi, Paul. What a lovely society we have ahead of us. In looking at some of the more prominent ideas pertaining to media and communication in 2020, I am struck by people's ability to manifest ideas. What are the steps people must take right now to make that transition from thinking about something to living an idea?

Paul: We have already discussed how one makes the leap from experiencing love to being loving himself, so why don't we take another idea, like treating others equally. And as long as we are talking about it, why don't we talk about treating all things equally, even abstract ideas?

Jenna: Yes, what can you tell us?

Paul: That perception has to do with feeling energy and that feeling energy comes about from knowing how to ascertain your own truths.

Jenna: Well let me backtrack then. How do people know their own truths? Are you not saying that manifesting ideas has to do with knowing your own truths which has to do with perception?

Paul: Manifesting ideas has to do with feeling energy and making some sense of it. The way to feel energy is to allow for your own flow. When you do that, you will meld with the flow of whatever else. Do not worry about how to make meaning from something that just happens—things come into your awareness. What you need to be concerned with is your ability to feel.

Jenna: Well, how do you allow for the flow of energy within yourself?

Paul: You are wondering what you can do to flow more. Just focusing on it would be the first step. This entails knowing what flow feels like. Some might call it a sense of well being, being in balance, or where nothing is forced. This is what people need to be in touch with. Let me say that you may be making this harder than it really is. For example, with no explanation of what flow is, I'll bet if you went around and asked people to indicate when they were flowing or not flowing, most, if not all, could tell you intuitively. This is a perfect example of what people need to learn; they need to learn to get information from feelings, not just from the intellect. Do you see? I am not talking just about emotions, like sadness, grief, or anger. Of course those need to be felt deeply, too. I am talking about the sensation of all moving energy, within yourself, as well as "outside" of yourself. Sometimes it's very subtle. I am telling you that people already know what flow feels like, so all they have to do is get in touch with it; for when they do, there is manifestation of ideas.

Jenna: I was following you perfectly, but that seemed like a big leap, that last point. Can you word it any differently?

Paul: Manifestation of ideas is giving credence to ideas and you won't perceive them if you are not flowing. Think of it this way: You want equality in your life? Then you need to feel it. There is no other way of knowing equality than immersing yourself in it, by practicing it, by *being* it, in essence. This is what direct experience is about; it has to do with feeling the energy of what you are experiencing. If you don't do that, then you are only partially experiencing, on a cognitive level.

Jenna: Okay, let's take another idea. How about something like honesty? We have a big problem in our society today with people talking about honesty but not being honest themselves, politicians, for instance. Give me some specifics on how a person such as this becomes honest.

Paul: Let me tell you something. The person who is talking about honesty but not honest himself is not flowing. In order for him to become

100

more honest, he will first have to be aware of his own lack of flow—and change those circumstances. People know when they are not themselves—and they know how to recreate that feeling of themselves. They know this intuitively. When one is flowing, there is insight. Do you get this? When one is flowing, when the energy is moving around the body with the appropriate speed, in just the manner unique to that person, one has great ideas—ideas that work!

Jenna: Paul, I understand what you are saying, but it seems so abstract.

Paul: That is because we are not discussing how you can be more honest and treat others equally. I am not trying to pick on you, but I think this is a good point. Let me just ask you right here how you might be more honest and learn to treat others equally. Do you think it is related to the flow of energy within you?

Jenna: Absolutely. Oh, my, I think this has to do with methods of learning, perception, interpretation, intuition, general awareness, fear. Paul, this is massive. I couldn't begin to tell you all the steps involved in becoming more honest and treating others equally.

Paul: Nor can I! But what I can tell you is that each one of you will become increasingly more honest and treat others equally—and I am talking about all things, not just people—if you live your lives in such a way as to experience energy more fully. The steps you will take will be up to you, but the single most important idea here is that you need to be flowing to be growing. Energy flow within you is the key to greater awareness; why don't we just start with that? Learn to know when you are flowing, which is a feeling where nothing is forced. It's kind of like you are just floating along; you have put no constraints on yourself—you just *are*.

Jenna: Okay, thank you very much. And now let's flow into the next question.

Paul: By all means, let's

Jenna: I have noticed that love-based ideas, rather than fear-based ideas predominate in society in 2020. This is wonderful, but I'm afraid today people do not recognize when their beliefs are fear-based, which makes it awfully hard for people to move beyond them. What can you tell people about fear so that they might recognize it?

Paul: Again, we are talking about flow. When there is fear, there is a constriction of energy. This means what people experience will be from a very narrow perspective. When there is flow, there is direct experience, which means there is a melding of energy, a totality of viewpoints—a much broader perspective. When you are looking through just your own eyes, you miss a lot; you are in fact coloring what you see with fear, and the perspective is minuscule. When you incorporate others' views, you will be taking on a greater awareness. Taking on others' views means more flow of energy, yours and theirs. So the answer to knowing when you are carrying around a lot of fear-based beliefs has to do with whose point of view you are living. If you do not consider the needs of others, if you never speak of others, only of yourself and your own needs—and your behavior exemplifies this, which it will— then I can assure you that you will be carrying around a lot of fear- based beliefs.

Jenna: Is there anything people have to do, or be, besides being loving, that will create a loving society?

Paul: You are wondering how this happens, I think. But to answer your question first. You do not have to manufacture those loving ideas. They will just happen on their own. Again, I think at some level you are saying to yourself, "Hmmm...let's see. How is it that I am going to stay focused on how I feel, on my energy, so that I can spew out all of those beautiful thought forms, which will be embraced lovingly by everybody?" Well, maybe your thoughts aren't exactly like that. But I'll bet I'm close, even if it is barely conscious to you. Let me assure you that the more you are aware of thinking how you're going to cre- ate something, the sooner you'll be able to release those kinds of thought forms so you do spew off quite spontaneously lots of loving ideas. Let us start with that. To get beyond the idea of having to do something in order to create, first notice that that is what you are thinking, that you have to do something. Everybody asks, "How do I just *be*," you know? My advice is this. You *be* first of all by starting to notice when you are trying to create something. When you find that you really are creating something, then you *be* better.

Jenna: Paul, I love you. That makes me cry; I can feel your love so. Some- times I laugh with you; other times, I cry. I guess it's all the same. I feel your deep caring for me, and others.

Paul: That's because you just *be* now.

Jenna: I wonder if anyone else can feel this, or if it's just me, your caring.

Paul: Let me just say that I can also feel your deep caring, and it is why this society will be created, okay? And it is nothing that you have to create, so to speak, for your creations will emerge quite naturally from those tears.

Jenna: Yes. Thank you...Well, let us go on. What can you tell us about releasing false beliefs about ourselves?

Paul: Here is what I think. I think it is extremely helpful to be close to others, to have intimate relationships because you can learn a great deal within them, such as we just experienced here. You felt my love for you. It fed into your love for yourself. The more you feel that, the less likely you'll be to hang onto false beliefs about yourself. Instead of analyzing it, or even trying to understand it, I would just like you to truly grasp the value of closeness with others. Every time you feel love from others, it feeds your own self-love and puts another crack in those stalwart but frightened beliefs about yourself you carry. How's that? The term, I mean! Oh, sorry for getting off track. Sometimes I think it's better if you just notice patterns, and here is the pattern that I want you to notice. When you are close to others, sharing love, things are better. When people truly feel that, then all will change.

Jenna: Yes, and the beliefs will leave on their own.

Paul: Yes!

Jenna: Paul, how did you yourself experience giving up fear-based beliefs when you were on earth? Is there something memorable or something you might share with us?

Paul: It felt as though balloons were floating away; there was a definite sense of form leaving me. That's what I would expect people to experience, something that has an infinitesimal amount of weight breaking away from them. Let's see, to what would I compare it? A snowflake melting in your hand? Yes, that would be perfect. There is a sensation of joy, an elation on the part of the physical senses, and a sense of oneness associated with the breaking away of beliefs. And I would add if people are experiencing all of these things now, or any combination of them, that they themselves just might already be in the process of releasing fear-based beliefs.

Jenna: Oneness, as opposed to separateness.

Paul: Yes, right now people keep reinforcing their own sense of separateness. It's manic. I would call it the worst plague of all time. When peo-

103

ple notice they are not doing this so much anymore—and trust me, this is in the process of happening—it's a good sign that they might be casting aside negative beliefs about themselves. Now I suppose you are wondering how exactly *this* is going to take place, or what you have to do to give up negative beliefs; well, don't, okay? Just for once notice when you do feel at one with the universe, then learn to maintain that feeling. It's easy, and it's indicative of fewer negative, or might I say, false beliefs about yourself. I am just trying to get you to notice that you do much intuitively, and that you don't have to plan what to do. Just notice those times when you feel terrific, and I can assure you it has to do with coming from a deep sense of self, instead of trying to prove something to yourselves or others that you are not, which as you know emanates from those beliefs we are talking about.

Jenna: That was neat, Paul, thanks. What kinds of insights are needed for people to grasp the idea that a better representation of reality—or truth—means more than their own viewpoint?

Paul: Again, that they are one of many people. When people get their love needs fulfilled—to love and be loved—which comes with flow, remember that word?…they will notice others more. I am saying that when people's own energy is flowing that there will be an automatic exchange of love. Right now people are caught up in getting and receiving love, as if they were goals in life. On an unconscious or perhaps semi-conscious level, here is what they think, "Let's see, how am I going to get love today?" Then on a slightly less conscious level, they add, "Well, I probably ought to be loving, myself." Honest, this is what is going on—moment to moment all day long. Their goals ought to be, if they need them at all, just being themselves, for when that happens, they do not have to plan for love. It just happens. Can you believe how simple this really is? All the answers lie in your own energy flow.

Jenna: Yes, it seems that way…well, I don't know about how easy it is, but thanks!…Paul, it seems to me that one of the key issues in growth and getting to 2020 will be realizing how limited our identities are. Do you concur, and what will it take to view ourselves in a more expansive way?

Paul: I concur totally. It will take the ability to discern very high vibrational energy, for this is what allows into the conscious mind the eternal you, or to use your terminology, you in many time frames. This kind of discernment is vastly different from a belief-oriented reality, which can be lived quite adequately with slower, interrupted energy flow. Here is an example of a slower-moving energy: people who are externally focused, always wanting to change what is outside of themselves. Now here is a faster, more highly evolved form of energy: people who realize that change has a lot more to do with their own growth! Of course this kind of insight does not occur unless one is in touch with one's own divine essence. Beliefs, on the other hand, even loving ones but even more so, fear-based ones, are constrictive of energy, not allowing for this kind of insight. So if people want to know which identity they are operating from—and it varies from moment to moment—they need to be aware of their own energy. When they feel constricted and tight, they are coming from a belief-based identity. When they are feeling loose as a goose, and joyous, they are coming from a more authentic identity.

Jenna: You're too much…I love that whole concept of eternal joy, because that's what we're talking about.

Paul: Yes, eternal joy, very good, as opposed to fleeting moments of it.

Jenna: We are talking about fear-based beliefs dissipating and also love-based ones, right?

Paul: We are not talking about giving up loving yourself. First of all we are talking about letting go of negative ideas you carry pertinent to yourself because they get in the way of feeling your true essences. Then we are talking about getting beyond beliefs altogether. It's kind of like language, really. Have you ever thought about it in that regard? When people start to love themselves more, two things are going to happen, probably more, but we'll start with two: language will disappear and so will all beliefs because people will be able to feel their true essences more. Beliefs are just made up, you know? You're real, okay? Don't worry about losing your beliefs. They'll take care of themselves. All you have to be concerned with is the continual process of self-discovery, to quote you.

Jenna: So you are saying it is not necessary to distinguish between beliefs and me.

Paul: No, I am not saying that. But if you can, then you are doing great. If you can see when you are being, shall we say, a belief, versus being yourself, that would be excellent. And guess what would happen? Bye, bye, belief. Do you see?

Jenna: Why is it that I keep getting tears in my eyes?

Paul: Because you can feel the teamwork here. At first you think it is because I give a special little twist, the way I explain with humor, but then at a deeper level, it's the love you feel. Now tell the reader that! I didn't have to tell you that.

Jenna: That's true. You explained it perfectly. I just liked the connection at the heart level, so I put it in a question form. I wanted to feel your energy again, Paul.

Paul: Well, that loop that you wrote about, that occurs during communication...I think I'm going to lasso you with it. Just teasing. Besides, it was our energy that was such a thrill. Get it? Just what we were talking about...

Jenna: Yes, I get it, Paul. There is something I am wondering...is there one big idea people will need to grasp in order to get meaning from light, as opposed to say, words?

Paul: That there are more ways to get information than humans are currently using. One big revelation will be the insight that language is actually holding humankind back. This will be learned through the feeling of constricted energy, not only in the ideas expressed but within one's self when using language.

Jenna: So then you are talking about perceiving from an idea's point of view too, in 2020. You started to talk about that earlier but said it was too abstract.

Paul: I am just playing off of what you have said about 2020, but yes, that is exactly correct. By 2020 people will be able to perceive not only from the eyes of other people but also from the ideas of theoretical ideas. Oh, dear, forget I said that...let's go on. These concepts are so enormous; I'd hate to lose a few readers who are now thinking, theoretical ideas? Give me another question, why don't you?

Jenna: Well, I used that term myself.

Paul: I know...but for now let's just lump all ideas into one category; I think it would be easier for the readers. It's hard enough to grasp idea, let alone theoretical idea. Let's go on.

Jenna: Paul, what obstacles do you see ahead for people in giving up language?

Paul: The biggest fear will pertain to their own identities. Language itself is a means of reminding people who they are, so to give it up means to give up what they know about themselves. Every time language is used it is a reaffirmation of who people are; their energy constricts and that is how they know themselves, based on beliefs about themselves. So to give up language means facing these fear-based beliefs and releasing them; something we have spoken about a great deal, already. It will be both scary and exciting for people.

Jenna: Anything else to add about the absence of language and how it will affect people's lives?

Paul: It will allow people to focus on their experiences, and those of others, rather than descriptions of them, which is the whole idea here, to get more deeply involved with energy because it's a deeper involvement with life.

Jenna: In conjunction with that, what can you tell us about telepathy, which is very prominent in 2020? Why will people turn in that direction, and what specifically will be the skills needed to communicate telepathically?

Paul: People will turn to telepathy when they realize that what they are doing isn't working, the way they are communicating, the way they relate to ideas. In other words, they cannot keep up with what is happening. Things are happening right now for you faster than you can conceive of them in your conscious mind. Your use of language takes too long. By the time you spit it out, write it out, think it out…the problems have intensified. Again, emotional pain will be your first clue that you must change, that you must learn new ways of grasping information and relaying it. The skills needed will be a better ability to feel, better learning methods, largely.

Jenna: Is this why communication in 2020 is so much more interactive?

Paul: Are you saying because the old ways with language didn't work so well?

Jenna: Yes, I guess I am just wondering a lot of things at once.

Paul: Such as?

Jenna: Well, people will be totally frustrated as problems mount; they already are to some extent. Solutions will be few…it's that insight that escapes me. I am not totally clear on how that works.

Paul: That is because you are trying to understand insight; you must feel it, just as you must feel much, much more in your future in terms of gathering information. You need not understand everything; it need not fit into neat little categories. People in 2020 don't do it, you don't have to either! It just happens. Forced understanding prevents flow. It's a way of controlling. Understanding happens naturally when it is not forced.

Jenna: You are talking about my propensity to define.

Paul: Yes, yours and all humans'! You need to learn to let that energy wander a little; it needs to do its own thing, take its own path. When you are able to let go of definition, you will have better experiences—more direct experiences—and more love. Try it, and thank you for letting me chip in my two cents worth!

Jenna: Thanks, Paul, you are fabulous.

Paul: That's not a definition now, is it? Just teasing. You are fabulous too, as are *all* humans. Believe me, I sincerely believe that—and so will you from the very bottom of your heart, as time goes on.

Jenna: I have one more quick question. What is the value of knowing something like how people perceive horses in 2020, as if they are right there in front of them, when they are thinking about them?

Paul: Something seemingly incomprehensible?

Jenna: Yes.

Paul: Are you wondering if that really is possible, actually true in 2020?

Jenna: Well, it's true for me, as I have experienced it through my time travel.

Paul: That is the whole point here. People will have to tap into their own well of knowingness. Ideas you have presented about 2020 are very valuable, whether agreed upon or not, because it stretches people, it makes them attempt to discern their own truths about the future. For some it will feel "right," for others, not so "right;" it doesn't matter. What does matter is that at least some are bringing the future into their awarenesses, are they not? And is that not part of your thing? When you first started this project, you said many would not believe *any* of this, "because the future hasn't happened." Now you are saying some might not concur with some of the ideas you have presented pertaining to the future. Well, that is all right; they have their own truths. It doesn't matter what the details are. The fact is, some are starting to think about these details, yours, theirs, whoever's....now that's pretty interesting for a society that has been imprisoned by the past for millennia—now don't you think?

Jenna: Yes, Paul; I get your point. It is important for people to bring the future into their awareness, whatever the details.

Paul: Well, it is your point, your issue, my dear, that humans are out of balance time-wise—and I totally concur. Bring on the future.

Jenna: Yes, and thank you, Paul. Thank you very, very much.

Paul: You are most welcome...most, most welcome.

REBECCA

Jenna: Hi, Rebecca. And how are you this fine day?

Rebecca: I am quite well, thank you. And what can I help you with?

Jenna: As you know, I am trying to figure out the path to 2020. What kinds of insights do you think humans will have to have in the years between now and then in order to manifest ideas, using honesty as an example?

Rebecca: People need to be able to distinguish between their own flow—or who they are—and their own familiar emotional reactions. How can you have direct experience with honesty, or be honest, if you are focused exclusively on your anger, sadness, and so forth, but not really expressing those feelings. I help people become aware of their own flow, so it is very familiar to them. I want my clients to orient themselves around that, rather than familiar "feelings," which are quite different from their own natural flow.

Jenna: Give me one insight you had in ascertaining your own natural flow.

Rebecca: When I first discovered my own flow, it felt as though I had no feelings at all. It was very faint at first. Your own flow does not come to you in a blast of energy, the way emotional reactions do, so the accompanying insights are picked up at a subtle level. One insight then was that I had to fine tune my perceptive apparatus. There are a couple of big ideas I want to point out to you here. One is that there is information in both emotional reactions and your own flow. Both are valuable, but in the case of the former, it has more to do with the nature of the emotion. Your own natural flow is constant, that is, if you don't

109

block it—it just *is*; whereas emotional reaction comes and goes. One needs to be able to tell the difference between the two.

Jenna: Can you relate this to some of the ideas pertaining to communication in 2020?

Rebecca: Interactive communication, as you so describe in 2020, can only occur when people are aware of who they are. This has everything to do with your insight that the way people relate to their own beliefs is the key to their loving natures. If people are overtaken by an idea, such as an emotion, they are not relating congenially with it, or as you would say, equally with it. This is when the trouble begins: when they lose sight of themselves. This is why feeling who you are is so important in perceiving the world. If you don't, just as it is possible to perceive through fear, it is also possible to perceive the world through rage, sadness, jealousy, hysteria, or any other emotion which has "bullied" you in the first place into its point of view. Of course there is fear in all of the above emotions, but my point is love begets love, and if you are not coming from a point of love, you will not see the world as loving, and your communication will reflect it.

Jenna: That was great, thanks, Rebecca.

Rebecca: Now that is not to say that you cannot learn about yourself in the context of full emotional flow; you can, as there is much memory pertinent to a more expanded you within it, but my point is not to lose track of who you are, for only then will you know the truth.

Jenna: Yes…Rebecca, people in 2020 understand that reality is a totality of viewpoints. What do you see happening between now and then in order for people to grasp this?

Rebecca: First of all, people will have to be aware of others' views, then they will have to have direct experience with them. Right now what people do is contemplate ideas, their own, primarily. Their scope is extraordinarily small, considering the amount of viewpoints in this world. Here is the kind of thinking that will need to occur in years ahead: "I have my opinion, he has his opinion, she has her opinion; are these not all valid opinions? Rather than trying to figure which one is best, why not let all of them be?"

There will be a gradual realization that allowing what is makes a lot more sense than assigning importance to everything, in other words, judging everything. People will gradually understand that an enormous amount of time is spent labeling, when it could be, in fact, spent experiencing. When you are labeling something, or judging—this even would include comparing—you are not having direct experience with anything. Let me give you an example. You are absolutely sure about something. You are trying to convince another of your point of view. What are you focused on? Yourself and the logic of your belief. That is not direct experience. What energies are melding? Certainly not you and the person, or even you and the idea. When you are not experiencing energy fully, but rather backing away from it, then you are not using the faculties you have. This prevents you from incorporating the views of others.

Jenna: People need to recognize when they are backing away from others.

Rebecca: Or anything. Yes, that is the feeling of being overwhelmed by something or someone and should be a red flag to each person which says, "Get in touch with myself!"

Jenna: Sometimes I literally forget what I'm talking about when communicating telepathically.

Rebecca: Yes, not coming from a sense of self can manifest as a blank memory.

Jenna: Actually, I do that when speaking too sometimes. I wonder if that is the source for all forgetfulness…well, I'll think about that later.

Rebecca: No, wait. You know that's true, now don't you?

Jenna: Yes.

Rebecca: And you don't have to study it later or think about it to verify it. It just came to you.

Jenna: Yes, instantly, or as you would say from a very subtle level.

Rebecca: In a flash! Well, I just want the reader to have an example of inner knowing because that's *exactly* what that was.

Jenna: Yes, and I knew too at the time, but I wanted to stay on course with my questions!

Rebecca: Okay, well, I just wanted to make that point, that you know for *sure* that all forgetfulness comes from not being in touch with yourself, because as Paul would say, that is a big one. Not only the point but how it happened. So let us go on now, if you want.

Jenna: All right, thanks for pointing that out...Rebecca, I am wondering, have you ever had emotional reactions to your own beliefs, and if so, would you be willing to share them?

Rebecca: Yes, of course...yes to both questions. Well, let's take the issue of equality. When I realized I was carrying around beliefs that I was truly better than others, I was astounded by it, actually feeling revulsion toward myself, but it was beliefs to which I was reacting. People have self-hatred today, they think toward themselves, but the truth is, it's about beliefs about themselves. I was disgusted with the belief that I was better than others—mad at it! Where did I get the impression that I was better than others in the first place? From fears, which I learned. That is right, I learned how to feel fearful about myself and in order to avoid feeling it with any depth, I incorporated compensating beliefs about myself, such as being better than others. All beliefs have some fear in them, but some have more than others. Most people do not enjoy feeling fear, so they go with the less fearful beliefs—identifying with them, actually. In my case, feeling better than others wasn't nearly as painful as feeling inferior to them, which is what I suspected, so I became attached to feeling superior to others.

Jenna: So are you saying that the emotional responses that people have towards themselves have to do with beliefs about themselves?

Rebecca: Yes, and emotional responses toward others, too, have to do with beliefs about themselves.

Jenna: Could you elaborate, please?

Rebecca: Often when I reacted emotionally towards others, it was because the issue of inferiority/superiority was at stake for me. I became so intertwined with the idea that I was superior that I spent years defending that position. Oh, yes, I am attractive, smart, happy, efficient, a good person, and so forth, because the alternative implied inferiority. Here is what I mean. One time someone said to me, "You are so dumb!" Of course I responded, "I am not!" Don't you think that almost everybody does this?

Jenna: Yes.

Rebecca: It is an effort to align with the belief that one is superior, or smart, good looking, whatever...Then there are the people who respond, "Yes, I am dumb," with sad dog eyes. Although it may appear to be just the opposite, or more self-assured, that is not true. It is just a

112

position of being more deeply imbedded with one's own fears, on an unequal basis, or letting them have their way! Neither is coming from any depth at all, in terms of identity. Now the person who knows that neither of those beliefs is true—dumb or not dumb—is the person who is a bit more on the ball. He simply does not react, and stays with himself. We are talking about judgments; that's all. And we are a long way from zeroing in on our own subtle judgments about ourselves.

Jenna: So you are saying that all emotional reactions towards others are indicative of judgments about ourselves?

Rebecca: I would say that's true. So the answer to learning to love ourselves is to become more aware of the beliefs we hold, so we can move them on their way, and get more in touch with a deeper identity.

Jenna: Could you distinguish between a true hurt versus, say, a manipulative kind of hurt?

Rebecca: There are beliefs emanating from a false self, and there are responses, or interactions, emanating from the real you. Genuine hurt from a deeper level is different and more apt to be expressed and released quickly. I am talking more about beliefs that pile up, which eventually become who we think we are. You know, I am fat, I am ugly, I smell, I am not smart, or the opposite…I am the perfect size, I am gorgeous, I smell great or have no odor at all, and so forth. We are just talking about different levels of reality, really,…When *those* identities are questioned, we are apt to have feelings of revulsion toward ourselves, but as I say, they are actually emotional reactions toward beliefs we hold about ourselves, and it is not a harmonious exchange. In order to have a harmonious flow of energy within yourself, perception must come from the point of view of the real you—even toward the beliefs you hold about yourself, so that they may be transformed and released. A manipulative kind of hurt where people try to elicit love from others would fall into that category of nonharmonious exchange between you and the beliefs you hold, coming from a flimsier sense of self. This is because you are giving them the power to stay there when you are coming from, for example, a point of view of self-pity. You are letting that point of view have its own way as if it were the real you, which it is not. It is just a false impression which you've learned to operate from—to get love, which you don't seem to think you have. But this pattern just seems to go on and on for almost all humans. People think they have to get love, which they see as coming from outside of themselves in order to be, literally. But by

2020 people's emotional reactions are more as you described of being genuinely hurt, emanating from a deeper level of identity.

Jenna: Is this anything you help people with later this decade in therapy that would be pertinent, and if so, could you describe it?

Rebecca: I help people feel the difference between themselves and the beliefs they hold. That is why knowing their own energy is so important. They cannot, in fact, know the feel of what they believe until they know themselves. Knowing their beliefs is not at all the way it is today where people rattle off what they believe in, as you would say, from a very removed point of view. My clients learn to discern what they believe in by feel, not remembering what they've been taught. They can feel when their energy stops and beliefs take over, or when they are coming from the point of view of the belief. As we evolve, we will all need to become increasingly aware of energy movement at finite levels, our own and that of others. This is the kind of thing I teach my clients, how to feel relative motion. That's all it is, really.

Jenna: Oh, boy, and I suppose that's all intuitive, too.

Rebecca: Well, if you can talk to me like this, don't you think you are already doing it?

Jenna: Well, I hadn't thought of it that way.

Rebecca: Well, you are.

Jenna: Are you saying it's not even conscious?

Rebecca: That is right, and I'm also saying this applies to emotions in the sense that you need to feel both yourself and the energy of the emotion. You will need to recognize all ideas, including emotions, apart from yourself in order to relate to them in the first place—or have that harmonious exchange you have written about. Look at it this way. Just keep feeling who you are, and as Paul says, everything will turn out fine!

Jenna: Well, one quickie here. Are you saying that stuck emotions, in beliefs, and the fear of feeling them, are the reasons for maintaining belief-oriented identities?

Rebecca: I did not say that, but that is true. Let it be known to you and others that details unfold when communicating telepathically. When you stay in touch with your own energy, and mine, and feel the relative motion, that is just what happens, when the ideas unfold. Within whole ideas are details, which actually make up the ideas.

Jenna: When you come from a sense of who you are, a truer sense, rather than beliefs.

Rebecca: It's the only way it can happen.

Jenna: Well, thanks, that was a good illustration…Rebecca, this communication doesn't feel as fluid as it does with Paul.

Rebecca: That is because you cannot feel yourself or me as clearly as you did with Paul and yourself.

Jenna: Relative motion.

Rebecca: You see?

Rebecca: You can define perfectly and grasp this at one level, the way humans communicate now, but if you really want to feel as close to me and others as you do to Paul, you are going to have to stop defining to know, for when you stop defining, you will feel love. You will feel the energy behind the original message. I do not mean to criticize.

Jenna: I know.

Rebecca: It is easy to get wrapped up in trying to understand, by way of words, just as you have written about. Go beneath them or behind them, whichever you prefer, dear one, for then you will feel love. To use your terminology, if you let people's words move more, even mine, you will have taken the first step toward feeling the love that underlies them.

Jenna: Yes. Thank you; that was nice. I send good feelings to you.

Rebecca: Thank you. I send them back to embrace yourself.

Jenna: Rebecca, is there one big idea people will need in order to grasp the importance of getting meaning from light, as opposed to say, words? This is fascinating. I am now "pronouncing" my words differently—a bit more softly—even though it is all telepathic.

Rebecca: You have just begun, dear, to notice the finepoints of telepathy, rather, they are just coming into your conscious mind. Excuse me, for defining! A human habit. Let me see, is there one big idea people will need in order to grasp the importance of getting meaning from light, as opposed to words? Yes, that there is more clarity with light. This will come after people have become increasingly frustrated with their inability to communicate what they really mean.

Jenna: You are speaking of telepathy, then, just as here.

Rebecca: Yes. Do the details unfold in language-based communication?

Jenna: No,…I know I've asked you this before, but it's difficult to grasp. When you say light, what exactly do you mean?

Rebecca: Coming from a sense of who you truly are, attracting to yourself light, or the true nature of whatever. Sometimes I think I'm Paul, but here goes: Light is you!

Jenna: It's so easy to get Paul down…Tell me something about your clients, as you deal with them in the latter 1990s. At what stage are they in terms of experiencing highly interactive communication, say, to people in 2020? Even more to the point, how do they perceive horses later this decade in terms of thinking about them?

Rebecca: There is no way I could specifically answer that because each client is different, but I can tell you that there is a longing that is apparent in my office, a longing for more authentic experiences. People are maxed out by superficiality. They are at the stage where they are truly recognizing the importance of the heart. They want to be closer to other humans, and they can feel the ineffectiveness of their habitual ways, their tools. They vacillate between depression and longing. I am helping them tap in to that longing.

Jenna: You sound sad yourself.

Rebecca: I am trying to tell you the task at hand; it is not easy. When people learn about their own flow, they do not learn just good things; they also learn what they have been avoiding for years, for within emotional flow is much memory. As we head toward 2020, not only will we experience many wonderful things, but we will also experience much tragedy and much despair. We will experience a wide range of all that is. This is what happens when we discover ourselves, and it is why so many are in therapy with me later this decade. For some, all that came flooding into their awareness in the 1990s was too much, too fast. People are spinning. They are trying to align themselves with beliefs that work, and they can't find them. So much is in their minds—too much. They can't decide. Or for some, it's too little.

Jenna: And so that is why you are teaching intuition.

Rebecca: Yes, I am helping them learn about the process so they can figure out how to get their own answers. Today answers seem to be outside of people, still, unfortunately, with many therapists being problem solvers. The answers lie in the process, which originates within the people themselves. That is where light is. Yes, I think that would be a wonderful concept in helping people learn about light right now…and where meaning comes from…if they can think of it as inside of themselves. Of course I mean feeling it, but starting with first steps first, people should think of light as inside of themselves. They want more meaning in life? Turn to the light inside of them-selves…think of it, feel it, whatever it takes, but recognize that the perception of light throughout the world—and in all life, actually—begins with recognizing it within ourselves first.

Jenna: Yes, that's good. I like that. How does one remain aware of a more authentic self? This point has been made repeatedly.

Rebecca: By knowing who you are, by taking on those negative beliefs you are carrying around about yourself and confronting them with love, then releasing them and letting them go. Then you will be left with a feeling of who you truly are, which will become increasingly more clear to you as you learn to recognize how you relate to your false self—or defenses—which is a feeling of jerky, interrupted energy flow which is emotionally painful. I want to repeat this because this is so important. The way the real you relates to your defenses or false beliefs about yourself is the key to expanding your own awareness and identity. You will need to resolve this struggle. You will need to learn to create, rather, allow for a harmonious flow within yourself. If your false beliefs about who you are lead the way, then you will stag-nate. Fluid energy flow must occur between the real you and the false you if you are to grow in the upcoming tumultuous times. Ironically, you will need to love what you hate about yourself first, in order to release it, for only then will your light emerge.

Jenna: That was great, thanks…Rebecca, do you have any insights on the physical body and communication?

Rebecca: The physical body wants to communicate itself. Allow it to. Notice what it is doing. It has its own sense of beingness, without having to be "told" what to do. If people would actually get in touch with their bodies, they would notice something quite remarkable: they're already doing things, on their own, without the dictates of the ego! Guess what? They're communicating. Have you ever just watched

117

your body? You'd be surprised the kinds of things it's up to! In fact, I challenge you, Jenna, and all the readers, to just sit down and watch your bodies. Try it!

Jenna: Do you have any particularly hopeful concepts you can share with us about your therapy and the near term future?

Rebecca: As people increase their awarenesses, they will want to reach out to others. Many are in the process of becoming more aware. Not all people need to go to therapists for help; some do, of course, but many don't. There are many highly skilled people in society who are very willing to lend a hand. One of the first skills that people have learned in bad times is to trust. This is incredible to me, to watch people learn trust, even after all they have been through—and many have been through very trying times, with massive changes just in terms of surviving. I speak to you now, looking back at the years around 2000. These are the kinds of things I hang onto as a therapist. I see it in my office; I see it outside of my office. It seems quite miraculous sometimes to see trust pop its head up amid such confusion and fear, but it does. Paul is right that our answers lie in increasing awareness; I am just trying to lend a hand at helping people grasp this idea.

Jenna: Rebecca, thank you so much for all the wonderful insights, tidbits and love.

Rebecca: You are most welcome.

Author's comments

I am gradually learning myself how I don't trust all that much, and here all this time I thought I was so trusting. I have found that I trust Paul and Rebecca a lot more than I trust my most loved ones with whom I deal on a daily basis. Actually, I think I trust Paul the most. One day he had me do an exercise to show me what happened when my partner and I quarreled, and it all came down to trust and my own identity! He had me go back and tell him, word by word, a conversation we had had which ended in a stalemate and some harsh words. He then had me delve into my unconscious and bring forth the reasons for at least my input into the blocked communication. What I found was that I didn't trust who I was—or who I thought I was—or who my partner was—and that I was trying to control both of our identities during our quarrel!

Then Paul and I looked at one of our telepathic conversations, and not one issue that I was dealing with on an unconscious level with my partner was applicable to him and me. I had a totally different identity with Paul! In the case with my partner, I felt less knowledgeable than with Paul, not as flowing, more afraid of judgment, more frightened of responsibility, and afraid of losing something. Well, none of these things was true when communicating with Paul, even at an unconscious level! Well, that's not true. I have felt a bit burdened with responsibility with Paul at times, but generally that's not where I'm coming from at all. I might also add that when I first began communicating with Paul, some ten years ago, that some of these things were true, so I don't think that it's just because he's a spirit guide that there's more trust. In other words, I communicated with him the way most of us communicate today with our fellow human beings, a bit more cautiously and controlled, to say the least! But the funny thing is most of us don't even realize what we are doing. We think we are coming from a very deep, deep part of ourselves when we are communicating, but we aren't. Once our fears get tapped, thanks to inaccurate perceptions of ourselves, we get totally sidetracked, distancing ourselves from loved ones.

What does this all mean? That maybe we're spending an inordinate amount of time today preoccupied with a false sense of who we are—trying to prove that identity, actually—when we could be dealing with something slightly more meaningful, like, ah…the truth? Just wondering if anyone else has noticed how they might be trying to control their own identities, or anyone else's This is what we are doing when we define who we are in any way whatsoever—or take on the project of defining others. All we are doing is maintaining these crazy ideas about ourselves.

Amazingly, Paul helped me realize that when I was communicating with my partner, all I was doing was saying essentially this: "Now this is who I am! Don't you forget it! This is who you are. Don't you get that?!" Unfortunately, I think that this is where almost all of our breakdowns in communication begin today. When we don't feel safe, we resort to our most superficial identities, ones we've learned and memorized but aren't true—someone else's depictions of who we are, actually.

When communicating with Paul, or telepathically, I have gone beyond this, trusted more who I am, who he is, which has allowed the setting free of our true essences. As soon as this happens, there is an exchange of information that occurs naturally. All we do is think something and the other knows it. How do we make this giant step of trust? How do we get cozy all the time with our loved ones, others too, the way it is with Paul? Rebecca's suggestion is to feel our beliefs as if they were Paul. That is what she said will allow us to give up those negative beliefs about ourselves. Odd, how everything comes down to love, isn't it? If we loved everything, just think...even the stuff we hate about ourselves, we'd all be telepathic. Something to think about.

Business and Economics in 2020

• Absence of money • Loving businesses whose purpose is to create love and harmony in society • Jobs emanating out of natural skills and talents • Technology powered by love and light • Innovative business meetings fueled by participants' loving intentions • Absence of numbers • True efficiency in business through natural energy flow • Awareness of energy at all levels, including in products • Investing in consciousness

Because energy flow is so highly valued by 2020—cherished, in fact—there have been monumental changes in business. For example, some of the things that are no longer around are: profits, predictions and forecasts, analyses, goals, planning, competition, taxes, money, and ownership! Why? Because in some way all block the natural flow of energy, which is just another way of saying none encourages love. All entail a constriction of energy at the cellular level, something people can feel by 2020, preferring instead the more expansive energy of love. Concepts such as these, where energy is bound up in unhealthy ideas and not allowed to flow, make people themselves feel awful—tight and constricted—which shouldn't be surprising since they are more reflective of the human ego than the human heart. Therefore, in the years leading up to 2020, these ideas died a natural death. The idea of profits is gone because all of society does not benefit from profits directed toward only a few; predictions, forecasts, and analyses are gone because others' opinions rob people of their own insights; goals and planning are gone because they discourage people from broader experiences, focusing them instead on expected targets at the exclusion of other possibilities; competition is gone because it defies the more loving principle of "uniting with"; taxes are gone because they are punitive and don't take into consideration people's wills or their ability to produce themselves what they

121

need in society; ownership is gone because it implies possession of another, or some thing, creating unequal flow; and money is gone because it discourages authentic love, relegating it to a symbol, when in fact it could be the real thing, live and in person!

Alive, Vibrant Businesses, Just Like the People

The kind of energy that is so highly valued in 2020 is love. And it is just this kind of energy that makes up all of society, from the people, to the institutions they have created, including the businesses themselves. Businesses in 2020 thrive on fluid energy flow, unlike today's businesses, many of which labor under the illusion that they are in charge of energy—controlling it, either by depressing or forcing it—believing this to be true power, as would be the case in obsessing about corporate identity or manipulating "consumers" to think they have certain needs rather than serving the whole. Fortunately, by 2020, businesses have evolved beyond this kind of egotistical control, and allow for energy to flow its own natural way. As a result, businesses in our loving society reflect the values of the people, which is to say they are much more alive, just like the people. Even today, our society reflects the values and traits of the people, depicting most accurately their energy flow. Like the media then, and all other creations by people in 2020, businesses are loving, naturally flowing, interactive, balanced, nurturing, changing, honest, and growing. This is contrasted to businesses of today, many of which are arrogant, nonresponsive, nonflowing, inflexible, with a superficial flair to them.

It could even be said that businesses in 2020 come more from the heart, that they are in touch with their feelings, their thoughts, even their "sense organs," as well as being more integrated than today's businesses. Like living entities themselves, they can see, hear, taste, touch and smell well; they are not asleep—*as both people and businesses are today*—but interact with that of which they are a part, valuing how they impact society as a whole. Not emphasizing their states of separateness like today's businesses which pride themselves in this regard, businesses in 2020 reach out to other businesses…and customers…the way people reach out to people. They are loving and "hold hands" with the products and services of other companies! This is what is meant by love being everywhere in 2020—even within businesses, which by this time sparkle with their own energy, apart from the people who run them. Another way to look at it would be to say that everything has its own identity, even businesses, apart from anybody else's defi-

122

nition of it. This is what has allowed the business community to come together in the first place, as one, with businesses finding *that* more compelling than "beating out one's competitor."

So by 2020 much has changed. Supply and demand is more like a spontaneous flow of love between business and customers; profits are more like energy toward the beingness of all; and competition is the exact opposite of what it is today, having more to do with integrating *with* other businesses rather than *against* them.

Of course all of these changes have come about because of changes in people, who by now have incorporated new ways of perceiving. *Today* people perceive largely based on their own needs, or from only one perspective, bringing into their minds only what is useful to *them*. As an example, today when shopping, a young person would probably not even experience the presence of a product used by an older person. In 2020 people do not block out this information. What they perceive is much more, with a great deal more actually being in their awareness. The result is increased love in their lives. When one perceives something because someone else needs it, there is an automatic connection with that person, a loving link to him, if you will. In addition, by 2020 people are not having to struggle so with identity issues, not having to prove themselves, being far more secure than today. So naturally the same holds true for businesses, which now flow more gracefully, much like the human body. So it should not be surprising that the purpose of all businesses in 2020 is to promote more love and harmony in society. After all, just as love and harmony are the *natural consequences* of uninterrupted energy flow in people, the same holds true for businesses. Incidentally, by 2020, with the absence of time, the purpose of a business, or anything else for that matter, is virtually the same as the result. Now that is true efficiency!

Absence of Money

What is money today? It is love that has been literally stuffed into currencies throughout the world and then presented in a most confined and unnatural way. When a person pays another with money for something he or she has accomplished, it is like saying, "Here, this is the best I can do," when in fact the two of them could be embracing and exchanging love from the heart. Today the tradition of exchanging money is nothing more than a formal, rigid method of thanks, which acts a barrier among people. And what a distraction from love it's been all these years! Used as a form of control to maintain a sense of inequality among management and labor, reminding workers continually of who is in charge, money has kept people focused more on their position in society than anything else. In 2020 there is no money because there is no need for it. People do things for others because they want to, out of reasons of love, which is motivation enough. And in the process of loving, that loving encourages another's love, which in turn encourages another's, which yet again encourages another's, and so forth. In its most refined and delicious form, this is interactivity at its very best: an ever-increasing accumulation of love.

Today businesses have very little emotional fiber. Something is missing. That is because people are coming from such a sense of intellect, and fear, frequently feeling little while doing business. In all facets of life today people are tight, fairly removed from the directives of the heart, which means businesses are tight, which also means there is no true interaction, as in 2020. As an example, today businesses *tighten* when there are problems, an effort to control, which is the complete reverse of what is being done in 2020, when there is flow. The way of relating to energy today is through intellect, which *discourages* love in society. There is no greater way to miss love than not to feel it—and this is what the logical mind is doing today, the CEO of most businesses! It is trying its best to understand love, but it is missing the experience of it.

For a moment, sense this loving business atmosphere, as a person would in 2020. Imagine the following. You are shopping for a new pair of shoes. You look them over and feel the loving energy inherent in the product itself. You can feel who made the shoes. One enormous difference in the "work force," between today and 2020, is that people who are "working" enjoy what they are doing! Like all people in society, they have been encouraged to be who they are, develop their own natural skills and talents, which they have done so to a high degree, taking pride in themselves, so that people who are making shoes, for example, are being themselves, which they enjoy. What a difference this is from today. By comparison, now we are practically still in a slave stage, where few people truly enjoy what they are doing, which is true for both management and employees. We are slaves to the idea of low cost goods, at the expense of being ourselves.

Natural Skills and Talents Being Utilized

How many people today are actually using their innate talents? And why aren't they? Because they have not been encouraged to by their parents, who weren't encouraged by theirs, who weren't encouraged by theirs—to be who they are. Everyone ends up just trying to get love, with little knowledge of who they are, including knowledge of their own innate talents and skills. Fear has bound us all up into a frenetic control game. People are not using their talents and skills because energy is being controlled somewhere by somebody at the expense of everybody else. Or the people *have* to do their jobs, as if they were their only choice, again due to fear, and unfulfilled love needs. In 2020 people are encouraged to be who they are, and when they are, jobs are *created*; somehow this just happens (not planned, just the result of). Happy people are actually the "cause" for new jobs. Today people conform to the jobs and the current marketplace. Now that is a big difference from today. When people are who they are, which they are in 2020, they create their own destiny in a more purposeful, joyful way.

The concept of people flowing right into their jobs—or creating them from their own beingness—would be quite laughable today for some, but this is indeed the case in 2020. And in the case of this society, niches get filled, things get done; everything gets done—and more! And the economy is viable, enormously "successful," in fact. Growth is not in numbers in 2020 (now that's a new one); it's in relationships that are filled with love and fueled with love at all levels of society. People interrelate with *everything* lovingly, as if they were human beings: with jobs, with businesses, with ideas, with products of the companies, with energy itself! It is why this magnificent society works as it does in 2020, because of true equality.

Today people routinely feel superior to just about everything, moment to moment, "inanimate" objects, intangible concepts like jobs and businesses. People nowadays feel there is no comparison between themselves and a "job," for example, (they are superior to it)…with no idea whatsoever of what they are doing to themselves by carrying around such an idea. Feeling superior automatically shuts down energy in the human body, but it is the way of the ego: always better, always in charge. Talk about laughable; this concept of inequality is dead as the dollar in our society of love, for by this time people realize that the flow of energy is not just dependent upon who one is but who one is in conjunction with others. True interactivity only occurs when there is equality.

Today, for example, when people think of themselves as superior to, or more important than something else, or someone else, they seem to be invested in maintaining this identity. The same is true for feeling inferior to someone or something else. It is as if we have learned these identities, which include inequality, and it is more important to hang on to those than it is to interact with our environment lovingly and directly. When our thoughts and feelings are bound up in identity issues, that's where our focus is. Sometimes they are unconscious, sometimes they aren't, but the result is the same—we are walled off from our world. Most people would say they relate equally to others, but this is totally untrue and much more subtle than we realize. Few people relate equally to *anything*. It is important to see this in ourselves first if we are to create this loving society, how we are not relating equally to others, starting with our closest and dearest, perhaps.

But back to the shoemaker and you, the customer, in 2020. What happens is that when you look at the shoes, you feel the joy of the shoemaker who lovingly made the product for others because you are such an expert at feeling energy, both yours and others'. You do not just look at the price of the shoes...well, there isn't any...or the durability...or the style, as you would today. What I am trying to say is, you do not *think* so, as is the case today. You *feel* the love, you *feel* the experience of the shoemaker, and you *feel* a connection to the craftsman. To say that people's awarenesses have expanded by 2020 is the understatement, but then this is the reason for the ever-presence of love in society. Love is everywhere, even in shoes!

For those wondering how you get your shoes if you do not pay for them, or where they are purchased, you get them from the people who made them, and the where depends on where the two of you decide to make that exchange, not permanent places like shopping centers but more personal places conducive to the exchange of love which has replaced money. There are farmers' markets of sorts, as we might view them today, where people come with their wares and go, but it includes all merchants. Often these places are temporary, just a meeting place, although people's homes are favorites for the sharing of goods and love. Think of it this way, you get your "things" in 2020, like shoes, or whatever you need out of the hearts of others, just as you supply to them what they need from your heart. "Creating" what you need in 2020 includes the hearts of others. This is something that can be counted on—a given! Amazing, huh?

Equal Energy Flow Among People, Products, Materials

Expanding even more on how energy feels different to people in 2020, consider the following. When you, as a shopper, feel the energy of a product, it doesn't feel as confined as today, not only because it has been made by more loving human beings but for another reason. You yourself are more flowing and less confined, which is apparent to you. In addition, no products have labels on them anymore, with names on them, or directions. Today manufacturers suggest to their customers the use for the products because they have designed them with certain purposes in mind. By 2020, however, this would feel extremely limiting and constrictive to people since they have their own ideas about use, considering the fact they have different needs. In 2020 people are very much in touch with their needs, unlike today when others, i.e. advertisers, routinely remind us of what our needs are, and we often concur! Labels are also limiting to the products themselves who also have a say-so in their beingness—or "use." As mentioned earlier, the concept of use by humans is not even around in 2020, since it implies unequal energy flow between a manipulating human and a manipulated object. Today labels are clear signs that the manufacturers feel superior to consumers, and their products, as if they were in charge of them. Some would argue that this is being helpful, but help doesn't come when you feel superior to the consumer or the product, because *you* designed it. The product has flaws in it which are "ironed" out by 2020, no longer sitting on the shelf, in bright yellow and blue plastic but truly radiating.

Many of the products in the contemporary workplace are in a word, dead. What would you expect from unhappy, repressed people? Also, the products themselves in 2020—in a template, nonphysical version—are consulted before physically manifesting, as are all materials that go into the products. Both the manufacturers and the "consumers" consult regularly with the products to jointly decide use, which is always from the standpoint of the highest good. Today manufacturers think they create products all by themselves, with little knowledge at all of other potential, beneficial forces, which would make the products stronger. Maybe this is why in today's markets manufactured goods often don't work, break down, or have estimated years of "use."

Manufacturers also honor the natural flow theory in 2020, meaning their products are made from natural ingredients only, for by this time people realize that anything in its natural state is generating its own energy, and therefore is stronger and more durable than that which is contrived by humans, as would be the case with synthetic products. By the year 2020 synthetic products have been broken apart by love, actually dematerializing.

Products in 2020 are much like the human body, and people know this; that is, they transform. Today we do not even realize this, thinking instead products, like all objects, are static, without life. Because time is so slow now, and because we do not live long, we do not see this transformation. Also, we are not focused long enough on any one product, since we're apt to get caught up in the latest version of it, forgetting about what preceded it. Take a camera, for example. Think of the changes it has gone through. If we were actually focused on earlier models, we might see light emanating from it, a small change, perhaps, but we could see this in our lifetime. And if we believed the camera had its own consciousness, we would see a bit more of it in these years—more radiance to be exact. But for the reasons mentioned above, our lifespan, the speed of time, and our focus, we miss all of this—the change taking place within the camera.

In the future, however, specifically by 2020, the earth's vibrational rate is faster (time has speeded up,) all processes have speeded up, and we are living longer. In addition, human beings have made the gigantic leap of accepting themselves versus perfecting themselves, which has spilled over into the workplace. Let's put it this way. Redesigning a product is about as passe as redesigning yourself. People perceive differently and are more aware. Products actually transform much the way the human body transforms, discarding dead cells and replacing them with new ones. Light is replacing physical matter, and it is visible. This is just a fancy way of saying people have accepted the aliveness in everything everywhere. Synthetic products are no longer around, as they were filled with people's combined ideas of imperfection and also viewed that way, not allowing interactivity—or the loving energy of the people, as fuel. Natural products bloom like flowers. There is a faith in what is. Today people don't realize what an enormous factor love is in another's growth, or transformation. They barely realize it in regard to themselves, even less in regard to other people, and are totally unaware of it in regard to "innate" objects.

The natural state has affected numbers in a sense, since they are anything but natural, being like labels, used to control by those who have chosen the numbers. The truth is, anything symbolic is gone, because it is not necessary to be redundant, with people preferring instead to tune in directly to the energy itself. Anytime there is control, there is the element of confined energy, so therefore numbers are also gone by 2020. Just as language has disappeared for the most part by 2020, so have numbers. Definition, or amounts, imply lack of flow, not allowing for process, or change. Besides, people don't care anymore about how little or how much.

Let me explain. There are many new operative concepts and realities by 2020. For example, people take what they need in the moment; they don't decide ahead of time. And it is given freely by those in society. Not a struggle to get what you need. Faith that you will get it. You help others get what they need. People's energy is what identifies them, not social security numbers or phone numbers, or rank of some sort or income. Yes, there is a natural order in the universe, but it is not viewed with numbers but as what is. Today, in addition to signifying amounts, numbers are used to assist in memory, or faith that something will be, that order, for example, in the universe. But as we start to accept it, it will just be, and it won't be necessary to define with numbers. That order will just be felt for what it is, which of course will be viewed somewhat differently by each person.

How can you run a business without numbers? Look around, they're doing it in this loving society. Oh, is one of the businesses yours? Perhaps it has evolved from the very business you own now, or work for—but by 2020 you are the "owner,"…or the one who *loves* it.

Businesses with Hearts

What exactly are the businesses in 2020? They are businesses whose goods and services promote love and harmony in society, not tap in to themes of hatred toward others, which unfortunately is true for some businesses today. Therefore, what is around are businesses promoting people's growth, like food manufacturing and food related products (containers, utensils, bottled water), clothing manufacturing, shoe manufacturing, certain kinds of "natural metals" needed for building homes and other buildings, very basic kinds of things needed for survival, not diversions from who one really is. Also thriving is the leisure/entertainment industry since relaxation and emotional expression are so highly valued in 2020. People are entertained profusely—and they participate themselves in various body-related activities, such as dancing, singing, and "sports" of sorts. What is around is that which enhances life, which means for businesses, focusing more on people's total beingness, not just trying to make people feel better. There is a world of difference between helping people feel good about themselves (today's pitch) and piquing their inherent good feelings, which is the natural result of the products of 2020. Some of the more flourishing businesses/industries in 2020 are: musical instruments; ocean-related products, such as diving equipment; art supplies, especially those relating to touch, i.e. sculpting substances; glass making; and cotton clothing, especially hats.

129

However, the clothing industry has diminished considerably because by this time people don't wear so many...no, not because they are all walking around nude, although there is a lot more of that by 2020, but because they have learned how to keep themselves both cool and warm through the generation of their own energy. In other words, they don't have the same need for clothes that we do today.

Even though there are businesses in 2020, they are much different from what we know today. This has largely to do with how people are living. People are living in smaller, rural-like communities. They don't travel as much, being more intimate with neighbors, rather than superficially close to large groups of people through television, newspapers, telephones, and so forth. In 2020, because of tremendous telepathic skills, people are very much aware of others throughout the world but have chosen to remain closest to those people physically close to them. In terms of how the businesses themselves are different, not only are there fewer of them, compared to today, but they are not nearly as structured, being more casual, creative, and spontaneous, again, like the people who created them. Operating in the moment, with little need to plan, goal set, or regulate in any way, emphasis is put on what is being learned, not on what has already been learned. Businesses and people in 2020 use current data to trust in the process of inner knowing, not the antiquated method used today where the past is highly favored at the expense of all other "time frames"—and reality.

In terms of energy flow in businesses, energy flows outward in concentric circles, unlike today's businesses where energy flows upward, to ever higher levels of management. In practicality, what this means is that the ever-increasing amount of love generated in business has created equal power among people in business.

Everything is on a smaller scale in 2020, but it is richer, and more heartfelt. Few businesses have offices, or specific places where they do business, operating instead in areas preferable to both the business and customer. Places in nature are often chosen for business, where people set up their wares, with many preferring to conduct business in the out-of-doors. Sacred places are favorites. Actually, most people get their goods and services from their friends, especially their neighbors, which means homes are often places of business; even in business, people prefer intimacy. There is an ever-present exchange of "goods and services" going on all the time, among people. And because time has collapsed, just about the "time" people realize that they need something, it is highly possible that they already have it—

130

because someone has already given it to them! This is especially true for children, whose knowingness is often some of the most developed of all by 2020. It also illustrates how physical manifestation in 2020 differs from today, being a heck of a lot faster. Also, there are some people in society who are able to physically manifest "out of the air" what they need in the moment, but not everyone can. Some are definitely more skilled at this. People do have choices where they can go and look at the creations of others—not everything comes by gift—but there are few if any permanent areas where people shop. Most business is done in one's own community in the moment it's needed, with people just finding a way to create what they need from native materials. Of course by 2020, people don't "need" nearly as much, with "things" having lost much of their charm since people no longer use them to enhance their identities.

Two thousand twenty is not a bartering society. When a person says, "I will do this for you if you do that," there are conditions placed on the trade. This happened prior to 2020. By 2020 people do things for others quite naturally, expecting nothing in return, but of course that is what they get, often in the way of handmade items, which are virtually everywhere and treasured in this society of love. Although technology is around, compared to today it is infrequently used, but when it is—to inspire human growth rather than to mass produce—it is powered by light and love! Now *this* is virtual reality. People's intentions fuel what they have made, and what they have made would be quite crude by today's standards. "Bigger, better, and faster" has definitely lost its glow by 2020. The human mind has been rediscovered and is being used profusely, along with the heart, which can be lovingly felt in the products of the day.

Technology That is Alive

Technology in 2020 is not just a gatherer of data and knowledge, inputted by others, such as today's computers. It has a sense of its own beingness, interrelating with people, as equals. The light machines and love machine would be good examples (more on the latter in the next chapter). Many of the products around in 2020 have to do with stimulating the physical senses. Hand stimulation is particularly popular. There are "squishy" things, for example, which people put between their fingers to stimulate sensuality—truly a part of them they revel in, and cherish. There are also items to assist skull and brain relaxation! There is no rush in our society of love. After all, rush means forcing energy.

131

It is interesting to note that experts have seen their better day by 2020 because by this time people have expanded so much they are able to tap within for essentially any kind of information they want, although there are some people who read energy, helping businesses with perception and interpretation of it. People do help others, but it is not as today where people are trained in one trade for life; they are much more expanded and versatile than that. People in 2020 have many trades, many natural skills, and are encouraged to "switch careers," with the idea of increasing their awareness. Actually, the "business consultants" who do come in to businesses are like therapists, who help people discern energy flow in their products, their philosophies, their interactions with others, and how they relate as a group. They don't provide answers but insights into how people and businesses can have their *own* insights! As for the economy, it has new meaning by 2020, referring now to the flow of energy in society rather than the accumulation of wealth. So in this regard, the economic condition in 2020 is excellent.

Today there is an obsession for fixing everything in the business community, trying to "make" it just a little bit better, with little regard for the actual inherent nature of whatever it is that's being fixed. In our loving society, everyone allows all to be—just as it is—which is why there is such a vibrant economy, and it is also why society has been unable to lift itself out of "bankruptcy," the slow demise that plagued society previous to 2020. People learned about flow—or allowing. Bankruptcy, incidentally, is just another name for nonflow in society, and it is what happened prior to this rejuvenated society. When people or businesses don't flow, they die, or get sick, bankrupting themselves, essentially. Well, by 2020, the people themselves are flowing, all of society is flowing, and there is a passion for being in the air—a crackling in the air—that makes energy emanating off the billboards of today seem lifeless. By contrast to this sparkling energy, are today's businesses and business people, both, exceedingly flat, even depressed…yes, many of the businesses today are emotionally depressed, just like the people who run them.

One of the biggest differences by 2020 in business is the actual business meeting itself. People sit around in circles, hold hands, and together form a "gold ball" which is an accumulation of their collective loving intentions! Their energy creates a giant, vacillating idea which they can all feel, and which feels like an enormous loving, nurturing mother! It is the group's creation—what to produce and how to do it. Each person's energy is a part of it...with everyone's emotions unraveling within the context of flowing ideas. There is a huge transformation going on, and it is thrilling! The idea of everyone's energy contributing to the whole in 2020 is literal. The ball is spinning off static electricity, which all can feel, near the ground, along with a lot of moisture. Light comes off people's third eyes in the shape of triangles, meeting in the middle, to form the gold ball. People can also feel energy coming off their own bodies, and others', repeatedly, concentrically, and in regular rhythms...and there is a sense of figure eights dancing around people, which is the energy pattern people feel when they connect from the heart. All this happens while children play blissfully in the background, aware of all that is going on, and synchronized themselves with the rhythm of the group. A fine pitch is discernible, even to the children—maybe I should say *especially* to the children—and there is a "roar" at finite levels when people join at the cellular level, which is what is happening moment to moment. This is all very familiar to them...the shivering cells...for it is truth, and as regular as their breathing. Indeed the children know they are a part of this powerful group, invested in consciousness, for this is what humankind has done, invested in everything, everywhere, and the children know this, too, trusting deeply in their hearts. They trust in themselves, others, and everything, as do the adults in this loving society. Everything is done by feel, spontaneously. And there is a sense of peace, as people gather there in 2020, for reasons of "business."

PAUL

Jenna: Regarding 2020, it's difficult for me to envision a society operating without money or some kind of exchange, where records aren't kept. Aren't records for accountability? And numbers are gone, too, by 2020. How can this be, with things changing so fast? Is trust the main issue? And if so, how can it be learned in such a short time, only 20 some years from now?

Paul: I think what's really bothering you is that you are worried people won't believe you, that they will say that what you say is impossible, and I'd like to comment on that first. First of all, it doesn't matter whether people believe you or not. I know that is easy for me to say. Please understand that humankind would make very little progress, indeed, if there weren't people like you, plowing ahead with unconventional ideas. Let me be the first to confirm your suspicions many will not believe you, but so be it. Now my point here is that I don't want that to influence your ideas, those wonderful ideas, that keeping pouring into your conscious awareness. They are wonderful ideas, flowing ideas, and just the kind that need to be embraced to get to that loving society you envision. It is first necessary to acknowledge ideas, before they are implemented into society, before they are manifested. And for those people who throw out your ideas as impossible, let them note that what they are saying is that those ideas are *wrong*. They are making a judgment, which will close them down "good." Allowing more into one's mind, as possibilities, is where it starts. One need not say, "Now those ideas are absolutely ridiculous," because they are indeed not.

It is not ridiculous to work toward a society that is more loving, where people trust others, and money and numbers are not necessary. And why don't you truthfully tell your readers now, just what is happening, that you actually have tears in your eyes, because you feel my love so and feel us working as a team? Let them know what it is like to join up with another—even a spirit guide—and work together on behalf of humankind and all the rest of the universe. It feels good. It brings tears to you, you who are so intellectual! Is it the ideas that make you cry? Is it the exchange of love between you and me? Is it your vision of many more humans joining with you and me and together carving out this path to 2020? Whatever it is, it is thrusting you forward, so stick with it. It is you!

Now, as to your inquiry about trust; trust is just allowing, as we have spoken of so often before. When you allow flow in your own body, trust is what happens. You need not trust first, as if it is something you are supposed to learn. This can really throw people for a loop. My approach would be quite different from Rebecca, and that would be when you allow flow in your body, you automatically start trusting others more. This is because you are letting ideas and behaviors associated with fear die. Do you think that money and numbers are fear-related? Of course they are. You were exactly right when you said money and numbers have to do with accountability. They have come into being for protection. That is, people wanted to protect themselves, they wanted to get their due, or what was owed them. They are just a form of control, where people have something to look at, reassuring themselves of what *ought* to come their way. Do you follow me? I am not just talking about material things, although that is part of it. I am talking about love, largely, which they feel they are not getting enough of—and they are not; nor are they "giving" enough.

When people get over focusing on what's in it for them…or at least stop seeing themselves as more important than others—you will begin to see numbers and money disappear. It will be a process, though, and not happen overnight.

You are wondering how all this can happen so fast. My advice here would be to just notice the feel of numbers and money. Do they not seem to confine energy? When people start flowing more, they will begin to notice where energy is confined, also, when it is allowed to flow. So once again, I say to focus on the flow of your own energy, for it is what influences how you perceive. Then things will fall right into place, including acceptance of unconventional ideas about money, numbers, definitions, and yes, even time.

Jenna: Thank you, Paul.

Paul: You are welcome. Maybe the problem here is that unconventional ideas have too much flow in them, for people now. They are just not used to them, the feel of them. They are causing the people themselves to flow more—and that is scary for people. As an example, think how often people turn away from love. It is not just because they think they don't deserve it. It is because the energy is too intense for them.

Jenna: Yes, I think that's true; thanks, Paul. It will take a while for people to get used to their own energy flow—and love it, I guess you could say.

Paul: It will take as long as it is important to them.

Jenna: What do you mean by that?

Paul: When they care, and realize it, they will go zip, zip, welcoming that intensity. They will make the association between caring and intensity!

Jenna: Yes, that's good. It will have meaning for them.

Paul: Just as you understood what I was saying here? Are you aware it was a bit more intense?

Jenna: This is happening so fast; I can't believe the subtleties involved.

Paul: The subtleties of caring, is what this is all about.

Jenna: I like that, Paul.

Paul: The more you care, the more intense it gets. Have you ever noticed how often you back off from your own caring? Do you not see how this all fits together? When you do that, you back off being. And in the case of businesses today, as opposed to 2020, it would never even occur to people that businesses could care, so of course they're not alive, or coming from the heart, as you would say. They don't *have* a heart.

Jenna: Let me be the first to say that your caring has tapped in to my caring.

Paul: And do not worry *how* your businesses form hearts. That is not the way it works. They will form their *own* hearts, if you will just allow them to. If you have the intention of bringing about more love in the world, begin by trusting that that *is* what will happen. Then notice all that you do to go against that intention.

Jenna: Can you give me some specific examples?

Paul: You treat a business as if it were there to *serve* you. Do you not think that doesn't have an effect on the flow of business?

Jenna: Paul, I grasp what you are saying, but this is so abstract.

Paul: Then let's take one thing at a time. Remember this, how you think of another affects its flow, which emanates from heart. Not only are you affected—your own energy slows down—but so does that which you have defined. Now that in itself is a concept rather unfamiliar to people today, but it is the same as your whole pitch on how you relate to what's in your head. You must honor another's beingness, a thought's, a business's. Emotional flow is the guts of an entity—and what you *think* of anything affects *it*. Now of course there will be many who will say that in itself is ridiculous. But just as I tell you to notice now what you are thinking in regard to businesses—any thoughts you have about them—the same is true for people. You need to recognize the effects on them. So before you choose to judge him or her, remember you are affecting his or her heart.

Jenna: Wow, I guess you just gave me a good lesson on thoughts.

Paul: I don't mean to scare you, but I do mean to be emphatic. Thoughts go right to people's hearts. They go right to the very core of a being. So, I am not saying thinking is all bad; I am just saying, send those thoughts with love. Wrap them in caring, for when they are wrapped in judgment, they *hurt* others, even something as abstract as businesses. When you put a business into a category of a servant, what are you doing? Well, I'll tell you one thing, you are not sending it a message of love. You are not encouraging its flow. You are in fact challenging it to stand up to you. Are you not saying, "You will serve me, or else"? In fact, any time you think of anything, without love, including products, even the government, this is what you are saying, which is to say you are acting as a counter force to its beingness.

Jenna: You are saying how we perceive something actually affects its energy flow; and if we love it, it can feel it and will be more flowing and loving itself.

Paul: Exactly.

Jenna: Wow, that sort of puts interdependence and responsibility into a nutshell.

Paul: I sense you are a bit overwhelmed.

Jenna: Well, the magnitude and implications of that…

Paul: Well, you can look at the flip side too, and that is that you count. If people truly believed that, what do you think? Do you not think that in itself would get the ball rolling?

Jenna: And now I suppose you're going to say that that comes at a feeling level.

Paul: Do you not feel you count with me, at a feeling level?

Jenna: Yes.

Paul: Well, make the assumption you count with others, and before long you'll be feeling it! Do you see how this works? If you bring the future into mind, or what you want as a possibility, I'll be darned, you've already started the process of creating it.

Jenna: That was really good, Paul, and thanks. With that in mind, I'd like to ask you about the personalities of businesses in 2020. At that time they are loving, naturally flowing, interactive, balanced, nurturing, changing, honest, and growing. In addition to developing those qualities in ourselves, as people, what advice can you give to create such magnificent businesses?

Paul: If you acquire all those qualities, the businesses will create themselves! And you will have little to worry about. It will just happen. But the trick is in developing those traits, so let's just backtrack a minute. You are wondering how this all works, how human qualities can manifest into businesses. Well, they can. You are just not used to seeing them as such. Human beings are not the only ones who are loving, naturally flowing, balanced, nurturing, and so forth. These are qualities inherent in energy. Do you get that? Let's look at that list: loving, naturally flowing, interactive, balanced, nurturing, changing, honest, and growing. There is not a quality there that doesn't just happen, if you allow whatever to be. So whatever is—in its natural state—has those qualities. The problem is, humans learn a great deal, so that the natural state is "shaped" according to human egos, or misdirected by, maybe I should say. So the idea is to discern what is natural. What is hard for you, is perceiving businesses with human qualities, such as products holding hands, for example, with products of other companies. Well, do you think that humans are the only ones who hold hands? This is just language, you know. And you know how I feel about that. So I am saying two things here, that humans and businesses both need to flow, for in the flowing state the qualities you named will all be there, and observable. The problem with humans is that they are so literal. Again, I say that acquiring those traits has to do with your own energy flow, for none can exist without it. As for businesses, try to perceive them differently. Try to feel their aliveness, their worth equal to you. When you recognize that businesses have not just been created by humans—but truly have energy of their own—you will not perceive them so as objects, to be used by humans, to use your phrase. It is a matter of recognizing that you are truly not the center of your own universe; for if you are, you are missing a lot. Each is the center of *his* or *her* own universe, too, you know.

As for what you can do to acquire all those traits, besides developing yourselves? Let me see. You can help others flow more by letting *them* be, which in turn helps *you* flow more. You do not have to fix others. You do not have to change others. All you have to do is let all be. Applying this to businesses, why not start by noticing when you bad-mouth a business, or anything, for that matter, also, products, just as you might a human, for in doing so, you are saying, "You do not have a right to be." You are doing a disservice to anyone or anything—*and everyone*—when you judge. This is the opposite of allowing something to be. Rather than spreading your message of your superiority, which is what you do when you judge, why not use your energy for something more productive, such as inputting another's flow by sharing love? When you do this, you are being quite creative, now don't you think?

Jenna: Absolutely; I must say I have never thought about bad-mouthing businesses before. Paul, I even experienced something recently where I bad-mouthed my alarm clock because it didn't go off!

Paul: And you're wondering why alarm clocks don't go off sometimes?

Jenna: Talk about using something, without respect. I am gaining a new perspective on how I "use" things, and trying to change that perspective.

Paul: Yes.

Jenna: Well, thanks, Paul.

Paul: You are welcome. I just felt like putting my two cents worth in about the human propensity to comment on, or judge everything! It is a waste of energy. Enjoy what is there—instead of trying to reshape it!

Jenna: Yes, I get your point…the human narrative, which is an attempt to control, no doubt.

Paul: That it is.

Jenna: Paul, in today's society, people go to where the jobs are. In 2020 people's energy creates the jobs, with natural skills and talents being utilized. This sounds wonderfully ideal. How do we make this transition?

Paul: By recognizing that people have natural skills and talents. People hardly know *their* natural skills and talents, let alone develop them. Let me ask you this, what are your natural skills and talents? Do you know them? You need not respond; I just want you to think about it.

When people get to know themselves, they will have a much better concept of what they can offer society. It starts with parents' encouraging their children to be who they are, even if those skills and talents are not in vogue, shall we say. Parents need to encourage their children to discover who they are. This of course comes largely through love. When children feel love, their energies rise to the surface, in the most glorious ways. For parents to be most effective with their children means they know their natural skills and talents. Since this is often not the case, I suggest starting with love. Notice when you are not being loving, and I say this to all people, whether they received ample love in their childhoods or not. All people can notice when they are not loving. When one is not loving, there is a blandness about one's life. There are few who cannot be more loving. Think about it. When you are more loving, honoring those as equal to you, you are helping them discover their own natural skills and talents, and you are also more apt to discover your own. Helping others discover who they are is not just the job of parents. All can help in this regard, by being, by loving.

Jenna: Thanks, Paul; that was really touching. To increase awareness of energy in physical objects, as in products of companies, or in anything, for that matter, do you have any specific advice?

Paul: You are talking about over-all increased awareness. One does not selectively learn how to note energy in objects, without noticing other things. One learns how to increase the flow in his body which helps one feel faster energies everywhere. But if you want to know about objects, per se, you need to first notice them, as you would say, apart from how you might use them. This is what people do in 2020. They notice that which is not particularly important to their needs. This has to do with not looking *for* something, say, as in the case of looking for your coffee cup when you want to have some coffee. What else did you notice? I cannot tell you every step, but I can tell you that noticing objects first comes before feeling the energy within them. In the case of the coffee cup, try to experience it more broadly than just providing something for you. See if you can experience it, without use. Also try to experience more than what you need. As is, people today filter out almost all that they don't personally need, which is a heck of a lot. That is because they look *for* something. When you learn to allow what *is* to come to you, rather than reining in what you need, you will have opened a much more expansive world to yourself. Try it. It is a matter of relaxing the physical senses more and using them more fully.

Jenna: That seems strange, looking at a physical object, apart from how I might use it—or what benefit it brings me, but I am already starting to do it, as I mentioned earlier in the incident with my alarm clock.

Paul: Well, get used to it, because if you want to be a leader in our "movement," you will need to do just that, perceive from the object's point of view.

Jenna: I just tried it again, noticing something apart from its use—and I started spinning.

140

Paul: That is because you are letting go of control. Remember when you talked about the ego assigning meaning to things? Well, that is what you are giving up. When you can allow whatever to be meaningful in the context of *its* own energy, then you are on the right track. It will give you a spinning effect because you are not stopping its energy; you are melding with it—and both of you are moving. This is quite different from a highly defined you and a highly defined it, now isn't it?

Jenna: How did we ever get into all of this?

Paul: With our intent, dear one, and we are *so* glad! Let's keep going.

Jenna: Paul, what about equal power among people in business?

Paul: Equal power will come about when a lot of people have a lot of spinning experiences, when they can view others as equal to themselves, even objects, nature, animals, everything! Here is my guess as to how it will happen. You will notice more and more movement in what you experience. As you allow more into your mind, you will be forced, frankly, to give it room to do its own thing. Forget the details on that one. Rather than only latching on to that which is highly defined, or form, you will learn to acknowledge "moving form." Another way to look at this would be to say that what you haven't liked in the past, or maybe haven't noticed, will creep into your awareness—in a new light. Not only that, it will begin to feel "good" and meaningful. You will be attracted to it. This will play out in the business place. You will be open to more and more, as your favorite ideas will be allowed to flow more, welcoming more ideas into your awareness, also more people. Let's see, what would really be helpful here? In terms of perceiving others as equals, I would give you similar advice to what I told you before. Notice when you are labeling, defining, judging others, for when you do, you decrease your own flow and discourage theirs. Every time you do this, you slow down evolution, you push away love. Start with this, why don't you? Notice when your behavior is less than loving—when you are judging—for it is a good example of not treating others equally. When you treat them equally, you love them unconditionally, which is our goal, right? Well, there can be no equal relationships in business until people actually relate to others that way.

Jenna: Yes, which leads me right into the next question. Sometimes I don't understand the difference between defining, just to understand, and judging another.

Paul: There is a difference in energy, in the energy of the intent. When you come across from a point of superiority, trust me, the whole universe knows, as it is felt on many levels. This is inherent in judgments. People will learn how to discern subtle judgments—ones they are not so clear on now—the more they learn to increase their flow. Then eventually they will be defining less and less, as you say, to understand, for understanding will come more and more by feel. When you feel, you take into consideration a lot more movement. When you define, you depend more on what you've learned.

Jenna: Do you have any ideas on what it will take to develop what I call investing in consciousness?

Paul: Awareness. Awareness of what one has suppressed—of what one is! People are starting to realize this more and more, how far they have strayed from their "true selves." I guess you could say it will go like this. As people realize what they're capable of, it will thrust them into greater awareness, realizing they are capable of even more. This is the spiraling upward that is so often referred to. It is the whole idea of eternity, which is at the heart of the timelessness of which you speak, or new ways of experiencing time. If there is always more, then how can time, as you know it, be accurate? How can time—with its categories—represent eternity?

Jenna: It can't, and it is necessary to transcend this kind of time if we are to increase our awareness.

Paul: Indeed, for just focusing on what you know as "now," is quite limiting. Here is my point. Investing in consciousness comes about through the experience of investing in consciousness.

Jenna: Talk about experiencing time in a new way! Thanks, I liked that answer. Cause and effect all in the same time frame!...Paul, your expertise from former human lives lies in the area of economics and finance. What else can you add which will bridge the gap between investing for material gain, say, to investing more in humankind and the consciousness of all things?

Paul: I love your simplified version of explaining timelessness, cause and effect in the same time frame. If you can state it so simply, why don't you try answering that last question, with a simplified response, no less?

Jenna: No, no, you don't. You have to answer this.

Paul: I am just teasing you, pointing out that you probably don't even need me, with your own innate knowledge. But in any case, investing for material gain versus investing in humans and the consciousness of all things. Let me see. What is material gain? Material gain is more for yourself. Let us start with humans because that is where it starts. More for yourself is okay. The problem is, people feel guilty about having more than others; yes, I would say this is true. When they feel guilty, they shut down—because they do in fact have more than others, and it doesn't feel right to them, some at a conscious level; some not so conscious. Then they rationalize that they worked for it, or whatever. They figure out a way to feel okay about themselves, but not in truly loving ways. They shut down themselves. The answer is not in taking less for one's self but figuring out a way to increase the flow of energy everywhere so that all have everything. I suppose you are thinking that that is impossible. How does that come about? I would say this to people who are good investors today, who have much. Love yourselves. I would say this to people who are not such good investors, who don't have so much. Love yourselves. Then the energy created by all those people will build quite naturally into a better flow of energy throughout society, so that more comes to more.

Jenna: That was neat, Paul. Talk about pinpointing something!

Paul: Investing *is* energy flow. Have you ever thought about that?

Jenna: No.

Paul: Well, it is, and don't let anyone tell you what is the best investment for you because only you know that.

Jenna: Oh, I thought you were going to tell me the investment itself would tell me.

Paul: Sometimes I don't know what I am going to do with you.

Jenna: I'm getting it, I'm getting it…

Paul: That you are, dear one. May you and all your investments flow.

Jenna: Paul, I have one more question, pertaining to goals, if it's okay to ask you.

Paul: Of course.

Jenna: How is it that there are no goals in 2020? I find this quite peculiar. It would be like not allowing the future into your awareness, which is what I am promoting now, or striving for anything, even growth? Am I off base on this, or what can you offer?

Paul: I would never say you are off base on anything. I would say that when you interpret the material you get about 2020, you use your logical mind. Now that is not to say there's anything wrong with that. If there is no time, how can there be goals? Do you see? It is not always easy to grasp concepts in the future, then communicate them in the present because in order to express something to people today it is necessary to use terms familiar to them. I would say you interpreted the idea of goal, as we know it now, meaning it would take away from people's beingness, not trusting that goals emanate *out* of beingness. Now that is true. If people are focused on the future and not in the moment, that kind of goal *is* no longer around in 2020. You were talking about businesses. Where they fall down today is to value too highly the past, just like people, as if the answers were there. They are not. They are in the present. Goals, let's see…the energy to reach one's goals and the goals themselves—emerge in the now. Now if people can truly get that, well, we have really made some tremendous headway here!

Jenna: I would truly love more on this.

Paul: Goals are what you are intending now. They are the same thing. Why would you set goals and then try to create the path? That is backwards. Just learn to see where your beingness is taking you and you will *have* your goals. Goals are a natural result of, or part of your flow.

Jenna: If that is true, then my thinking is a little off that we are a team creating a path to 2020, because I *do* think of it as a goal.

Paul: By today's standards it is a goal. By 2020's standards it is reality. Can you follow this?

Jenna: I am getting mixed up with my time frames.

Paul: Take all the time frames and lump them together. Goals are there, right, but only if you are viewing from the past. Do you see why language will have to go? You keep having to know from what time frame and which definition of goal we are talking about. The problem with that is you never get to the heart of the matter. Let me try to sum up. To make this transition, cause and effect are the same...see how smart you were earlier?...you will need to recognize that you naturally create goals as you *be*, okay? So notice where your *being* takes you, because those are the goals. The important thing is to tap in to your own inner knowing, because that is where your intentions are, rather than trying to create them as if they were step one, step two, and step three—apart from you.

Jenna: Oh, my, I just had the thought, rather the feeling that everything *was* a part of me. I have read that often but never felt it so.

Paul: And remember that my love is a *part* of you, too. If you can feel *that* in the same way, then we are really chugging right along.

Jenna: I'll be working on it. Talk about the feeling level...

Paul: Yes, please do!

Jenna: Paul, thank you again for your love, and your comments.

Paul: You are most welcome.

REBECCA

Jenna: Hi, Rebecca. Is there anything you would like to comment on before I ask you my questions?

Rebecca: I wonder if anyone is tapped in to us, as we talk.

Jenna: I have never even thought about it, have you?

Rebecca: Well, I was thinking, with all the monitoring going on who knows where. It wouldn't surprise me if someone were sitting at his or her computer somewhere, just registering our comments!

Jenna: Are you serious? Do you really think so?

Rebecca: It is certainly possible.

Jenna: Excuse me, I think I'll ask Paul. What do you think, Paul?

Paul: So what if they were?

Rebecca: I'm not saying they are, just that they could be.

Jenna: What do you mean monitoring? You mean the government? They're still trying to figure out what they mean by the information highway.

Rebecca: Tut, tut...judgment. You're talking down to certain people who are creating the information highway.

Jenna: You're right, I take that back...and apologize.

Paul: I'll leave you two now, to figure out the realities of communication. Ha! Ha! Bye, bye.

Rebecca: Did what I say scare you?

Paul: Heck no.

Jenna: I can't believe he said that, when we weren't even talking to him.

Rebecca: He did it on purpose.

Jenna: I know.

Rebecca: I didn't mean to scare you or even imply people might be aware of us. Maybe it's just the usual paranoia most of us carry around.

Jenna: Well, I did have kind of a tightening of my stomach when you asked me about that, but don't you think if someone had an evil intent, as in monitoring, they wouldn't be able to link in to this at all, you know, without a loving intent. Is that right or not?

Rebecca: You tell me...you know quite a bit about telepathy.

Jenna: I'd say it's possible but unlikely. I'm not going to worry about it. Actually, my guess is that my comments about the information highway, since they were less than loving, could be picked up. Or the other comments, I don't know, they probably could be registered somewhere.

Rebecca: So you do care.

Jenna: Well, I had assumed all this was private. I can't believe you are asking about all of this!...Okay, okay, I can see that this has scared me a bit.

Rebecca: I'm not trying to alarm you. I was just wondering if you had ever thought about it.

Jenna: No. And I can't believe I'm acting like this, emotionally. I don't know why I would care.

Rebecca: Because it is not easy to be open. Learning to be open in spirit is quite different from learning to be open emotionally, as you can see yourself, by your own behavior. Did you see how you got angry at

146

me? I just use it as an illustration of what anger is often about, the fear of exposure. Most people are really quite frightened to show others who they are and certainly prefer to be the initiators of this process. Well, let us talk about 2020. I don't know why I got off on that.

Jenna: Because you care, too, about others' being in on this. I can just feel it.

Rebecca: Well, I'll tell you something, I think we better get used to it because having people aware of our thoughts and feelings *is* the name of the future.

Jenna: Yes, this feels very unresolved…

Rebecca: Let me just make a suggestion. Certainly there are some who might be tapping in to our conversations telepathically, but so be it, as Paul would say. I think we should just relax and be open to our own self-growth in this regard.

Jenna: Yes, simply put. It does sort of act as an inhibitor, though, doesn't it?

Rebecca: Truthfully at some level, yes, but let us proceed to that deeper more trusting level. And let this be an illustration to the readers that once fear sets in, bye, bye, to good clear telepathic messages. So…would you like to take a breather and return in a minute?

Jenna: Yes.

Jenna: I am back, more centered, and able to make out what you were saying. I really lost my focus there momentarily…Rebecca, what advice would you give to people, as they learn to let others know who they are? And can you apply your response to business in 2020?

Rebecca: Be prepared not to like yourself, when you first start to be open, or allow a fluid flow of thoughts and feelings, which *will* be easily discernible to others. Most people do not realize how much they have covered up negative feelings about themselves, truly deep ones, I mean. As we take the chance to know ourselves more, we find out all sorts of yuckiness we are holding which we need to be aware of, which acts as a buffer to those incredibly *good* feelings we have about ourselves. When I say be prepared not to like yourself, I mean be prepared to see that part of yourself that does *not* like yourself, because it is baggage. Also, recognize that increasing irritation at others may be just an avoidance of these so-called bad feelings toward yourself. As for 2020, and businesses and the economy, when people can pare themselves of this baggage and see it for what it is, then they themselves will have more fluid energy flow, creating a more efficient economy with more efficient businesses.

Let me see, I want to say something emotionally about the businesses. Okay, if people notice that their businesses are not flowing, loving, instead sluggish, nonresponsive to customers, as we head toward 2020, I would suggest they step out of themselves, putting them in the position of viewing from the businesses and look back at themselves. The whole art of stepping outside of yourself and looking back from another's view will be greatly increased in the intervening years. This is what I would suggest people do when things are not going so well for them, "when the system is not working," which I strongly suspect will enter people's awarenesses here pretty soon, if it has not already. And yes, you can look at yourself from a business point of view. Although that might sound extremely abstract, in some ways it might be easier than from another person's point of view, because the emotional issues are not as likely to be as intense, although for some they could be more! In any case, in these times of opening ourselves up, when you can look from another's point view, feeling the pain of exposure and fears associated with it—we are apt to develop compassion for ourselves. And when that happens, we are well on the way to tapping in to those deeper loving feelings we have for ourselves that we have been talking about.

Jenna: That was really nice, Rebecca. And comforting too.

Rebecca: It is one of the benefits of clear communication among people, such as telepathy here; it is emotionally comfortable, because it unites people.

Jenna: Yes. That is exactly the comfort I felt, a uniting with you when you said that…. Hmmm, so this process of communication is quite a bit more than the sharing of ideas.

Rebecca: Yes, unless you want to call us ideas!

Jenna: I hadn't thought about it quite like that before…Rebecca, could you comment, please, on the absence of money and society in 2020?

Rebecca: First of all, I would like to talk about numbers. Numbers link people to something. The same is true for money. The problem is that they act as buffers to feelings, removing people from a more accurate depiction of reality. They're middle men! When we remove these symbols, we experience reality more clearly.

Jenna: It is easier for me to understand how money could be gone by 2020—and why—than it is for numbers. It's hard for me to conceive not knowing how much.

Rebecca: You can know how much without numbers, just from the energy of whatever. Are you wondering how you explain to another, in communication, how much or how little?

Jenna: Yes.

Rebecca: I think it gets back to what Paul says, that you are worried you will not get your due. Tell me, if you can go to a deeper level, as best you can, what you think your emotional needs are, when using numbers.

Jenna: Well, I could tell you, for example, how long it has taken me to write this book, or how much food I have in the house, or how old I am.

Rebecca: First tell me how you feel when you use numbers.

Jenna: It feels weighty to me. It feels as though I am carrying extra baggage.

Rebecca: Well, you are.

Jenna: I think it has to do with reconfirming who I am.

Rebecca: Now that's an interesting thought, isn't it? Hang on to it for a while. Regarding your comments about your book, your food, and your age, well, I'll tell you something. I have a pretty good feel already for the amounts, without your stating the numbers.

Jenna: So you are saying that quantitative messages need not even be stated in telepathy.

Rebecca: Perhaps I am making a value judgment. Excuse me if I offend you, but the truth is, I don't care about any of those things because those things get in the way of our love.

Jenna: But we are communicating right here, about "important" stuff, and words don't seem to be getting in the way, at least as much. But you are saying that numbers get in the way?

Rebecca: They are not really necessary to the core message, neither are the words. We have sent and received these messages long before words appear. Besides, as you know, if one really wants to know numbers, they are just *there* within the greater message.

Jenna: Yes, but this still is confusing to me.

Rebecca: I am trying to help you grasp the rather insignificant role that numbers play. You will not grasp the need for more sophisticated perceptual techniques if you do not see the reason for them. How much or how long are just human narratives; they are just comments on what is. They are not experiences at all, of what is; they are just opinions. And I suppose now you are saying numbers are opinions? And that one is one, two is two, three is three, and everybody would agree with that, and therefore, it is quite accurate.

Jenna: But not necessary.

Rebecca: Numbers, money, words, labels, definitions, and no doubt a host of other things, are not necessary. They encourage people to focus on symbols,—rather than on the flowing energy among people, or among people and objects—the direct experience about which you write.

Jenna: Yes, I get that.

Rebecca: So my advice to people would be to notice first of all the absence of loving feelings when focused on definition. And I include time in here, too; for it, too, is just a collective opinion. Whenever one gives one's attention solely to something outside of one's self in order to know, which is how time is perceived today, one removes one's self from one's own being, which as you know is necessary for clear perception. Let us presume you and others begin to discern when you are turning away from love, or focusing on something like numbers, for example. Only then will it be appropriate to speak more of actual perceptual techniques. But for the record, I will say that it involves keeping love in your awareness more. If you are not aware, at a very subtle level, of what you are doing now, you will not gravitate toward more sophisticated techniques, because frankly, you will not know what you are missing.

Jenna: You are saying that people don't even realize now that they are turning away from love by focusing on definition, so why would they be motivated to learn more sophisticated techniques to keep more of it in their awareness?

Rebecca: Exactly. People must first recognize what it is they do to break the flow of loving energy between them and whatever, or whomever, and feel the agony of that—for many, it might be emptiness—for only then they will have the intent to fulfill their longings, which will also become more apparent to them, namely, their longings to connect with others. Numbers and money are great examples of how people distract themselves from the more noble game of love! The hard part is people don't know what they're missing if they are not aware at a feeling level, which sadly is the case for most today. So I would say, first notice what you notice, and if you are constantly drawn to that which is highly defined, which I suspect most of you will be in order to maintain your highly defined self-concepts—then know that you are missing love. I will just tell you that. And secondarily, when you *do* feel love, notice what is in your awareness. I doubt if it'll be anything highly defined, like numbers! And if it is, then you have not experienced true love yet! You're more apt to be experiencing love of what you have, which is quite different from 2020 where love has more to do with bonds among people.

Jenna: Now that was really poignant, Rebecca, thanks. I felt your caring.

Rebecca: Yes, it is the way of the future, not so much the words but the caring.

Jenna: Well, I experienced both.

Rebecca: You experienced both because you are getting better at feeling your own love for yourself. You do not feel you *need* my love so, in order to be, which ironically allows you to feel both your own *and* mine. Now how's that?

Jenna: It is at the essence of all that we have been talking about, I think, you, Paul and I—feeling from our deepest, more refined selves.

Rebecca: Yes.

Jenna: Let us continue. In your estimation, what are the most important things we will have to learn in order to create the loving businesses in 2020?

Rebecca: It will become necessary for people to recognize that learning is a process, that it will not all happen at once. In order to believe that a society like 2020 can exist, people will have to have the faith that one step leads to another, that a series of steps will be needed for completion. My example there would be in regard to what I have just said, or the need to grasp what one is doing right now. Focusing on numbers or money, or any other highly defined whatever is a turning way from loving feelings, but it is also a first step toward change, toward a more mature love.

Jenna: You are saying then that love also evolves, just as everything else.

Rebecca: Of course.

Jenna: I am getting a little mixed up here. I often hear about the importance of just tapping in to whatever is already there, but I also hear it is necessary to *create* whatever, which is what I think you are saying here in reference to love.

Rebecca: You are asking what love is, essentially, and what you have to do to get it. Are you aware of that?

Jenna: No, but I think you are right.

Rebecca: You have lost the perspective of who you are; it is as simple as that. Getting mixed up or not understanding today has to do with thinking you have to *do* something in order to feel something, as in love for yourself. This is largely unconscious, of course. In 2020 people don't feel they have to *do* anything to get love, and you are wondering also how to bridge the gap between now and then. Now I suppose you are thinking, "Just when I thought I had a solid feel for something, meaning love, now I have to allow for *it* to evolve!

Jenna: This is fascinating to me, how well you read me, unconsciously. And yes, it is a strange sensation, accepting that one, that nothing has consistent meaning or feel.

Rebecca: Well, do not start to worry about that because love has many surprises, starting with getting to know its true nature.

Jenna: But you are saying that nothing *has* a true nature.

Rebecca: To grasp that concept and not feel panicky, trust me, is an accomplishment. But why don't we just start with this? Know love as you know it and all will be well. You need not create it, you need not even create those loving businesses you ask about. Just allow love to create them, okay? You are getting caught up again in what you must do. Do you see? You are the one who is talking about people controlling love, when they put it into currencies in 2020, right? Well, your energy tells me *you* are trying to control love, yourself...because you are afraid you might not get yours! Now I say this to all of the readers. *Love* knows what to do! So you need not be in charge of it, yourselves.

Jenna: Do you think that everybody tries to control love when they don't understand?

Rebecca: It couldn't have been better said. And I say this to the readers, too. Notice when you are controlling love.

Jenna: Rebecca, I asked Paul about the emergence of people's natural skills and talents, in the upcoming years. Do you have any thoughts about this?

Rebecca: It will take some learning to be able to discern between what is natural and what isn't. What one has always wanted to do involves natural skills and talents. If there is some question about one's deepest yearnings, I would suggest looking at what makes one cry; tears of joy, that is. Do you remember when you cried with Paul, when there were tears in your eyes? In addition to feeling love, I would say you were tapping in to purpose—a deep purpose you have here on earth—which would certainly be related to your innate skills and talents.

Jenna: So you are saying that purpose, natural skills, and talents all go together.

Rebecca: Without question.

Jenna: Rebecca, what kinds of concepts do we need to grasp to improve our ability to discern energy in objects, animals, minerals, nature, all the things that we filter out because we feel we don't need them as much as people?

Rebecca: Well, first of all, you will recognize that you do need them as much. But as a therapist, of course, I would emphasize loving all parts of yourself first. If you are stewing around about who you are—rather than lovingly discovering yourself—I can assure you that you will miss the rocks, the animals, the minerals, and so forth, since you will be looking *for*, as Paul would say, that which will enhance your self-concept. I think what you are wanting to know most is, how does one have direct experience, with say, a physical object, as is the case in 2020? How does one feel this loving energy? What skills are involved? What I do is teach essentially what you have done to get your material about 2020. I teach people to get information from the experiences themselves, by melding with them, by *being* there. Just as you put yourself in 2020—time travel, as you call it—to experience business, for example, I help people do the same kind of thing. The problem for most people is that they do not know when they have reached that more authentic part of themselves. They doubt themselves, which is normal, but what often happens is people dismiss what they receive, that inner knowing. I act as confirmation. Of course the best source is one's self, but I have become highly skilled at helping others know their own inner truths, based on my reactions. I can feel *their* direct experience, so in this regard I am very helpful to them. In regard to objects, my clients learn to transfer what they have learned in my office, to their everyday experiences.

Jenna: Do you, too, then have direct experience when your clients do?

Rebecca: Absolutely, yes. I feel both the energy in my cells, as well as theirs, but the actual perception or experience of it is highly individualistic.

Jenna: Rebecca, do you have any "inside information" on how to bring about equal power among people in business? I should have saved that term "inside information" for Paul!

Rebecca: It will all come about by learning how to entrain with energy, as we are talking about here. People are not able to entrain with those they perceive as unequal to them, which is the case now. As years go by, this will begin to feel worse and worse to people; it will feel like a big chasm, a well of emptiness. This will be the incentive to learn more about energy—and love. People will long to connect, as I said before—and they will do it through the process of feeling equal, which will carry over into the workplace.

Jenna: Thanks, Rebecca. I can't believe how comforting this all seems. And it all sounds so easy. Do you have anything to add here?

Rebecca: Yes, the reason we are able to communicate like this, telepathically, is that we see each other as equals—and there is much love between us.

Jenna: Telepathy is a good example of direct experience in communication, isn't it? I had never thought of it that way! And the same holds true for any direct experience. This is what equality is all about.

Rebecca: We would not be connecting if we disliked each other, so let that be a lesson, too. If people learn how to communicate telepathically, they are going to have to actually like the people with whom they are communicating—feel love for them, in fact—and not be "above" them in any way...or beneath them.

Jenna: Rebecca, do you have any real life experiences of the joys of "true" energy flow either in yourself or business?

Rebecca: People will not *have* business if they do not improve their own energy flow in the upcoming years. What will happen is, they will feel pain. Then they will think, "What am I doing wrong?" It will be a blatant reminder that self-judgment is a part of them.

Jenna: When businesses slow down?

Rebecca: Yes. I would not say self-judgment *causes* business to slow but would say it is more noticcable during slow business times because of the propensity to reflect upon one's self. As for me, I felt joy as I peeled off beliefs of doubt such as, "What is wrong with *me* that has caused my slow business?" I was able to see myself more clearly. In great business times we're not as likely to discover those parts of ourselves we don't like so much, so in that regard slow business is a window of opportunity to know one's self better.

Jenna: I am wondering if you have any ideas, or again, any experiences of your own, that might help people grasp what they will need to undergo themselves, as they move toward 2020, and greater awareness.

Rebecca: Paul has mentioned panic, so have you, and I concur. There will be more of that. Getting to know one's self better actually has to do with letting go of a rigid identity. People will experience this differently.

Jenna: Go on. These are the real things people will want to know about.

Rebecca: Let me give you a list then: eating new kinds of food, things you never thought you'd eat before; changing residences less often or more often than you expected; sleeping at unusual times; bizarre dreams; noticing animals act strangely; increased paranoia; thinking certain things are moving, then deciding they're not; hallucinating; thinking you are a totally different person than you are; crying at "inappropriate" times; thinking you are moving faster than normal, for example, when walking; noticing bugs.

Jenna: Wow...Are you saying these are all things you've experienced in giving up a rigid identity?

Rebecca: Many I have. I am just relating common experiences of my clients. They have stated these things quite clearly to me.

Jenna: This is almost too much. Is there anything else you'd like to add?

Rebecca: Well, I think it's important for me to point out that that remark you just made indicates to me you are scared, also the fact you changed the subject so abruptly. No one wants to give up what she knows—and that is the bottom line here. When people give up their identities—and all these strange experiences start coming into their lives—they get scared. I hope I didn't offend you, by stating your feelings that you are scared, by exposing you so.

Jenna: No, no, not at all. In fact, I'm glad you said something because that did scare me, all that change, the loss of control. Just as you are sharing some of your experiences, I feel strongly about sharing mine. I do feel a little shaky, though, right now. That part about the bugs…for some reason I felt myself being *invaded* by bugs.

Rebecca: It is okay; I didn't mean to frighten you. As we have talked about before, for some, it's going to be too much too fast, this increased awareness. I think I'll call Paul in here.

Paul: I wrap my arms around both of you. We spirit guides love you. We see you two, huddled together—reaching out to each other—and trust that you will learn much from your experiences of fear, for in them come great lessons of love.

Jenna and Rebecca: We need you, Paul.

Paul: And we need you, too. Did you know that the arms of spirit guides literally go on and on forever? Honest to God, it's true!

Rebecca and Jenna: And we send our love to you, too, Paul.

Jenna: It feels so good to get comfort when frightened.

Paul: If you remember that, 2020 will be here in no time! Take care and remember your own wings!

Author's comments

Well, I guess I just had my first truly noticeable reaction to giving up my rigid identity, when I got scared, as pointed out to me by Rebecca. How *do* we comfort ourselves when faced with what's ahead and the anxiety associated with it? I know what I did. I changed the subject when talking with Rebecca, telling her clients' stories about their experiences during difficult times ahead were just too much for me. Noticing bugs? Talk about paranoia. Somehow *that* sent me into a mild state of panic, if there can be such a thing as a mild state of panic! What was I going to do, is what I experienced on an unconscious level. Clearly, it would have been better to actually feel my anxiety, even the underlying fears, but no, like most humans, I tried to avoid the emotional pain.

Whether or not Rebecca's claims of what's ahead are entirely accurate is irrelevant. The point is many of us need to change the way we react to our own feelings. Avoiding them removes us from our own authenticity—and love. It was only *after* I recognized I was afraid, that I was able to truly feel the comfort of Paul and Rebecca, and I cannot tell you how deeply I felt their love. It is the connection that both Paul and Rebecca speak of repeatedly, the human longing to connect with others, and then the connection itself. There is nothing quite like it. I wanted to melt into their arms and share love with them forever—and I will. Evidently this is what it takes to feel this kind of loving connection—facing our fears, then feeling them, facing all of our feelings, actually, then feeling them, but especially that old nemesis, fear. It is a good example of the importance of getting to know ourselves—to improve our experiences of love! Otherwise, we might just go through life, ah…changing the subject. I don't know about anybody else, but I'd rather have "true love." Besides, hiding from one's self and others, is ultimately more painful.

Learning, Education and a Day in 2020

•Harmony •Physical senses and intent •Teleportation •Experiential learning •Soul-based identities •Emotional flow and learning •Grasping eternity •Physical bodies and learning •Love and learning •Community schools •Physical manifestation

Imagine yourself in 2020. You wake up one morning and smell food, you see it, you hear it, even sense its fine textures in your mouth... no, no, not because it is right there in front of you, in your mouth, or nearby... but because you are hungry, and this is what you intend to do, eat! This is what you desire, and your physical senses are relating with the thoughts you have as to what you want to create! Yes, you are going to create very quickly what you want—food— either by physically manifesting it, or bringing it to you by teleportation. Or perhaps you are more in the mood to just go get it, as we do today, by walking, or as they sometimes do in 2020, by floating, which is a bit faster walk than today, or something that is even thought to be possible now. The more you use your physical senses, the quicker things happen for you. In 2020 people smell, hear, taste, see, and feel the textures of what they want in a big way *before* it is actually "there." That is how they are able to create what they want so quickly. It is more like becoming it, though,—its true essence—than thinking *about* it, as we do today, when we want something. So physical manifestation has more to do with awareness than anything else, which is done with thought and expanded physical senses. Today people think that their physical senses bring them external data only, or what's outside of themselves. By 2020, however, people know the "important stuff" is internal, with the ability to sense their thoughts as having form.

Thought Power

In 2020 you create your circumstances by the nature of your thoughts, and how you relate to them—with no resistance and with great love. They are, after all, your means for getting what you want, in this case—food! By 2020 thought is much more relaxed, has more depth to it, and is much more integrated with the senses.

Also by 2020, your physical senses are now being used in conjunction with one another to such a degree that you do not favor any one of them, as would be the case today, which has limited our ways of learning, keeping us all essentially shut down. In favoring sight, for example,—the very favorite today!—or any other physical sense, we use energy to hold in place fear that is trapped in the other ignored sense organs. Instead, by 2020, you use all of your physical senses always, honoring them equally, like all other parts of your body. Along with your new identity, one that is based on and fueled by self-love and love from others, this new way of using the senses has allowed you to have an open mind and an open heart, two of the most important aspects of learning in 2020. By allowing your senses to come alive, or to flow, not only are you more focused in the moment—on what you are creating— but in this case you are seconds away from fulfilling your desires for a yummy meal! So when you wake up on this morning in 2020 and have all of these physical sensations, you do not think to yourself as one might today, "Gee, there must be some food around here," but instead something more like, "Whoopee, I am going to eat here soon because I know how to manifest the food that I want!" And you do it, which is to say, you feel who you are. In short, you have incorporated your desire more into your thoughts and used it as firepower.

And when you do this—which entails a true flow of your own thoughts—you magnetize the food right to you. And if you were a child, you would manifest it instantly, for by 2020, children have come "equipped" with phenomenal thought power, which they have been encouraged to use. You, however, produce very quickly what you want, even though it takes a few "moments" longer due to more inaccurate concepts about yourself. By today's standards, however, you have come a long way in getting what you want. You produce exactly what you want to eat, either by actually creating it out of "thin air,"—physically manifesting it—or by moving it from one location to another—teleporting it.

Learning Harmony Through Self-Love

How in the world did you figure out how to do all these things by 2020? Well, the first thing you learned in years previous to 2020 was to actually feel your desires, in depth, entraining with them. Then you learned how to allow all that you related with, to flow. This came about by first learning to feel resistance, then eliminating it, then learning how to feel the sensation of surrendering to the life force, or to feel harmony in all of your experiences, including the experience of relating to all parts of yourself, such as all that is in your awareness! You learned this in school, actually,—or maybe *from* your children—sometime after the year 2000, by learning to feel a "balanced teeter totter," which was not static but had a harmonious, up and down or back and forth motion to it. By entraining with energy you learned when you were sitting on your end of the teeter totter too hard, and you were taught to move up toward the center to allow others more flow, rather than forcing energy in your favor. Forcing energy is what people do today, feeling the need to control it, as if it were their only means to love. By 2020, however, you know there is plenty of love if you just are, so you don't try to force. You have also learned that when you are too far towards the middle of the teeter totter, you need to move back a bit, toward your end... again, allowing for more equal energy flow, instead of pushing and pulling energy the way people do today.

Now, in 2020, you do all of this spontaneously, just by feel. You even know this feeling of harmony pertaining to everything that takes place in your mind. You can tell when, for example, you are resisting your own thoughts and feelings, and you stop it by surrendering to them! You can also tell when you are resisting your desires, and you stop that, too, by surrendering to them...since by now you know that self-love means trusting all parts of yourself, even if you might have viewed these thoughts, feelings, and desires selectively in the past, perhaps even judging them or prioritizing them. Anything that is resisted is the same as not sitting on the teeter totter right!... which *feels* bad. Resisting the whole then—or resisting harmony—feels emotionally painful to people. No, you do not get off the teeter totter and walk away when you feel bad. To restore your natural state of joy, which has to do with harmony, you just readjust on the teeter totter to *input* that harmony, which is done intuitively by 2020.

But back to you... after eating then, you think to yourself, "Hmmm... wonder what I'll do today?"... and immediately you know, because you do not have to be anywhere or do any particular thing. Without intrusive

161

thoughts like those, you can feel who you are... and you honor that being. Following spiritual laws instead of societal ones, of which there are none, you realize you would love to go swimming, so you ask your family members to join you, and off you go! And how do you experience it? Just as with everything else: with grace, with a sense of surrender, and a great deal of joy. As an example, you do not hit the water the way you once did many years ago, when you were an aspiring executive, attacking it, as if it were your competitor. Instead you meet it as an equal, literally reaching out to the water with love. In the past you would have vigorously controlled the water, with hungry, aggressive strokes, as you swam, thinking *that* was sheer pleasure, but now you meld right into it, as it surrenders to you—with both experiencing the ecstasy of knowing the other's true nature. Luxuriating in your own well of everything, you remember when you used to feel empty, but you do not berate yourself for less evolved thoughts, accepting that part of yourself, too. Now you just float there, feeling, allowing all parts of yourself to meld, including memories of yourself in the future... and in the context of that, the most amazing thing happens. The ideas you have been wanting pertaining to your "work" pop right into your mind. Ping!... like mini explosions in every one of your cells, you are flooded with just the right ideas, as you float there, feeling yourself... a true example of experiential learning. It is common to you and to others in 2020, which just means that when you are being, you are aware—and when that happens, you "learn!" People go in and out of being in 2020, or levels of awareness, and when they are most true to themselves, they not only grasp what they specifically need to know but also eternity. At this time then, when at one with the water, you feel at one with everything. Yes, your "work day" has gotten off to a good start.

At one with the Divine, you are also feeling the joyous experiences of your loved ones, as they swim. Telepathically, you know "where they are." And you send love to them, which they feel. In fact all of you feel intimacy, as you explore your own worlds; that's the way it is when you feel your own godliness. But then suddenly you find yourself angry. Splashed by your child, and you don't like it! Your body restricts, your aura turns red.... then you remember... wait... this doesn't have to do with my child, it has to do with me. It's something inside of me that has caused this emotional reaction. Relaxing your body... and your mind, you then allow those beliefs about yourself to flow. For you have been here before, where you accuse others of doing something *to* you. Once relaxed, your heart re-opens and into your mind comes what seems like the ever-present internal struggle between the eternal you and your own beliefs. At a very deep visceral level you sense a conversation going on: who am I if my child splashes me? Dead?!!!" Somehow, though, knowingly, you embrace that part of yourself. You have heard *that* before, too. Allowing yourself to totally relax now, what comes to you from yet a deeper part, is: No, no, I will never die, ever… at least not the *real* part of me… and you begin to see your child quite differently now, as you go on with your peaceful swim. Taking place in a matter of seconds, at a feeling level, not a language-based one, you have just experienced allowing the entirety of your ideas and thoughts to flow, including the emotions within them. Your child, by the way, has far fewer of these experiences—the internal struggle within—having fewer false beliefs about himself.

Then your child goes off with a plan of his own. And you do not stop him, telling him what to do. He knows what he needs, as do all of you, and you all part, your spouse, you and your child, taking the love of the family with you. Incidentally, your choices for transportation are to walk, float, ride a horse, or to dematerialize, then materialize yourself elsewhere! High-tech transportation, even cars are rare, and if they are around, they are more for the sake of curiosity.

Your spouse goes off to the mindcare clinic, your child to the community school because he "wants" to, and you, to implement your ideas into your "work." Along the way, you meet friends who offer you love and support. You stop to share yourselves, for in every way this has to do with your "work." Time is taken by all of you to dangle your feet in a nearby stream and gaze at birds. The loving exchange affects everyone positively, to such a degree that even your family elsewhere senses your joy, which they share with you. You do not need to produce materially as you once did since there are no longer so many *things* around, so you bask here in love…sharing ideas and encouraging one another…then what happens? Because of this loving exchange, each one of you experiences even more energy flow and inner knowings. And there are tears, and sadness, and euphoria, as you feel one another's essences, for you are acutely aware at the heart level that your joy is enhanced by others and shared by others.

You even do "business" with one of them, accepting a newly made basket of reeds, and one of them accepts "advice" from you, since you yourself are an authority on energy. Offering information on process, you offer it unconditionally, as to her home business of glass making, telling her about the power of light and love, pertaining to her "machines." But even more

163

than that, she picks up from you by osmosis what you know about so many other things. You can just feel it, by her questions. Then you take what she knows, still unconscious to her, what you know, what some other beings in different dimensions know, which you tap in to immediately, and offer it to her. After that you thank her for bringing even more into your awareness. It is implicit in the hug you give her.

Next, you visit the new granddaughter of a friend, a new baby. When your eyes meet, you can tell that she is attuned to you. You can feel her presence acutely as well, as can your family, again, elsewhere, but also sharing in the joy. Telepathically, you can sense her future, her purpose and needs, as she can herself; and the two of you send love to each other, by just being. Spontaneously, you touch her, and just as if they were happening all over again, you reexperience the birth of your own child and also the death of another, with great sensitivity and vividness that cause your heart to open even more, as by this time—2020—your emotional flow is so profound that painful memories inspire you. You hand her back to her father, whose clarity toward the baby is sharp but nothing compared to the baby's clear perceptions of him. When you leave, you notice that the baby is communicating something telepathically to her father. He only partially "gets" it but grasps the bigger message, snuggling her in his arms, lovingly.

The Community School

You are on your way now to the community school, a pleasant place in nature where you will join the children who wish to be there, which all of them do, most of the time! They hang out, and it is more like a friendly gathering place where people come to know others and share themselves. The closest thing to organized education in 2020 is these "schools" spontaneously formed by members of the community. No one, per se, "runs" them, and certainly not from afar. Today you have been invited with great pride by your son not to tell what you know, but to be who you are. Since you are an energy expert, you will show them what being in the moment truly means, but you laugh to yourself when you think about that, knowing it is they who will show you. The last time you were at the school you never even got to what you thought you might say because a giggling response to something started, and it never stopped. You used it, to illustrate the now... never once saying *anything*.... The "learning" was incredible.

As you approach the school, you are in touch with everything in your surroundings, not being lost in thought but rather being brought into the moment by it. In the past your thoughts would have taken you *away* from your environment, having to do with your needs predominantly, but now you are able to take the perspective of all that you experience—*and* think about it. You notice the animals, and you contact them telepathically for nurturing support, sending love back to them, too. Stopping for a moment you sit by a tree. Both relaxed and abuzz with energy flow, you marvel at your own physical body, which by this time is lighter and more translucent, touching it... then you touch the tree. A perfect time to expand into the worlds of others: your grandchild; yet to-be-born, or even conceived; your deceased mother; perhaps the baby again; your spouse, guides,... or even the animals to which you have just opened yourself. You are always interested in being in contact with anyone from any "time frame anywhere." So you do it here. You do this often, integrating others' worlds right into your thoughts, whatever you're doing. But today for some reason, you wish to sit next to this tree, while you embrace the loving energy of others... so you do, feeling in particular the loving energy of the tree. You are clear that you would not be able to experience such beauty if you were time-bound, as in the past. How else would you know eternity if your world didn't include the future? How else could you know the true magnificence of this tree if it were not for your vibrant memories of its bare limbs next season? Or its past, of its golden leaves of "yesterday." You would not, for you would only be experiencing a fraction of it. Just as you have learned to integrate yourself, you have learned to perceive in an integrated way, honoring process. The tree's energy field surrounds you, and yours, it, in a glorious display of scintillating sounds and colors, as memories embrace you, of different seasons, and the tree. Even space has become more integrated so that you are in the middle of all things, or *around* all things, never apart from them. And as you head off to the school, you are certain you sense music. Many years ago, you would have wondered what the source was, or why, but now you don't care about either... you just immediately entrain with the music, becoming it! And again, your cells explode... which feels good to you.

Focusing in the Moment

In 2020 the process of learning comes about through interacting with one's environment, direct experience with it, truly allowing one's self to flow, which in turn encourages the interacted with, to also flow and learn. Rather than focusing on the past, as in remembering what you have been taught before—or hearing from others what they've been taught before—

165

you allow emotional flow to guide you. Where it takes you is what you automatically focus on. Your own flow is what allows meaning to come directly from your experience, for this is what you need in order to perceive accurately. When you love, your whole world opens up, allowing you to tap within, where truth resides—your truth. It is the flow of love in the moment that allows one to use current data, making new discoveries. It is also current data in 2020 that allows one to know much more about the process of creation than today. Now we are almost totally fixated on the past. We only consider things that are already in physical existence, smelling them, hearing them, tasting them, seeing them, and being aware of their textures. This is what interests us, instead of what we might create in the moment. In other words, we miss potential. Likewise, we carry the fear of our parents, their parents, their parents, and so on, so that our perceptions of what we do experience, are distorted even further. For example, we carry around a continual tape, both unconscious and conscious, reminding us of what we should or should not be doing. We also, at a subliminal level, judge ourselves moment to moment as to how we stack up to another, actually rating ourselves as either superior or inferior to everything we interact with, most prominently with people but also with animals, objects, nature, even intangibles like ideas. We go through a process of saying I am worse, I am better, I am worse, I am better, constantly, in order to give ourselves some kind of identification and sense of safety. Then what we do experience we try to control. Our judgment of ourselves also manifests into thinking that others are looking at us, also judging us, making us all to a degree paranoid. All of these things affect learning since this is where our focus is, rather than on what is truly happening to us in our environments.

By 2020 people learn a great deal with, and from their own physical bodies, being able to communicate directly with all parts of themselves. They can do this by talking to their body parts consciously—or just by feel, which is faster, more fluid, and more common. Knowing what the body parts perceive—including the cells—helps people grasp in a more integrated way what they are experiencing. They are not just their heads by 2020, deducing, analyzing, objectifying, categorizing, prioritizing! Since they feel themselves more, all parts of themselves, they feel safer, more secure, and learn more from others too. They *see* others more, *hear* them more, *sense* who they are more… because they know *themselves* more authentically. When people are aware of who they are from their cells' point of view—not their egos'—they have an expanded use of all of their bodies, the physical, the emotional, mental, and spiritual. When this happens, a sense of eternity permeates their beings, allowing an unlimited contact with all in existence, which means there is eternal learning and soul-to-soul contact everywhere. In short, by 2020 people are aware of all that is, including eternity—because their own bodies told them so! One lesson that is mighty clear by this time: Once you discover your own eternal nature, everything else is easy, including "learning." And for the most part, this is the mindset of people in 2020.

The Love Machine

As you enter the community school, which is small, since communities are small, but ever "open" since there is continual interest in knowing others, you see your son. He beams upon seeing you. Your spouse is there also, as this is not just a place for children to gather. There is nothing formal about this, so you don't come with a plan, but trust in your own knowingness. For some time now your community has been working on a love machine together, and it is currently here at the school. The concept of a love machine began years ago, a challenge put forth by Corporate America, during its years of rapid spiritual growth. Who could develop the most loving machine? To this day the challenge continues, not pitting communities against one another but uniting them, as well as the people within the communities. All know that all everywhere on the physical plane are attempting to perfect a machine that is alive, both giving and receiving love. It has been an idea that has unified people, fascinating them. It's been fun. Not surprisingly, the children are the most natural toward the machine, interrelating with it freely, like the closest of friends! Now *you* are here to explain how it works. As you begin to illustrate perpetual motion, a child who is in perpetual motion herself, teaches you something, rather, helps you tap in more to your own inner knowing. You integrate it right into your demonstration. Part of your demonstration utilizes group energy, something the children are well aware of, so you make sure that each child's perspective is known and shared, as you communicate sometimes with language, sometimes telepathically, since by 2020 truth is more like the combined experiences and viewpoints of all people, not just yours. The children love this, though it is not unusual for them to share so readily. It is not new for you, either, though your memories from past experiences in this lifetime make you perhaps a bit less flowing. Nobody is trying to fit into any system. People are just being, and in the process of that is creation. One child offers the "future" of the machine, which you use to tap into others' knowingness as to its future,

167

illustrating the process of this machine—its beingness. You integrate into your own thoughts your memories about the future of both yourself and the machine—even more evolved joy, which used to be for you just the absence of pain! Oh, that was "a long time ago," you think to yourself. But today you are immersed in the ecstasy of joy, just as the children are, and the place really gets wild with energy.

Also, there is a spontaneous joyous response to a troupe of improvisational entertainers which has suddenly shown up at the school. You also use this interaction to illustrate perpetual motion, not by explaining after the fact but by being a part of it. What you are doing with your own behavior is to illustrate the power of light and love, as you encourage love and all to share themselves. You are in fact a group leader of sorts, today.

Funerals

After the school, you go to a funeral. You knew him well, as you know everyone in your community. As usual, you are the one who reads at the funeral, offering solace to relatives and friends, as you are particularly skilled at knowing unexpressed beliefs, messages, and memories of the deceased. You share these idiosyncrasies with all at the ceremony which by contrast to today is upbeat. The future of the soul is mentioned, with "accomplishments" being more like reliving loving encounters together, including those to be shared in the future. Almost all will continue to communicate telepathically with this soul. There is pain in this society of 2020, often very evident at funerals, but it is transformed quickly into joy. Even at funerals, there is "business" accomplished, as many exchange food, clothing, "leisure-time" products, artistic endeavors, not so much to promote themselves but to reach out to others. No money is exchanged, just love, with all gathering together to honor not only this departing soul but also, themselves, making it more like a celebration of life—in all its dimensions. Again, you have gathered with others to create *the now*.

Consciously Creating

And this is the way the whole day goes. Just as others do, you create what you need and want by *being who you are*. In the morning you create exactly what you want for your breakfast. Then you create wonderful moments with your family, swimming,—and with friends, and with nature. You connect lovingly with others in other dimensions, and with the children at the school. You interact with the love machine yourself, and you go to a

168

funeral, honoring life. And now you return home where you and your family will experience even more bliss, for you are alive, and aware. Even in your dreams you will continue to consciously create, as you have a whole new awareness there, too. Creating in 2020 means tapping in to—and this is what you do in this loving society. This is what energy flow has afforded you: experiencing everything just as it is. Your own energy flow has allowed you to grasp eternity, it has allowed you to tap in to your own eternal self… it has allowed you to experience the joy of love.

PAUL

Paul: Well, you have really tapped in to something quite possible, quite authentic, now don't you think… this society of 2020?

Jenna: Yes.

Paul: I'd like to talk to you about creation. What is creating to you? Do you realize that at some level you must begin with these kinds of thoughts that this is possible? You must begin there. You could spend the rest of your life doing certain things, but if you thought they were for naught, you would not *get* what you wanted. Most do not realize this subtle level of sabotage they have created for themselves. Do you believe in what you are doing, or are you someone's else's pawn for what *they* want? Yes, creating a society such as 2020—filled with love—has to do with a certain balance within yourselves, where what you "do" coincides with your own evolvement, not just what you believe, but actually who you are. There are millions who spend virtually all of their lives—especially in their jobs—doing something that makes "sense" to them but not bringing joy. It is largely, I think, because they carry within them thoughts of impossibility, starting with the premise that what they truly want is impossible. Then they end up spending the rest of their lives just proving that to themselves! Of course, it's largely unconscious.

Jenna: Yes. That reminds me, speaking of concepts of impossibility, I myself have had a most interesting experience lately and I'd like to relate it to you. I have noticed that if I am aware of the possibility of something, then it actually seems to predispose me to experiencing it. Now how do you like that?

Paul: How do you? Yes, I'd love to hear more about it.

169

Jenna: Through my time travel and my follow-up discussions with you and Rebecca, I have learned much about the expanded use of physical senses in the future. Well, I think this was the critical factor for my insight recently in one of my own experiences regarding my sense of smell. Let me tell you what happened. I woke up one morning and smelled french toast. At first I looked around to see where it was coming from, but nothing was there. Then I considered the presence of a guide or someone of a faster vibration nearby someplace. Again, not much to go on. Then I realized I *wanted* french toast. I gasped because it was the first time I had ever considered one of my physical senses to be bringing me first and foremost, *internal* data. What I am saying is that I don't believe I would have had this insight if I hadn't known intellectually about the expanded use of the senses.

Paul: You are talking about a new kind of reality, aren't you, where people question what they are experiencing, where they have something within them which pushes them to do that. Let me ask you this. What do you think, to use a favorite phrase of humans, *caused* you right then and there to look at "reality" differently?

Jenna: That is what I am saying. I think it was because I had already accepted the idea on an intellectual level of more developed physical senses as we evolve. But it was more than that too. I *felt* I had hit upon something very important, as well. It was something I could feel deeper.

Paul: You are talking about a kind of depth of feel, your term, I believe, where you seem to feel your own self more deeply, allowing clearer perceptions.

Jenna: Yes, absolutely.

Paul: This is what getting beneath or beyond our own false beliefs is all about, where we don't see our beliefs so much as what we desire. And this is a great example of how learning and experiences will be different by 2020, which you are starting to do now. This *is* what being in the moment is, at least in regard to your sense of smell.

Jenna: What do you mean, at least in my regard to my sense of smell?

Paul: Well, what were your other senses doing?

Jenna: I don't know, probably in the past, I guess, focusing on external data! Oh, my, I hadn't thought about all of my other senses. Now that really *would* alter reality if all had been feeding me information about what I desired. *That* is mind-blowing.

Paul: You see, you have just begun... You may have even been eating the french toast right then, now don't you think?

Jenna: I can't tell if you are kidding me or encouraging me.

Paul: You could if you were tapping in to your senses more, because the more you do *that*, the more you'll know the "truth." I put that in quotes because it's so misunderstood now.

Jenna: You mean we doubt it all the time, I presume.

Paul: That, and let preconceived beliefs rule, which is what you were able to temporarily let go of there.

Jenna: Do you concur with me that knowing something intellectually might predispose one to the experience of it?

Paul: Now that is a fascinating question. Not only does it predispose one to it, but also its opposite. So how do you like that? What you are talking about is true open-mindedness, and when you have that, you have in direct proportion - direct experience.

Jenna: Are you implying that by the time we realize the possibility that all of our senses might be reflecting the moment that we'll actually be physically manifesting whatever instantly?

Paul: Now where did you ever get *that*?

Jenna: Now you've really got me going. I know that is what many people are doing in 2020, but I certainly don't have the particulars down yet for physical manifestation.

Paul: What was your inclination when I said that about your french toast being right in front of you about the time you took in data from all of your senses?

Jenna: That you were right, but also that physical manifestation entailed a heck of a lot more than just awareness of my physical senses. Kind of like I had to *do* something, you know.

Paul: But you knew what I said was part of the truth. Isn't this also what you are writing about for 2020, that people just know the truth when they hear it? This is what I'm not sure you grasp. Everything is happening so fast—our communications—and you are making inferences, I guess you could say, that are "right," then integrating them right into the bigger picture. If you were to ask your readers to go back and reread this section, taking your part, I would bet that none would sense the kinds of things that you are. That is because they are *reading*. As you have said yourself, reading is long gone by 2020 because it is too slow and nonreflective of high vibratory light. I want to help illustrate your new methods of learning by using you! You are not even relating to my actual words at times but tapping in to a far deeper, more significant reality.... Let's do something really quickly here, with no thinking, okay? Tell me immediately one factor of physical manifestation that you have not yet consciously grasped. Go.

Jenna: That intent will be as obvious to people as the physical manifested whatever.

Paul: Now that was easy, wasn't it? Okay, tell me another. Quickly now.

Jenna: That your desire is an important factor in my knowing.

Paul: Not bad... another.

Jenna: That tapping in to others' desires inputs the speed of physical manifestation.

Paul: Now what do you make of this? Are you learning here? What in the world is going on?... Did you see how you did that? You just knew certain things which you picked out of nowhere using "tomorrow's" thinking methods. Also, are you starting to get your thoughts and mine mixed up?

Jenna: Sometimes I do for just a second. But how is one to know or be able to trust what comes forth? Don't all of these crazy beliefs we carry affect how we perceive things?

Paul: Of course. That is why we have to dig deeper, to this level of feeling the truth, or what is. Your beliefs were bypassed right over, when you responded like that because you didn't run your responses through that belief check list! You just felt them entirely differently, much like how you felt your desires for french toast. You went deeper.

Jenna: I am starting to get a feel for this. I call it flimsy, lightweight energy versus I don't know what it is.

Paul: Well, you don't have to know. That is the whole point. Just feel it, and when you feel that flimsy energy, let it dissipate. You don't have to stick with it.

Jenna: Oh, my, those are my beliefs, aren't they? Hmmm…

Paul: Hmmm… you felt that, now didn't you? You didn't think that out. That is the kind of thinking that will prevail here, pretty soon. Now I want to get back to something we were talking about earlier. You said you started mixing up our thoughts. Maybe this will be a precursor to people's not having to *own* ideas. You have stated people do not own ideas by 2020. Well, maybe they will need to first feel what you just felt, mixing up their thoughts with thoughts of others.

Jenna: Yes, in fact I *know* that is accurate.

Paul: Here is what is important for you to know right here, that what you need from me is love and support, not so much information, as you think, for *that* is what is "helping" you get in touch with this deeper sense of knowing. Do you see? This *is* what that flow of energy is all about that all are living in, by 2020, this great interactivity, where one person's love affects another's entire beingness and where that great inner knowing just seems to pop to the surface in people's minds and hearts.

Jenna: Yes, and I can feel your love and caring once again.

Paul: It *is* the answer, don't you see? When you can feel that love and caring, not only *from* me but also from you *to* me, that is all it takes!

Jenna: Feel yourself and know. Feel yourself and love.

Paul: Just feel, and all else happens automatically! You don't even have to have goals like that. Something else. In regard to your question about your physical senses and intent, I think you should question every little bit of data you are taking in with all of your sense organs. You may have to start slowly, but do it!

Jenna: I think if I did it all at once, I'd go crazy.

Paul: Well, you don't have to do it all at once… but just keep going with it. Maybe one sense at a time. You are on to something; we guides agree! You know, we have talked about feeling so much, feeling what you experience, but you might need to consider this concept first, so that you can *feel* more… and that is, that what you see, hear, taste, smell or sense with your skin might be coming from internal happenings, not

173

just elements of what is outside of you. Just start with that. That ought to keep you busy for a lifetime! You might even say to yourself when you sense something, question it, "Now is that really outside of me?"… because you may be focusing on the wrong data, so to speak. If you assume that all the data you are dealing with is just reflective of what is external, how will you ever get to know yourself?

Jenna: Paul, you are great. Could you state simply then how we might look at reality in new ways?

Paul: If you question the beliefs you hold, you will question your own perceptions of reality, which is pretty much what you did. One way to question the beliefs you hold is to consider "opposite" beliefs, or perhaps just ones differing from those you hold. What happens when you hold exactly opposite beliefs? Have you ever thought about that?

Jenna: Not exactly, but I suspect it mutes both.

Paul: That it does. Now just ponder that for a minute.

Jenna: You are suggesting then to get beyond beliefs, all of which distort reality, that one actually add more beliefs.

Paul: At first it will be precisely like that. But in order to do that, you will have to stop focusing on why, when, where, who, how… for they are just diversions from what is, really. When you focus on those things, it is like a bee-line out of yourself, which is where, as you know, truth lies. I agree, you wouldn't have had that insight about the aroma of french toast being internal—or having to do with your own desires—if you hadn't previously allowed into your awareness that our physical senses will be used more expansively in the future—something you believed, a new idea in other words, a new idea for you. This is what allowed you that deeper knowing, or the ability to focus more deeply.

Jenna: Yes, that is good, we are mis-focusing or there is a lack of focus, or something. We really are hung up on the wrong things, aren't we?

Paul: That is the understatement.

Jenna: I want to be clear on this. Are you saying that we might consider the possibility that when we have sensory data that they might not be properties of what is right in front of us, as in looking at a tree, for example?

Paul: You are talking about two things. Experiencing a smell, for instance, with no external data, either physical or metaphysical, as was the case with the french toast, is one thing. It was only by a process of elimination that you considered something inside of yourself. Now you are also adding the possibility of seeing green, smelling the tree, whatever, experiencing it… and I think you are asking me, is it really there or could your experiences be coming more from your desires? I will tell you this. If you start saying to yourself, "Is it really there, and could this be more reflective of me than anything else, all sorts of exciting things are going to happen. One of the first things, I will be quite blunt with you, is that people will come after you. They will attempt to prove you wrong. They might try to hurt you. I do not tell you this to stop you from this exciting new way of looking at reality—where you focus more in the now—but to warn you. This will be both confusing and frightening to people.

Jenna: So the question is not really whether the tree is there but new ways of looking at yourself.

Paul: Exactly but it will not be received as such, rather, as disputing the existence of the tree.

Jenna: I see, and I can see how threatening that would be, as it would be so ingrained with what people believe, including who they are.

Paul: I will give you a little exercise, since it will be frightening to *you* too. Take one physical whatever, say, in your house and pretend it is not there. Each time you experience it, consider the possibility you are experiencing yourself, your intentions, as you say. When you see green, let's say it's a plant, experience your own green; when you see the sun shining through its leaves, experience the sun shining through you or your own internal sunshine. Hear the plant, then consider the sounds made by the plant as your own sounds, and so forth. Every time you see that plant, do that. Then tell me what happens to the plant and you! Take one object at a time. Do this for a month, why don't you? I can hardly wait to talk to you about it!

Jenna: You are a real partner in crime! I can hardly wait to talk to you! This must have something to do with the existence of vastly fewer objects by 2020 that I have written about.

Paul: Now *you* couldn't be a factor in this, could you?

Jenna: You mean, fewer objects in the future and new ways of perceiving?

Paul: That's what I mean.

Jenna: You're doing it to me again. All I wanted was a few little hints on what we have to learn and you bring me personally into it again. Do you mind if we go on?

Paul: We are, darling! Whoopee!

Jenna: Any advice, Paul, on how to feel balance, that feeling of a balanced teeter totter, or one where there is harmony, that is practically inbred by 2020?

Paul: Again, I would say look where your focus is. If you are thinking about why, when, where, who, how, then all you are doing is jumping right out of your own skin. At this time in history people experience everything as external, then they analyze it. Expand within yourself to know and quit worrying about defining so with stop-action focus. You cannot feel the movement of energy when you are categorizing it.

Jenna: Oh, boy, there is so much.

Paul: Let me interrupt you for just a moment there, please. When you say, there is so much… this is totally based on your concepts of space, which you also know will be changed by 2020. In short, your spatial beliefs are screwy, and you have gotten all caught up in them in limiting ways. Why did you sound so burdened, may I ask?

Jenna: There is so much to know.

Paul: And you fear that you will never know it all. What have you discovered about 2020 in that regard?

Jenna: I haven't.

Paul: Well, tell me right now. How will *you* be relating to knowledge by then? Do you think you will still be feeling overwhelmed by it? Again, I want to use you as an example.

Jenna: No, I won't be overwhelmed by it.

Paul: Okay, let's reverse roles. What concepts will you have learned by then?

Jenna: I will have learned that…

Paul: Don't think it out, just tell me, the way they do in 2020.

Jenna: I will be knowing, so when I feel whole, I will know. I will not focus so on what's outside of myself, I guess. I am not clear.

176

Paul: Integrate concepts of space. Do it quickly.

Jenna: Not something I have to do. Trust. There is not an amount of knowledge. It's all wrapped up in myself as process.

Paul: What are you, spatially, by 2020?

Jenna: I'm not!

Paul: Hmmm... now that's interesting, isn't it? Your own self-concept is less physical, as in amounts. Let's go on here. I wanted to make one simple point. The more you perceive yourself as physical, the more you perceive even something like knowledge as spatial. And when you do that, there is always an emotional threat to your own existence. Knowledge can be security to you, you know. It will not carry the same comfort later. It will be far more expansive, far more available, and will not be associated with something you must *do* to feel okay. As with everything else we have been discussing throughout this book, it is you. Knowledge is literally you.

Jenna: Although I understand that intellectually, it's a little hard emotionally. Maybe your response to my next question might help. Do you think there is one thing that would help us understand the importance of emotional flow to learning?

Paul: I would say if you are not aware of your own desires, you will be learning little, for your desires are what drive you, what cause you to interact with your environment in the first place. If you take a look at how you smother your own desires with self-judgment and truly acknowledge that you are doing this—you will have made a great step in grasping the importance of emotional flow to learning, which is just being, after all. You cannot learn without being. You think you are learning, but all you are doing is "mis-focusing." Recognize that you are stopping your desires—or emotional flow—by judging them as wrong. That is the same thing as judging yourself as wrong. If you asked a large group of people today what their desires were, I don't think they would know, giving what would be more accurately described as instant gratifications. It just goes to show you how truly unaware people really are of their own desires. To block desires is a common way of blocking your own energy. Also, there is something to be said for allowing your mind to direct you. It will focus on what you need to know if you truly allow it to function as it is made to. It is important to allow it to unravel rhythmically in the same way you would your heart. Some people think the mind is all intellect; that is totally false. It has the same longing to be as everything else... and its vehicle or means of doing it is through more relaxed thought.

Jenna: Oh, that was great, Paul.

Paul: Thanks, I got it from you.

Jenna: You are so funny sometimes. I feel embarrassed and self-conscious. You sound like my agent.

Paul: I am, darling. But it is not so much that I am trying to promote you personally. We are a team, remember? Our thoughts are one, our hearts are one. We are on the same teeter totter!

Jenna: Why am I always crying with you? You say something so simple like that, and the tears just come.

Paul: It is because you are often not thinking who, when, why, how, and so forth. You are truly feeling the intermingling of our hearts, and so am I. You probably think this is a little bit sappy, but I cry too when you do. Although we are more used to the feelings of love, it is still the most glorious feeling that we experience; and when we share it with others, we too get mighty teary. I know when I cry, something happens inside of me that says, "Okay, I surrender... here I am, with no pretenses," and that is the unraveling I am talking about. And when I can share it with another, it is more delicious than ever.

Jenna: Thank you, I am touched. I cannot believe all the years we have been focusing on those journalistic principles, or whatever you want to call them—analyzing!

Paul: Like money, the whos, wheres, whys, hows, and whens have acted as barriers. I prefer the tears.

Jenna: I also can't believe all the years I've spent holding back my own tears.

Paul: Loving is not a big part of your society. Go easy on yourself. Love your analytical part! It will not be totally absent here as we create the path to 2020. And love your tears too! Now what is your next question?

Jenna: I have noticed something about myself I wanted to share with you. It seems I am becoming far more flexible about just about everything. For example, in the past I would often make a decision, then stick to it, practically no matter what. Now I don't feel so confined to what I decided previously, trapped by it, and am more likely to bring in new data, maybe even reconsider the decision. Some might say this is fickleness, but it seems to me like being in the moment. What are decisions all about, and how do they relate to learning?

Paul: Your questions are terrific. Okay… anyone who makes decisions without reconsidering new data later is truly in the past. Why do people make decisions in the first place, and what are they about? People decide just how they're going to feel safe and how they're going to get love. When they feel they have those things, then they want to hang on to them. I would say that is what decisions are all about, trapping a concept of what one wants to be—safe and loved—which obviously emanates from *not* feeling those things. As for learning, let's see… for most, those two conditions are huge in terms of what people retain. They are also factors in what people notice in the first place. So when people increase their feelings of safety and love, which will come through their own self-love, largely, then they will "learn" a great deal more. In fact, the whole nature of decisions will change when people are less fearful, enabling them to interact more lovingly with their environments.

Jenna: So it goes back to self-concepts.

Paul: The general trend will be merging *with* environments, as opposed to getting something *from* them. People will not talk so much about what they need on an individual basis. The "I need, I need" will become "we need" and the we will include everybody and everything! This will come about only after seeing themselves differently, namely, more lovingly.

Jenna: Boy, that's exciting.

Paul: Equal energy flow, to use your term. In regard to decisions, I would say when you find yourself making many decisions,—and very quickly—you are probably afraid. What I want to distinguish between is spontaneously making decisions in the moment versus making them ahead of time in order to feel okay. There is a big difference there. *It is important to start from feeling okay.* If you are truly in the moment making a decision, it will not feel as if a decision is being made, more like the decision is making itself. There is an equal flow of energy between you and whomever or whatever, including the ideas with which you are dealing. Today when people decide, this is not the case. There is a manipulation of the environment or the mind. Notice when you do not feel as if you are making decisions, then remember that feeling because that is *you*, when things just happen very quickly with great ease. Recognize that when you are clearly deciding something—laboring over it—that you are in fact resisting something—yourself. I hope that helps. Decisions, as you know them today, I would say, are thought forms, created from fear. You will do what you need for yourself and others if you trust your own flow, too. This is what it amounts to ultimately. Unfortunately, many have been taught they are not innately "good," which puts them in the position of *owing* something to a higher power. There is a world of difference between that and genuine respect and love for that higher power.

Jenna: Thank you, that was really nice.

Paul: You're welcome.

Jenna: Paul, how will people learn teleportation or moving themselves or physical objects to new locations by the use of thought?

Paul: I would be inclined to say they will learn it very differently. I don't think it's so simple as to say that one can go to school to learn the principles of teleportation. I think that is one huge "mistake" that has been carried on for centuries, that principles are taught from outside-in, or from others. Although one can learn a great deal from others, one's own being is an enormous factor in learning anything. Learning will be accelerated tremendously when the assumption is dropped that one person teaches another or that one learns essentially from another. This is really not true. There are many ways of learning anything. It is completely untrue in the first place that there are certain principles regarding anything. It is just that only those principles seem to be recognized. I can assure you that all people have their own principles which need to be expressed about everything. So when you ask me how people will learn about teleportation, I will tell you—any way they want. And for those who do learn in that manner, learning will be more "successful," more exciting, quicker, and the basis for many new principles for teleportation. Just as decision-making will be in the moment, so will learning. It will not be so static but much more explosive and dynamic. Those are the best words I can think of. Now tell me something. Right now, is your thinking more relaxed?

Jenna: How did you know?

Paul: In order to incorporate what I am saying, it *has* to be! I cannot tell you how excited we all are in regard to your new concepts about thinking, equal energy flow, benevolent relationships with everything in your minds, the perpetual motion of the teeter totter, the love machine…

Jenna: These are not all my concepts.

Paul: Well, they will be viewed, to a degree, like that.

Jenna: It was just a matter of tapping in to them.

Paul: See? There you go, 2020 thinking… and if you can get that point across, oh, my, well,… the possibilities are unlimited… just that concept alone, do you see?

Jenna: Yes, Paul.

Paul: Well, we spirit guides have enjoyed tapping in to you and your readers, and send all our blessings, along with much universal love. Do you know what that is? *Feel* it! We are always here, always open to you… and we thank you very, very much for including us in this magnificent team, this magnanimous effort to allow the blossoming of who we all really are. We need not create 2020 so much as just recognize it. It is *all of us,* you know, so it is just a matter of being, for truly *that* is the true path to this loving society. Thank you, and adios, from all of us, especially me, Paul, your friend forever and spokesperson from "above." I love you all.

Jenna: I swear, if others can feel your love a fraction of what I do, we will have no trouble at all tapping in to our own self-love. Thank you again, Paul.

Paul: You are most welcome, and let it be known that we are the true love machines, capable of… yes, *anything!*

Jenna: And we send earthly love right back to you!

Paul: And so you are starting to read the minds of your fellow humans, too, now… hmmmm. Interesting.

Jenna: Hmmm… it is interesting, isn't it? The team is growing, Paul.

Paul: Yes, it is, dear one. Think of us often, feel us often because we are all one. We send our hugs. Unravel, unravel… it's okay. We have a universal net of love everywhere! Did I tell you about that? Swing in it. Wrap yourself in it. Envelope yourself in a brilliant, scintillating, magnificent, radiant, sparkling apron of love!… hey, *that's* what you can wear on your speaking engagements!

Jenna: I'll do that, Paul. I've got to go talk to Rebecca now. Much love.

181

REBECCA

Jenna: Rebecca, what will people have to learn to be more in the moment, to learn experientially, in other words, elevating them to the position of realizing they are co-creators of their experiences, rather than hapless victims? And have you had an enlightening experiences yourself you might share?

Rebecca: I would say I learned a great deal about being in the moment when I allowed myself to defy conventional wisdom, much the way you are challenging the notion that your physical senses reflect more than external data. In my case, I had a surge of energy when I realized I was *not* who society or my parents said I was. I noticed a real conflict within, as if I was trying to be something I wasn't. I found out I was actually resisting my own flow, and it appeared to me in the form of hives.

Being in the moment has to do with accepting those parts of yourself you do not find so great, thanks to what you've been told you are. When you do that, you notice the unraveling of your own thought. My first sensations made me feel as if I were walking right out of my body, and initially I tried to stop that. It felt as though another being were stepping right out of my chest area and walking away, leaving a reluctant body. It was confusing. I thought I was breaking in half. Later I learned that this was energy of thought, reaching out, longing to lead me somewhere, but since I didn't know where, it scared me. I kept trying to stop it. What I would do is sit down and stop moving. But it kept happening. That's when I got the hives. I had to decide whether to let the energy flow or just sit around, feeling scared. In the context of feeling scared, I noticed that my body was spreading, or so it seemed. It felt both bigger but lighter. I then seemed to make the correlation that this was my fear expanding. Before I knew it my hives were gone, and I began to sense an ebb and flow in my own body with my breaths. The long and short of this is that when I allowed my thoughts to flow, and fear which was wrapped around them, so did my body. I became so fascinated with the effects of thought *on* my body that I began to stop focusing on how external factors were affecting me. I also noticed that almost immediately my life's circumstances began to change with virtually everything coming into my life that I had always wanted.

Jenna: That is fascinating. Are you saying then that you experienced thought as an expanded physical body?

182

Rebecca: It seemed that way at first, although I later realized it was just an increased awareness of my other bodies, my emotional and mental, for example. What happened was kind of like this. I noticed that every time I thought, energy at all levels in my body seemed to stop moving. There was an actual tightening which hurt. That was before I really got into recognizing the deep conflicts within me. When I realized I was not being who I was, I began to think differently. That's when it seemed as though something wanted *out* of me. And I am just saying this because others may experience the same thing in days ahead… and maybe even to expect it. We are so used to perceiving ourselves as only our physical bodies that this may come as a real shock to people.

Incidentally, I think you are right in saying that people simply do not grasp this concept of like attracting like, or that a stuck thought—and that is what we are talking about—wants completion; it seeks completion. People don't get this. They think things are happening *to* them, of which they have no part. I still struggle with this myself at times, but if you don't allow your own thoughts and emotions to flow, — what you feel and think, in other words—you will attract to yourself the complements of your own thoughts. Have you ever thought about it that way? It's as if your thoughts are looking for mates; and if they are not very mature, that's the kind of mates they get!… which explains this long, arduous, karmic experience we are all going through, where it seems to take us forever to learn. So, I guess, one big thing I would say to people is to recognize that perceiving yourself as more than your physical body will help you, and others, too. Maybe there is something inside of you that wants to expand. If so, let it, for it will bring to you just what you want.

enna: That was really nice. Kind of like the power of the heart.

Rebecca: And isn't it interesting that I experienced thought in the area of the heart, not the head?

enna: Yes, very interesting. And that's the first time I've ever heard you say that fear is wrapped around thought.

Rebecca: Stuck emotions are really just distorted desires, and I would say the same for thought. If you don't be, as Paul would say, you get all discombobulated in terms of who you are.

enna: Rebecca, I have to tell you what I have been experiencing lately. I keep having sensations of energies, lighter energies, passing right through my body, almost as if beings were walking right through me! Could this just be more expansive thought, on my part?

Rebecca: It does not surprise me that you might interpret those energies to be beings, which they could be, but you are quite astute to note that perhaps this is just a more expansive you. Did you just think of that?

Jenna: Yes, I assumed they were other beings, actually, until just this moment. Also, I keep carrying around this feeling that we are coming to a dead-halt right now in history before something explodes, leading us into a situation of massive chaos. Talk about defying conventional wisdom. How does this relate to the physical body and concepts we have of ourselves?

Rebecca: You yourself have a fear that you will come to a dead halt, then will burst violently out-of-control. It is because you think of your body as limited and needing to be constrained. But you are not alone, just more aware. Others feel this way too which inputs the possibility that this could indeed happen. When you have a more expansive view of yourself, this fear will dissipate. It is a good example of being aware of what you really feel in order to let it evolve. For if you don't, you could create it.

Jenna: That's a scary thought.

Rebecca: It's even more scary if it happens and you think you had nothing to do with it, in other words, you feel helpless. When you recognize you have these fears, it helps—as it is the first step in transforming them.

Jenna: Thank you. I have noticed something, Rebecca, in regard to being myself. Ironically, at times it almost seems as though I am *trying* to be myself; I think it is when I push energy, as I say, trying to prove something. Would you say that trying to create an effect is the same thing as trying to prove something to yourself, and if so, how do people learn they do not have to create any effects at all, just be?

Rebecca: I'm with Paul. I love your questions, and yes, I would be delighted to respond to that. Anyone who is trying to create an effect, yes, is trying to prove something to himself. Now think about that. Isn't that what virtually everyone is doing? They are trying to prove to themselves that they are effective people. If they grasped what we were just talking about, that there are certain magnetic forces at work in regard to thought, there would never be any need at all to try to *create* anything. This is what this merging with everything is all about.

184

When you flow, you automatically create, if you want to use that word, effects—your thoughts invite their mates, remember? If people understood this, they would be into unraveling thoughts like some kind of fitness program.

Jenna: Oh, that's great, Rebecca, the next self-help program. Well, would you say then that we are lacking basic physics in our schools today?

Rebecca: Absolutely, yes, on a practical level, such as thought energy. That might not sound too practical to some, but it will, as time goes on. And speaking of schools, I'm sure you want to know more about how to create those terrific community schools of 2020? Allow people to enjoy at all levels, including learning. The thrill of learning is around the corner when people, for one thing, realize the power of their thoughts. But I think first they must recognize it is okay to be happy. I think there is a large group of people today who feel if they are happy, someone else will lose out. Are you aware of this?

Jenna: Yes, what are you saying?

Rebecca: I think people need to become aware of this. I just throw that out as something for people to think about. Actually, they will encourage others' happiness if they are happy. Happiness does not mean loss for someone. That has to do, once again, with worrying about *effects* on others. People's happiness, true happiness, has a positive effect on others. The power of thought, yes. I'll tell you something about the power of thought—it has kept people from being happy because they are so certain it will cause negative effects on others, which will hurt *them*. That is the way they think it out. Hmmm… I tell you, it is essential that people grasp more of their own irrationalities.

Jenna: Do you think this has to do with these bodily fears, we spoke of earlier, harm to the physical body, in other words people's inhibitions about being happy?

Rebecca: Yes, I do, and I suggest people broaden themselves to allow those kinds of deep fears to arise, so they know they *have* them. It is hard to know much of anything if you don't have your own, as you say, direct experience. Once you start allowing that *thing* to walk out of you, what happens is all sorts of other realizations come to you, such as what happiness really is, or can be. People think they are happy today, but it is nothing compared to what they have ahead of them in the upcoming years.

Jenna: Yes, kind of an intellectual happiness now, I guess. It must be really something later... Rebecca, you spoke earlier about the concept of spreading beliefs in your therapy. Is this related in any way to depriving ourselves of joy?

Rebecca: Spreading beliefs has to do with bringing more points of view into your mind. It is a technique I use in therapy to spread the energy of the belief outward. When people can see how others view something, it changes their beliefs! So what do you think of that?

Jenna: That sounds pretty simple. Hmmm... let me think about that. I know that when I have encountered stubborn people who have tunnel vision, it seems impossible to change their thinking. They wouldn't listen to another's view if you begged them.

Rebecca: They might if they didn't feel criticized or weren't trying to create *effects.*

Jenna: So you are saying that people who aren't trying to change others are the ones who probably will?

Rebecca: That is absolutely true because there is more likely to be direct experience there, or merging energy fields, in your terms.

Jenna: So to help others open up their minds, what would you suggest?

Rebecca: Love them.

Jenna: It's so simple, isn't it?

Rebecca: That it is, well, most of the time! By the way, do you think it's possible that your wanting to change that stubborn person is a factor in furthering his stubbornness?

Jenna: Absolutely yes... creating effects, pretty ineffective. Hmmm... I hadn't thought of that.

Rebecca: Yes, and true interactivity. Now take a moment to grasp what I am saying, for you are no different from that stubborn person.

Jenna: I gotcha.

Rebecca: I'm not reprimanding, just illustrating.

Jenna: I know... I wanted to ask you something earlier when we were talking about our irrational thoughts. How do we get in touch with them? Certainly we don't grasp how irrational we are sometimes. Is there

186

some way you can state it, besides energy flow? I know that is ultimately true, but sometimes it is kind of abstract when we talk here.

Rebecca: How to get in touch with irrational thoughts? One way I would suggest is to be open to others' views of you. Now that may sound like going outside of yourself to know, but many become increasingly more irrational the more time they spend alone, or with just one or two others on an intimate basis. People feed each others' irrationalities because of what I just said, worrying about the effects they have on others, and it seems to be worse when one is with the same people over and over again. I would recommend people enlarge their group of friends, mix more with others, both with like and unlike interests. There is no better way of learning about love than from people. Now what I am talking about is true friendship, where people share and are honest, not superficial hoards of acquaintances. Love is what inputs energy flow, which clears up perception.

By the way, when you are trying to create an effect, you will muddy the bigger picture, or not see it, in other words. People in 2020 do not try to create anything, or change anything, instead, they're just there *with* whatever. Now this is an important concept because it starts very young, erroneously, with babies. Babies learn that if they cry, they get fed. That is not their original intention, did you know that?

Jenna: No.

Rebecca: What do you think it is?

Jenna: To express themselves.

Rebecca: And so what happens?

Jenna: Mothers interpret it to mean they are hungry and feed them.

Rebecca: Yes, when in fact…

Jenna: They are trying to tell them something else.

Rebecca: What?

Jenna: That they love them, that they love themselves.

Rebecca: And the mothers think it is something they must do. How many mothers think to themselves, "Oh, I love you, too!," expressing *that* emotion primarily to the baby?

Jenna: Not many since they immediately *feel* responsibility, which I suspect is why we have such convoluted concepts of love. I don't know where all this is coming from.

Rebecca: Oh, yes, you do. Go on.

Jenna: Babies feel love then as having a bit of a strain to it because they can feel their mothers'... who knows, unresolved stuff about motherhood, responsibility, or whatever.

Rebecca: But it is rarely just a response of love, right, to the baby?

Jenna: I would say that is absolutely true.

Rebecca: So these then are first lessons in love?

Jenna: I would think so.

Rebecca: Do you remember how you felt when you fed your babies?

Jenna: I think I felt very loving, but I certainly wouldn't say I was all that flowing because I think I did feel the responsibility, maybe even overwhelmed at times with motherhood and all that had to be done!

Rebecca: Well, babies feel this; it is how they learn about love, and who they are. Now let me ask you this. If you are feeding your baby, with intermittent thoughts about what has to be done, what do you think your physical senses are experiencing? And also, are you in any way thinking or feeling, "This is hard"?

Jenna: Yes. Wow. It's like giving my senses permission or encouragement to stop being, not to take in any more data, since I already *know* that it is hard! Oh, my, just passing thoughts.

Rebecca: That is exactly true, just passing thoughts, but they have indeed affected the rest of your body. I will tell you something, every time you say something to yourself like this is hard, you have made a decision based on fear, which manifests into a big no to your senses.

Jenna: It makes me feel the power of self-doubt and that I haven't been very nice to my senses!

Rebecca: If your physical senses are asked not to participate except to bolster your own beliefs, it is no wonder love is such an unknown today.

Jenna: That's for sure, love from only one point of view, your own distorted one... Are you saying that the baby doesn't feel unconditional love and the mother doesn't feel unconditional love largely because the physical senses have been so shut down?

Rebecca: Well, I don't mean to sound terse, but what do you think love is like that has elements of this is hard in it... or I can't do it, or this is taking too much time, or this hurts, in it?

Jenna: Yes, I see. Love is purer than that, solid feeling, I guess. But we all are thinking all the time.

Rebecca: It's not that thought, per se, is so bad; it's just that it is so... unintegrated, without unity, lacking wholeness at this time in history because people are so afraid to be, which results in rigid thinking which affects the flow of love.

Jenna: Now that is really something, isn't it? Could you elaborate more? What do we have to know in order to experience them more fully?

Rebecca: You will begin to smell your thoughts, emotions too, hear them, see them, sense them in totally different ways when you can feel better that lightness, which is you. Every time you feel doubt, you will feel a heavy veneer around yourself which keeps you from experiencing higher frequencies and a clearer reality. Let me sum up so we can go on with some other concerns about 2020. You will sense the bigger picture when you feel lighter because in the context of that, you will sense movement which will take you to new levels of perceiving, in this case a whole new level of relating to your thoughts. Now whoever heard of the physical senses being used like this before, in conjunction with your own thoughts—or energy flow?

Jenna: Not me. How does this all relate to learning?

Rebecca: People will learn when their senses are not being shut off or down. What happens now is, people get sensory data, then misinterpret it because it conflicts with who they think they are. How many people today think their thoughts smell? Do you see? Already they have all sorts of emotional trauma about the idea that their bodies smell. Do you think they are ready for smelly thoughts?

Jenna: Okay, so as our thoughts are allowed to flow more and we consider the possibility that our sensory data might be reflective of us, are you saying our thoughts will become more aromatic?

Rebecca: To steal a phrase from Paul, now where did you ever get *that*?

Jenna: Okay, I follow you, you are saying yes. This has to do with the evolution of smell itself as well as our other senses. In order to move ahead here toward 2020, we are going to have to accept what we consider offensive smells or sights or sounds—strident unpleasant sounds, for example—in order to be a part of their transformation, which is ours.

Rebecca: So here you are using both logic and feeling, so don't throw out deducing things altogether because it is still quite valuable to you. But yes, just as you say, there must be acceptance of all that *is*, not resistance to it; and for now there are some unpleasant smells, sounds, sights, textures—you know, just a lot of "yucky" experiences, as you see them *relative to you.*

Okay, now here is where contemporary therapists, I think, and I would disagree. I say that those thoughts about you smelly body and other irrational thoughts and fears about yourself ought to be embraced, not dismissed because as soon as you embrace them, they transform. You will learn in fact that what you believe about yourself *is* true. You will not try to throw out good and bad or appropriate or inappropriate thought in order to be sane, which just comes from therapists' and society's deep fears about craziness, unacceptability. If you take what you believe and embrace it, you will be right on your way to a deeper level of knowing yourself.

Jenna: I think you are right. I know you are right.

Rebecca: Let me ask you this. If you think you smell bad, is that true? Therapists today would be inclined to say it is untrue because *they* can't smell anything. But I say, it is *true* because your thoughts are a part of you, and as soon as you accept your own thoughts with love, guess what? You will begin to smell quite lovely, lovelier than those therapists and others who still carry around their judgments about smells. You see, as soon as you unite with your beliefs, something really quite miraculous happens, you *flow*, truly flow. And when you allow the possibility of smelling bad, then fear dissipates, changing who you are and how you smell, how you appear, your own textures, your sounds… your light body comes into being.

Jenna: You are talking about getting beyond an either-or kind of thinking, and embracing your own truths, correct?

Rebecca: Yes. There is no such thing as another person telling you what is true. That ought to be confusing to people, but it's "true." People find input from others, as to their own truths, but they are not *from* them.

190

In regard to what we were talking about, when you hear an awful sound "outside" of yourself, or a smell, your revulsion toward it is toward you. That sound is not something outside of yourself that you dislike so. It is you—it is that discordant, strident part of you, which you cannot stand.

So rather than reacting distastefully toward yourself, know that there are sounds and smells and textures, and so forth in *you* which you are rejecting. Just know that. I am not suggesting you embrace the next siren from a fire truck as it speeds by. You will automatically later—as you learn to love yourself more—hear the siren differently, or whatever the sound is. You will smell different things and also smell differently. But you need not worry how all this will happen.

You just need to recognize that what you back off from are parts of you. Much has been written about qualities in others you dislike as being parts of you. What I am saying is that all that enters your awareness is *you*—which includes sound, smells, tastes, light, textures, every little bit of data that comes in from your senses. I am talking about a leap in consciousness where you realize that everything you perceive—and the means by which you do it—is you. Why don't you just start with sounds and smells, recognizing they are not outside of yourself? Oh, yes, I am not talking about unpleasant sounds, melodic or pleasant ones. I merely bring this up to point out they are not outside of ourselves.

Jenna: Okay, I follow you, but I am back to where I was with Paul in our discussion about whether or not the tree is actually there, or if its qualities are just our own?

Rebecca: If you just start with that, questioning whether it's outside of you, you will go a long, long way. Begin, why don't you, when you experience something "outside" of yourself by saying: Is that me? I think if you just begin there, all the rest of this will fall right into place.

Jenna: You and Paul are saying basically the same thing, that when there is a natural flow within you, well… everything just works out dandy.

Rebecca: And you have said it too about people in 2020, haven't you?

Jenna: Well, yes. But I guess what I am wondering is, how are you and Paul different in terms of how you view things?

Rebecca: Paul emphasizes everything is intuitive. I tend to break apart serious misconceptions, explaining to people at times, so they can use

191

their logic, which they are used to. I use language more and am more involved with actual therapy with people. After all, I am still alive myself and dealing with all of these things myself. After we die, there is a certain amount that just falls aside because it is not "strong" enough to remain, allowing discarnate souls such as Paul to have the inside track on seeing the bigger picture, but most of us here have to learn that to a degree. Since I am human I am constantly being put in the position of tapping in to people's stuff reminding me of *my* stuff, unresolved issues, which are really just bogged down thoughts and emotions. So, in some ways we are the same, but others, different.

Jenna: Yes. Rebecca, I am curious… do you actually say to people, how are your thoughts smelling today, in your therapy leading up to 2020?

Rebecca: Well, maybe not exactly; they often discover these things themselves, kind of like you with the french toast. Sometimes I tell them *my* experiences when I sense they have become bogged down. That really brings a reaction on their part, and I find it is an excellent way of finding out the degree to which they fear what they fear. This is fairly taboo in today's psychological circles, with therapists divulging very little about themselves, which I feel is an enormous mistake.

Jenna: You are talking about love, sharing who you are. You are teaching them love, Rebecca.

Rebecca: Yes. That's all we are talking about!

Jenna: That reminds me, what do you think about the strict rules today not allowing therapists to touch their clients?

Rebecca: I think we have a long way to go in learning about love. It all goes back to that hapless victim concept, I think, as if others would take advantage of us, given the chance. The day will come when one will not legislate for fairness—or love, actually—or sue, or make demands for it… as it will all come very naturally, and I thank you for including me in this marvelous team, do I dare say, of lovers? Even that term will take on new meaning.

Jenna: You're welcome… Rebecca, do you teach physical manifestation, teleportation, or the walk that is "floating?"

Rebecca: I teach knowing who you are which leads to clear perception. I do not teach those things per se.

Jenna: Are you capable of doing these things, and if so, what can you impart that would help others?

Rebecca: Excuse me but are you relating to me now as someone in the late 1990s primarily?

Jenna: Yes, I am.

Rebecca: Do you realize that this is the way that almost all people today relate to one another, from specific time frames only? You see, that is very limiting. When you talk to Paul, you do not sense him so as only in one specific time. You do not inquire, "On Tuesday, Feb. 3, 1989, how are you, Paul," thinking of him as only then. No, you tap all of his past and all of his future, just as you share all of those time frames about yourself. Your souls communicate. Yet you communicate with your friends the way I just mentioned -- from tiny slices of time only. Here you want to know if I am doing these things later this decade, but I speak to you from a much more expansive view of who I am. I respond as an evolving person, much the way you presented the person on a "typical" day in 2020, you know? You showed that person to be vastly more aware than people now, with the now encompassing both the past and the future in terms of a self-concept. So when you ask me, am I doing these things at a certain time, yes, I can respond to that, but I would prefer to communicate differently, not using time as you now know it. I wanted to point this out to show how people use time now to understand. At the current time people have a great deal of difficulty understanding anything if they don't know when. But the truth is, that is very limiting. What happens is, they put themselves in that time frame only and do not tap the database of forever. I am talking about awareness. This might be difficult to grasp, but I would actually know more about later this decade, the specific moments of it, if I were not pulling information from only that specified time frame. Oh, boy, let's just move on. You don't have to understand it, just know it. How's that? You don't need time, just feel it. But even so, I will answer your question about later this decade. Am I teaching physical manifestation or teleportation, or that floating kind of walk? As of that time, I am not capable of any of these things, rather not doing them. I am capable of them.

I sense you would like to more about doing these things yourself. I would make this suggestion. Take something you know you yourself are capable of doing now, think of it, and become acutely aware of what you experience. I would note what it is you feel and think. Then take something you know you cannot do and do the same thing. What is the difference? Remember that feeling of what you can do, then strive through your intentions to find that feeling again. It is there. It is important to know that feeling—or those feelings—because they are you…and you are the one who will be doing these things.

Jenna: Rebecca, thank you very much for all of your insights, your experiences, your words of love. And yes, we are a team!

Rebecca: And I send you, Jenna, an enormous hug, which *will* be the way of the future in all time frames—even from therapists and other "professionals." Thank *you* for your love. And much love to all of the readers, too. And for those who want to communicate with me telepathically… I'm here.

Jenna: And so am I, for those who want to communicate with me telepathically… or maybe just be a part of the team in whatever way they choose. We're here, Rebecca, Paul, and I.

Author's comments

And so it was for the three of us, yacking with one another, over a period of years—and it continues, as we are still in touch and working on getting to 2020 in all time frames! I talk to Paul often, and Rebecca, too. They give me little exercises… and prod me along with love and encouragement. I even have my friends now turning to me to ask Paul about their problems. Ask Paul, they say to me, then they look toward the sky. My son even used him during a college exam and got the highest grade, using *his* answers. Oh… and guess what? Now there is someone named Soren in Scandinavia who wants to communicate—a human, I can tell by his energy; it's a bit tighter. This is new for me, another human instead of spirit guides. I have only known Rebecca before this. You know, I never really thought about it. I just got his name one day in my head. … maybe he wants to be on the team. Now I'm feeling a little shy. Oh, oh… there are Paul and Rebecca. They pick right up on my thoughts. Okay, okay, I'll get in touch with him; honest, I will. "We are *counting* on you." They just showered me with kisses.

Reference Libraries of 2020

A look at the process of awareness

In our society of love, people have available to them reference libraries where they can get large doses of information. The degree to which they can process this information leads to their own clarity of thought, and hence level of awareness. Although they can access much intuitively with their minds, and have their light machines at home to magnify "all that is," they also have the option of going to these places in order to sense red, glowing bricks of compacted information. Unlike today, where relatively few viewpoints are offered in libraries on one subject, by "authorities," the people of 2020 can grasp enormous amounts of information, or viewpoints, on any one idea. The amount of information "consumed," is purely by choice, with people usually taking small doses at a time, then allowing what they need to appear in their conscious minds naturally. People's own ideas on a subject are immediately processed so that the information is kept up-to-date, adding even more glow to the brick. There is no memorizing, or taking notes, at the libraries, as would be the case today, but a sensing with the chest and heart what one needs to know—which just happens, with the information from the brick reflecting purpose, or what's needed to know to keep one on one's path. Ideas adapt to the person! This is contrasted to today where control rules, and most of our interpretations of ideas start with definitions from the past—and stop there. Then people decide whether it is true for them, chucking it if it does not complement their identity. If they allow the idea to "live," they constrain it into a tight jacket based on preconceived beliefs, or that definition. No movement occurs, just a lock on the past. In 2020 people allow ideas to unravel, beyond definition, so as to guide them into the future. Once movement is felt within the idea and in the mind, greater awareness is achieved, with the bricks themselves serving as extremely powerful triggers to inner knowing. Two examples of information available at the library are depicted below (of course it is not in language, but in glowing light):

From the point of view of those attending the libraries in 2020:

Each person "takes" the information and "gets" more from it, in a very personal way by feeling the nuances of light and sound. Within the ideas presented are even more ideas, waiting to be discovered. As an example, inherent in the bricks is information that the Red Sea is the most vibrant body of water in the world in 2020. What this means for one person is very different from another, but it is processed at the time of sensing. This is where libraries of today are very different, since they reflect only the past and do not incorporate the "reader," or the interactive process. The libraries of 2020 reflect the bigger moment, or a compilation of the past, present and future (as we would see it today), with the "future" lending some insight on people's intentions.

World Levels of Awareness (which would reflect the degree to which the society of love has been embraced and implemented):

Tier One:

United States
Europe
Canada
St. Petersburg area of Russia
Ukraine

Tier Two:

Middle East
Eastern Africa
Southern China

Tier Three:

South and Central America
New Zealand
Australia

196

Mexico
Rest of Africa
Asia except Japan

Tier Four:

Japan

From the point of view of the author
All people are vastly more loving by 2020, but there are some areas of the world which are more evolved, which is always "measured" by awareness. Within the areas are even further degrees of awareness among people, with children of all tiers being especially aware. All four tiers are considerably higher than world awareness today. The equation is like this: the more aware people are, the more loving they are. Tier one represents the most loving. There is a *small* degree of difference between tier one and tier four but one that is discernible.

Relationships with what we now know as extraterrestrials, angels, devic kingdom, spirit guides, any beings considered "other worldly":

Tier One:
Highest awareness of ETs, spirit guides, and other beings, has frequent interactions with, experiences more of and more varieties, experiences more vividly, more radiantly, more colorfully, and more physically, as in right there in person—embraces chance to learn from, and work with, senses bigger picture of cosmos better, which includes relating equally with other worldly beings, or OWBs.

Tier Two:
Slightly reduced awareness of OWBs compared to tier one. By 2020 perception is more the degree of clarity, not just whether these beings exist or not, as we might view them today. Experiences slightly less of all of the above. In other words, has fewer experiences and perceives OWBs as less colorful, less radiant, less vibrant, and less physical. Experiences them more mentally, as would be the case in the earlier stages of an evolving idea—or the acceptance of an idea. Interactions with OWBs are controlled to a degree by perceiver based on belief. Tier two reflects a minor unconscious degree of skepticism which keeps the experience from manifesting more fully.

197

Tier Three:

Yet another degree of reduced awareness of OWBs but not greatly different from tier two. Experiences even less color, radiance, vibrancy, and physicality than tier two. Fewer direct contacts with them. When thinks about them, constrains ideas of them, does not relate as equally to ideas as above tiers. People love and accept OWBs in this tier, as is the case with tier two, but in tier three they started "thinking about them" at a later chronological time, and their belief systems are even more intact, which control even further their natural spontaneous experiences with them.

Tier Four:

Same, or even more reduced awareness of all of the above but not greatly different from tier three. More recent acceptance of ideas of OWBs. Possibly less influenced by children. Like above tiers, "believes in" OWBs but has not integrated the idea well yet in terms of themselves. They are very mental and somewhat controlling in terms of how they perceive the world rather than meeting it equally.

From the point of view of the author

People throughout the world by 2020 are experiencing other worldly beings, but their experience of them is dependent upon their individual awareness. The people in tier one are the most likely to have been thinking about and "believing in" OWBs for the longest time, resulting in the physical manifestation of the beings themselves. This is true for ETs, angels, spirit guides, devas, other wordly beings, all of whom appear as "real physical beings" for many by 2020. Perception is a gradual process with increasing clarity. It is not as if one day in the future people wake up and find that ETs or anybody else have inhabited the earth without ever having thought about it previously. This is not the way perception works, and people understand this by 2020. In fact the relationship between clarity of thought and physical manifestation is clearly understood by this time. Briefly, the clearer one is, and the more desire is incorporated, the faster the idea physically manifests. Everything is a process beginning in the mind. One of the most notable differences by 2020 will be that subtle energies, or as we know them now, will feel more "physical" to us. Another enormous change will be that perception is more by degree, not whether something exists or not.

198

APPENDIX

Guide to Telepathy

Communication of the Future

More and more we are moving into a time where rather than cherishing our privacy, we will cherish our self-expression. When we are truly open and loving of ourselves, we are naturally telepathic. Our walls are down and we are comfortable with ourselves and having others see us. Today we hide and don't want others to see us due to our discomfort with ourselves. In the future we will desire that others see and know us much more. We will seek it out, in fact, which will ignite our own telepathic capabilities. What is telepathy, and why is it so important? Learning something about it is a good start.

- Telepathy is a deeper level of communication than we are used to, more of a soul-to-soul exchange, where our true selves are revealed, versus a personality-to-personality exchange, which is frequently superficial.
- This deeper level means a clearer, more direct message.
- Technically, it is a transference of thought.
- One needs to be able to feel one's own true essence, then the true essence of another for the process to begin. Feeling one's own eternal, subtle vibrations will attract the same in another, then there is a spontaneous unraveling of telepathic information. Feeling one's own loving nature is a big part of it.
- Process begins in unconscious mind, then becomes conscious.
- Telepathy is an intuitive, natural by-product of being open and flowing.
- Messages come in complete thoughts or whole ideas. Are already "there" and just need to be tapped in to; the ideas are not created by you and your telepathic partner but chosen jointly in order to express what you

199

want to "say," then sent as messages "back and forth." Choosing happens intuitively, though not necessarily consciously. There is a sense that you and your partner are agreeing on something, rather than emphasizing your differences, as in "your point of view" and "my point of view." Although it seems that you are individually choosing what you are going to "say" and your partner the same, it is agreed upon in the moment by both of you. Feels as though you and your partner are one and that the topics slide into one another.

- Information comes instantly, faster than time as we know it, and faster than the speed of light. One does not think through what one is going to "say." It's more like zip, zip and the information is exchanged, with awareness (of the ideas) and the intention (to communicate) being "all that it takes."

- The process is done by feel...namely, feeling subtle movement of energy on mental plane. Movement is often felt in aura directly in front of the chest area, in front of the thymus (outside of physical body).

- The brain then processes information into words, voices, sounds, smells, textures, colors, pictures, symbols, "moving pictures," making it more understandable, which is when most people become aware of telepathy happening.

- Sending and receiving information telepathically triggers one's own inner knowing, or greater awareness.

- All senses are involved, although some people favor one or two of their senses, as in referring to themselves as clairvoyant or clairaudient. The more senses used, however, and used equally, the clearer and more abundant the telepathic material. Using all senses enhances ability to feel movement.

- It is important to allow information to come TO you, rather than reaching out with eyes, nose, ears...looking FOR it. Some refer to this as passive senses. Ideas jump out at you, toward you, like windows opening on your computer, revealing even more ideas. There are ideas within ideas communicated telepathically.

- It is sometimes necessary to "go through"...or allow into the mind extraneous material first, which feels flimsy, light weight, jerky, tinny, and brittle. Can be totally nonsensical. At this point it is important to be totally nonjudgmental of self, as in rebukes for making something up. Allow it to come forth. Frequently the "deeper," more meaningful telepathic material is "beneath," which feels more resonant, smoother, harmonious, rhythmic and whole.

- One needs to feel safe within context of one's self. For example, if you need to feel safe in the relationship first, as in needing proof of another's love, it will be very difficult to communicate telepathically. One needs to start from a point of safety, not elicit it. One *assumes* the love that is there and feels it, then the message can go through. Fear has a very low vibratory rate which colors perceptions and keeps love out. Some common fears preventing telepathy are fear of being judged, fear of not being worthy, and fear of not being loved (by your telepathic partner).

- Telepathy necessitates a high vibratory state and a new way of thinking— a more fluid way—which is what happens when one trusts what one feels and knows, along with what another feels and knows.

- One's state of mind affects whether telepathy "works." If you are in bad mood, critical of yourself and/or others, with stuck emotions, you won't be able to send or receive telepathic messages. You will be more aware of your own stuck emotions than the true essence of another, which will block the messages from reaching you. Your mind won't let them in due to your own lower vibratory state.

- Telepathy necessitates an open heart. The predominant feeling is love. One cannot connect with another unless coming from point of love and equality. If have a lot of unresolved emotional issues with someone, i.e. upset with someone, it will get in the way of telepathically connecting and keep one at a lower vibratory level. Must actually like the person with whom you're communicating (and the fonder you are, the better)! Also, one must feel equal to, neither above nor below one's telepathic partner, (both being equally worthy). This is the only way like energies can meet. Telepathy involves the merging of two beings, characterized by the essence of each being revealed in the flow of energy. The energy does not merge if you view your partner as beneath or above you. This principle also applies to communicating telepathically with an object or animal, or an idea like the future. One must not feel above, as in "better than." If so, no exchange of energy or information will occur.

- Telepathy has a certain rhythm to it, a kind of back-and-forth rhythm, until the proper frequency is met. It involves entrainment, or the locking in with your partner's sound waves. Feels as though there is a string between you and partner that goes zing when the connection is made. When loss of focus or concentration, feels as though the string sags, and everything is "too heavy." Happens when you lose touch with who you really are. Occurs when you are thinking and/or fearful. One does not "think" when telepathic; one feels the finer vibrations of thought.

- Telepathic material may tap in to own memories. Are different from messages sent. Can tell difference by feel. Memories have more constricted emotion in them, whereas loving messages feel more fluid. When telepathic, one is not going in and out of emotional reactions which is so common in personality-to-personality communication. Would lose connection with partner if did. Emotional reaction has to do with separation, whereas telepathy has to do merging with your partner, a coming together. True emotional flow is inherent in telepathy, but blocked emotion will prevent it.

- Telepathy necessitates an equal meeting of energies, a melding, where your energy and another's meet lovingly—at the point of nonresistance—where neither pushes AT the other, or pulls forcefully toward one's self. This describes direct experience, and telepathy is what happens when there is direct experience...and vice versa.

- For telepathy to occur, it is necessary to put your consciousness "inside" of that with which you're entraining, i.e. people, guides, nature spirits, angels, deceased people, souls yet-to-be incarnated, objects, animals. Connecting at the heart level, or soul level, means fusing the consciousness of both.

- The mental state is one of alertness, not a mellowed out state induced by drugs or alcohol. Fatigue and illness can be factors but do not make telepathy impossible.

- It is helpful to be in environment where can feel very fine vibrations. Very difficult to be telepathic on airplanes or where "big bumps" get in the way of feeling smaller ones! Need to be able to feel own very fine, internal vibrations to be aware of fine energies outside of yourself.

- Telepathy can also occur in dreams. Can be going on in your head too, when you have not had the conscious intent to communicate with someone, as would be the case where someone answers your thoughts. Example: You are thinking, "What should I do today?" Answer: Do such and such. This could be someone other than yourself speaking to you. Spirit guides try to reach us by responding to our thoughts. Telepathic information at first might seem misty, cloud-like, a bit elusive, much like a dream, until latched onto, at which point it clears up.

About Jenna Catherine

Not a prophet, but a proponent of the future, Jenna Catherine demonstrates a philosophy that the future—at least as much as the past—should be used as a frame of reference. This philosophy permeates her writings, speaking engagements and classes.

She has a Master's Degree in Mass Communications from the University of Denver, where her one-act play, "The Phone Call," was produced and televised. She also wrote, produced, and directed a first-place winning skit, "A Night at the Oscars," and created a short film about children's soccer titled, "Firebirds!"

Known as a clear and concise communicator, she appeared in 1995 on a panel of experts discussing time travel on NBC's "The Other Side". Ms. Catherine has published articles and games in the *Glenwood Post, Tennis Magazine* and children's magazines. Her first book, *Being is Enough*, which is unpublished, reveals the process of expanding awareness and communication with spirit guides.

Fascinated by perception, she has been a regular instructor at the International Women's Writing Guild's Summer Conference, held annually at Skidmore College. she has also has been a speaker at the International Association for New Science, explaining the effect of beliefs on perception. Her seminars include telepathy, psychic skills, the power of thought and time travel.

Her passions include: Elvis Presley, classical music, margaritas, and the Colorado Rockies baseball team. If there was one thing she would like to contribute to the world, it would be to help people increase their awareness.

Acknowledgments

I wish to thank Carlene Sampson for her encouragement and editorial assistance, and whose many hours of reading, proofing, and "thinking," made it all gel; Doris Jeanette for her companionship, love, encouragement and own unique work, which fueled and inspired me; Alex and Lindsay for not dismissing me as a whacked out parent but enthusiastically supporting me; Anne Price for her suggestions, comments and insightful editorial assistance; Pam Meyer and Brian Crissey of Blue Water Publishing, Inc., for their faith in me and suggestions for strengthening the book; John Warick of Red Mountain Computer Services and David Erickson of the Rocky Mountain Printer for their computer assistance; The International Writers' Guild and Director Hannelore Hahn for providing a nurturing place for me to express myself; Allen, my grandson of the future for his irresistible companionship and insights; Paul and Rebecca for their love-filled guidance; the idea of the future itself, for luring me into learning more about the nature of ideas--and the power of them; and lastly to anyone who commented that it was impossible to know the future "since it hadn't happened," because it spurred me on.

Photograph of the author is courtesy of Doris Jeanette.

index

of selves 166

L

labels 127, 150
language 96, 106, 150
    spoken 96
    written 96
laughter 68, 79
    as healing 72
    learning tool 72, 78
learning 13, 23, 30, 159
    and physical senses 189
    by osmosis 164
    experiential 162, 165
    individualistic 180
libraries 195
light
    as feeling 82
    smelling 88
light machines 95, 195
longing 116, 153
loss 52
love 3, 7, 17, 24, 25, 48, 53, 57, 60, 63, 151,
        153, 188
    controlling 153
    in business 122
    machine 167
    mother's 59

M

manifesting intentions 49, 99
manufacturers 127
Martin, Todd xvi
material gain 143
media 91, 99
memory 45, 60, 116
    future 84, 162
mental health 11
    care 12
    in 2020 11
Mexico 197
Middle East 196
millennium xvii
mind travel xx
mindcare 11
    clinics 13, 18
money 122, 133, 148, 150
    absence of 123
    misunderstanding of 98
    nature of 123
noon 45
motherhood 188

N

natural skills 153
    use of 124, 139
New Zealand 196
numbers 125, 133, 148, 150

O

objects
    awareness of 42–43, 61, 140
    businesses as 138
opinion 42, 150
ownership 122, 173

P

panic 52
paranoia 146, 155
Paris xvii, xxi
past lives 8
Paul xiv, 5, 15, 47, 73, 99, 133, 169
Pennsylvania xxiii
perception 20, 38, 43, 57, 64, 78, 88, 93, 123
    cellular level 166
    of emotional flow 75, 83
    of movement 26
    of nature 165
    of new things 82
    whole body 68, 166, 173
philosophy xxiii
    of new things 82
physical body 37, 69
    age of 68
    synchronization with 36, 165
physical manifestation 71, 131, 159, 171, 193
    food 160
physical senses 24, 63, 67, 70, 88, 159, 173
    expanded use of 67, 77, 160, 170, 174, 189
    hearing 42, 69, 191
    smell 170, 189–191
place xxiv
population 38
predictions 121
privacy 39, 52, 146
products 126, 127, 140
    natural 127, 128
    synthetic 128
profits 121, 123
protagonist xxiii
psychometric experiences 43
psychotherapy xvii
purpose 22, 153
    of business 123

R

reading 96, 172